AF470680

THE
MEGALITHIC
EMPIRE

Also by M.J. Harper

The History of Britain Revealed

Published in USA under the title
The Secret History of the English Language

THE MEGALITHIC EMPIRE

M.J. Harper

H.L. Vered

Nathan ⟣ Carmody

Nathan Carmody
38 Goodings Green, Wokingham
Berks RG 40 1SB

nathancarmody@aol.com

Published by Nathan Carmody
38 Goodings Green, Wokingham
Berks RG 40 1SB

info@nathancarmody.com

First published 2012

ISBN 978-0-9542911-1-2

Typeset by Bookcraft Ltd, Stroud Gloucestershire
Printed in Malta by Gutenberg Press Ltd

Contents

1 **Stone Circles, A Users' Guide** **1**

It is an unsolved mystery how reasonably advanced but illiterate societies made long distance journeys, as the archaeological evidence shows they repeatedly did. Stone circles, countryside markers and strategic trackways turn out to be the answer. Luckily the evidence is often still there.

2 **The Michael Line** **21**

The Megalithic navigational system required a 'base line' and the longest stretch of land across Britain, running from Cornwall to the Norfolk coast, was adopted. The most convenient point on this line, Avebury, became the main entrepôt.

3 **The International Dimension** **31**

The problem of sailing without charts in tidal seas as opposed to tideless ones and how menhirs and dolmens solved the problem. The *ankh* and the *Celtic cross*. Carnac explained.

4 **The Megalithics after Megalithia** **43**

The increasing demands of the Bronze and Iron Ages rendered the stone circle system increasingly obsolescent. The rise of The Hermits ('servants of Hermes') aka the Druids who developed the system. The arrival of the Romans and literacy displaced the non-literate Megalithic system which only returned to power when the Romans and literacy departed.

5 **The Megalithic Saints** **64**

After the Roman Empire Megalithia utilised Christianity by creating a counter-canon of saints: John the Baptist, Mary Magdalen, the dragon saints, the Irish missionary saints, etc. Former Megalithic sites were given a Christian veneer and monastery-scriptoria established to redevelop the old trading routes.

6   Festivals and Folk Beliefs   100

The significance of May 1st (Beltane) and its calendrical opposite
November 1st (Samhain) in the Megalithic Year. Animal domestication as
the origin of many folk customs: the maze as bird-snaring device, hobby
(hobbled) horses etc. Rogationtide festivals and boundary marking. The
original significance of pilgrimages. The folk-character Jack as Everyman
(Guy). The role of witches in contraception and abortion. Yuletide and
Boxing Day explained. The role of various sprites, piskies, green men,
etc. in the countryside and the wildwood. The importance of drugs in the
Megalithic economy.

7   Paying for the System   144

Salt as the main commodity. Relationship between villagers and drovers.
Payment devices embedded in modern lore: nuts in May, wishing wells etc.
Transport nodes and economic activity: fords, mill races, textile industry,
fish-on-Fridays. Problems of capital accumulation: advantage of 'celibate'
organisations over family firms.

8   Megalithic Terraforming   159

The possible human origins of various landforms: chalk downlands, forest
reserves, moorland. Megalithic structures that are recognised as such,
e.g. Silbury Hill, or not, e.g. Milk and Tan Hill. Avebury and Stonehenge,
compare and contrast. The artificiality of the Somerset Levels and Norfolk
Broads. Solving the mystery of the 'Iron Age hillforts'.

9   The Megalithic Control of Animals   179

The surprisingly small number of today's fully domesticated species. The
larger number of animals that have been exploited in antiquity. The true
history of falconry. The barn owl. The mustelidae. The natural history of
the rabbit. Water fowl and their relationship to Man. The extraordinary
corvidae. The bison: an exercise in historical revisionism.

10   The Origins of Megalithia   219

The first animal domestication, reindeer. The first plant domestication
and why. The development of grass products for animals and then people.
Explanation of 'cradle civilisations'. The gulf between nomads and farmers.
The Megalithics exploit the split.

In Greece there is a circle of rocks called the Hermaion, named in honour of the god Hermes. Hermes has an impressive portfolio of responsibilities; most famously he is the God of Travel, which is why he has wings on his feet, but he also carries his trademark caduceus, the staff with the two serpents twined round it:

This is because he is the God of Knowledge. Not ordinary knowledge—that could be handed over to Athena, Sophia or some other rank-and-file goddess of wisdom—but hidden knowledge, hermetically-sealed knowledge, knowledge not for public consumption. The red-and-white striped pole outside the barber's is a 'caduceus' because barbers used to be surgeons and Hermes is also the God of Medicine. Hermes was made the God of Commerce and Banking on account of his constant travelling, which is also why he is the first herald. So here's a nice mystery for any book to solve: what links Hermes, megalithic stones, travel, secret knowledge, medicine and banking? And what's it all got to do with Britain?

ONE

Stone Circles, A Users' Guide

Here's the problem. Archaeologists find a bronze foundry on the outskirts of Birmingham and it is dated to around 1500 BC. This means that regular supplies of copper and tin[1] were arriving at this spot in 1500 BC. A quick assay will show the copper comes from North Wales and the tin from Cornwall, so how did the Ancient Britons manage to get both here in 1500 BC, a time when there was no literacy, no maps, no written instructions, no signposts, nothing to tell anybody where to go? There is no point in 'looking it up' because archaeologists don't know how things were moved *purposefully* over long distances in Ancient Britain even though they know they must have been because myriads of objects have been found hundreds of miles from their place of origin and dating back as far as 4,500 BC.

Academics can come up with any number of ideas to get things shifted long distances *non*-purposefully by invoking exchange ceremonies moving things from one tribal area to the next or by positing pedlars wandering about the land like miniature tramp steamers, but what cannot be arranged is for copper and tin supplies to arrive regularly for the metalbashers of Birmingham. If pressed, prehistorians look vague and mumble about long distance trackways which is rather to put the cart before the horse since it is the making and maintaining of trackways that is at issue. Re-enactments often feature waterways but Britain is in fact peculiarly *un*favoured when

---

1 Bronze is an alloy of copper and tin.

it comes to inland navigation because its rivers tend to be short and to flow into treacherously tidal seas. In prehistoric times, when nature alone shaped the river bank, very few miles of waterway could ever have been regularly navigable nor even very suitable for walking along. The specialists are entirely silent when it comes to the question of how people would know *the way* from A to B when A is several hundred miles from B. They assume without much reflection that this kind of knowledge would be somehow *available*. Not that any of this weighs heavily on the academic brow because, one would have to say, the people paid to think about these things don't think it's a problem and therefore don't think about it at all.

So let's think about it for them. How would *you* get from a Cornish tin mine to Birmingham if you couldn't read, and couldn't ask anybody who could? You can appreciate the true difficulty of the problem by sitting in your white van *today* outside the Pentrithick Tin Mine Heritage Centre and considering how to get to The Brummagem Bronze Foundry Ltd. You can use all the modern highways but you can't use signposts or maps. Begin! OK, well of course you can't. Even if you happened to know that Birmingham is sort of north-east of Cornwall and you can tell by the sun approximately which way north-east is, you are going to miss Birmingham by miles. But help is at hand. You have beside you somebody who knows the way! And he is going to tell you, "Left, straight on, bear right onto the motorway, next exit...." All you have to do is memorise his instructions so that in future you can do the Pentrithick-Birmingham run by yourself. How many times will you need before you can be really confident of doing it yourself? Twice, three times ... quite a few. That's just the way it is when you can't write things down. So remember, according to orthodoxy, every time a prehistoric person needed to transport something from A to B, he first had to find somebody who already knew how to get from A to B and that knowledge is hard to come by.

So much for the task faced by white van man today with roads but without road signs. Now remove the roads. The difficulties which were many are now legion. "Once you're clear of the mineworkings, go east until you hit a fairly big river (ignore the small stuff), walk down the bank until you can get safely across. That'll depend on the state of the river of course but as long as it's not too far north, you should see a white-ish hill in front of you which you'll have to pass to the north of if you don't want to get lost in the jungly stuff … " and so on for several hundred miles as the crow does not fly to Birmingham. How many journeys to learn this lot? How many such journeys can one person make (at walking pace) in an active lifetime? Meanwhile your necessary co-transporter is setting out from Llandudno with his load of copper. It is unlikely you will meet at Birmingham any time soon.

It is not that all this is impossible. There are professional techniques for keeping vast quantities of information in one's head. Song-lines for instance, in which directions are rendered in memorable metre and rhyme, are found everywhere in pre-literate societies but these are only applicable in places like the Australian outback or the ocean[1] where there are few impediments and only a limited number of possibilities. When it comes to long distance journeys in somewhere like Ancient Britain there is always one insurmountable problem: there are an infinite number of journeys. Yes, after an apprenticeship with the present incumbent you personally could eventually memorise the Pentrithick-to-Birmingham route, you could spend your entire life shifting tin from Pentrithick to Birmingham, but what about Pentrithick to every other bronze foundry in Britain that needs tin? And then who shifts all the bronze to the bronze-casters after which a different set of characters would have to take the finished goods to the people who are actually going to buy them. That's the production of one tin mine catered for, each journey requiring a memoriser and a memorisee. If individuals are required to memorise every individual journey in Britain it will soon require the entire population to be engaged in the carrying trade. Or the memorisation trade, it's hard to tell.

---

1 The Odyssey was originally a song-line.

What is needed is what we have today, what every society that engages in reasonably sophisticated long distance trade has, *a navigational system*, some method which allows people to go wherever they want to go without knowing precisely how to get there beforehand. You accomplish this task all the time because you have a) maps and b) signposts so you can set off from anywhere to anywhere in Britain without having to find someone who already knows the way and then to learn and memorise the route before setting out. All that is required to solve the Ancient British transport problem is to find a system which does the same thing *but without the maps and without the signposts.*

The earliest evidence for long distance trade in Britain is from the fifth millennium BC in the form of flint tools, traceable to centres like Langdale in the Lake District and Grime's Graves in Norfolk, which were exported all over Britain. This is also the time when the earliest wood and stone circles start turning up, and these circles are the other chief mystery of Ancient Britain: what on earth were they for? With two problems linked by time and place, it is not unreasonable to try to solve both by linking them together through function to provide a preliminary hypothesis: *the fundamental route marker of the Ancient British transport system was the stone circle.* Armed with this provisional insight, the resemblance between a stone circle and a compass face stands out:

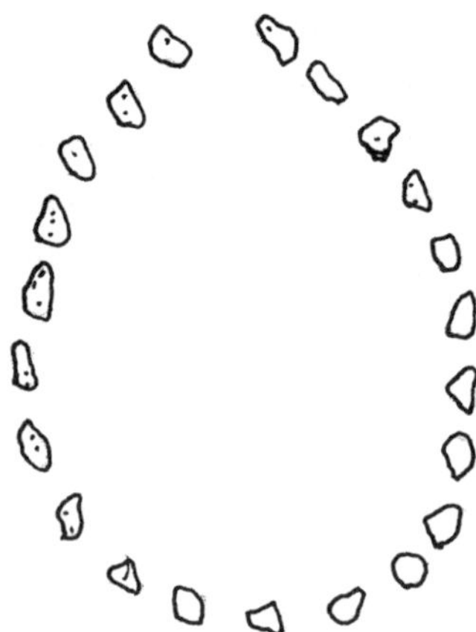

Megalithic[1] circles are either egg-shaped, suggesting the thin end is being deliberately differentiated from the fat end or, like the most famous of the circles at Stonehenge, circular with a *heelstone* marking the 'narrow' end.

Whether circular or ovoid, it is the *line of travel* that is being indicated. The reason for having two distinct methods is that Megalithia always uses devices that last indefinitely and a 'circle with a heelstone' runs the risk of becoming useless if the heelstone is removed, hence the employment in more out of the way places of an ovoid circle which is less accurate but more tamper-proof. The two models can be found extensively throughout the British countryside. Since more than three thousand stone circles are identifiable now in the British Isles, a vastly greater number must have been available to Megalithic travellers. Certainly enough to get from anywhere to anywhere, as long as the instructions can be 'read'.[2]

---

1 **Mega** = big **lithic** = stone Refers here to people that used large rocks in a characteristic fashion in Western Europe from about 4,500 BC onwards.
2 These 'circles' are overwhelmingly small, a few metres across and often barely recognisable. You should cast out of your mind for the time being the very large ones you may have heard of—Stonehenge, the Ring of Brodgar, Thornborough and so on—which have a different if related function.

If all that was required was the immediate direction of travel, other stones would not be necessary as this would be achieved by a single sighting stone plus the heelstone to identify a particular 'compass bearing'. So the fact that there are other stones arranged in a rough circle implies something else is also being indicated. The most widely held belief nowadays (by even the more antediluvian archaeologists) is that stone circles have something to do with astronomical orientation and this can now be confirmed. The traveller stands in the centre of the circle, faces the heelstone and that gives him his immediate path of travel; but by then turning towards the stone over which that morning's sunrise occurred, he knows his path of travel when he no longer has the stone circle as his point of reference. His direction of travel will always be at a given angle from that morning's sunrise. Actually, as we shall see, the traveller won't have to go to all the bother of waiting for the sunrise (much less judging where it is on the averagely cloudy British dawn) because the appropriate stone will already be singled out for him by having a *capstone* on it.

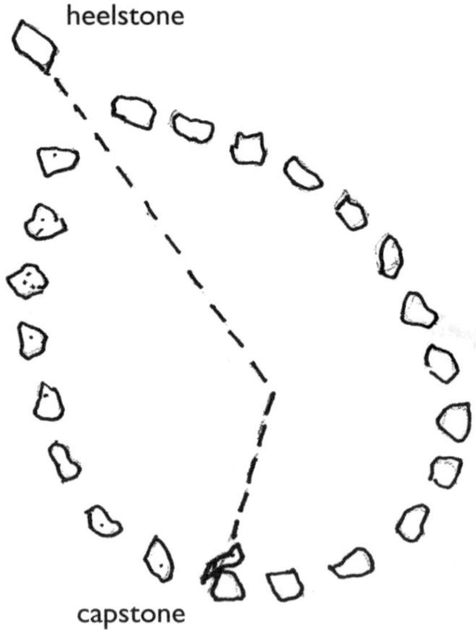

Two directions have now been created: one, pointing to the heelstone, marks a known direction from that particular stone circle and another, pointing to the capstone, indicates the direction of an astronomical event that holds good not just for that stone circle for that particular day but for anywhere in this part of Britain for the next few days. So all that is needed to travel in that marked direction *anywhere* in this part of Britain over the next few days is to stand at the centre of the circle and, using a sharp implement on a piece of leather, score two lines that represent this angle:

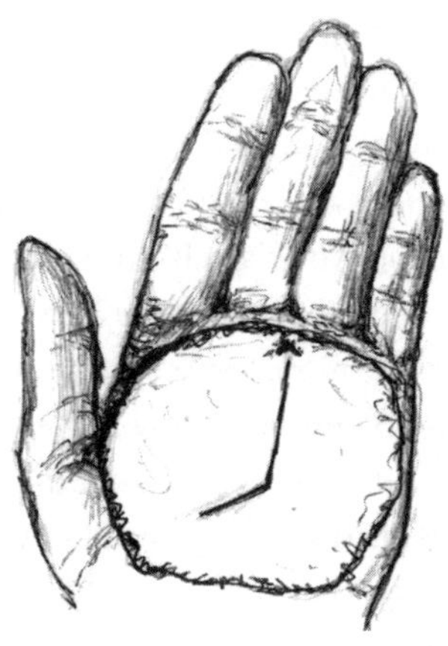

From now on, should the traveller get lost, all that is needed is to point one scored line at the morning sunrise and the other scored line will reveal the original direction of the heelstone, and thus the route ahead. In theory this would require waiting for the next dawn before being able to use the 'compass' but this is the case only for *us,* people who have lost the need for, and therefore the ability to use, sun position and elapsed time. For experienced *megalithic* travellers, for anybody before literacy provided maps and signposts, knowledge of where the sun rose that morning will always be a de facto cardinal point because the sun travels across the sky in a constant, predictable and observable manner. Nowadays we have to point the hour hand of a watch at the sun in order to compute south but the position of the sunrise is readily computable by anyone who can judge approximate time passed and the height of the sun. So for the megalithic traveller, the leather compass acts exactly like our own compass: he can consult it at any time to ensure he is still travelling in the same direction as the original heelstone because he will always have a fairly precise idea, judging by where the sun is and how far the day is advanced, as to where the sunrise had been. But, yes, if he is truly bereft, he can wait for the next sunrise.

Why is the direction indicated by the heelstone so important? It is because that heelstone points straight up the local *leyline*[1] and it is the direction of the leyline that the megalithic traveller should always be following. In popular reckoning, leylines are placed somewhere between flying saucers and crop circles in the realms of fantasy but in fact leylines are very prosaic. They have no mystical qualities, being simple sets of signals etched in the countryside for the purpose of telling long distance travellers how to proceed in an era when written directions were not technically possible. Leylines can be of any length—sometimes a few miles, sometimes stretching all the way across Britain—and they are straight for the very good reason that straightness is the one unambiguous direction telling the traveller which 'signal' to follow in a landscape full of such signals. In practice, leylines only have to be straight*ish* because so long as the next sign can be lined up with the previous two it is sufficiently clear to the traveller which mark is being indicated. Once the observer knows what sort of thing to look for and the direction to look for it, the 'sign' leaps out of the background clutter.

But what if the leyline does not happen to be going where the traveller wishes to go? The leyline is *always* going where the traveller wishes to go because the Megalithic System is constructed using the same trunk-and-branch principle as are all transport networks. As a matter of fact we ourselves encounter the exact same problem whenever we are setting out on a journey but it is so familiar we rarely recognise it as being a problem. For example,

---

1 Technically a ley is a line so 'leyline' is *line-line* but the term has stuck and will be used here throughout.

should you be in Central London and wish to go to Cornwall your overall direction of travel will be south-westerly but that is *not* the direction you will take if you ever wish to get there. You will go, perhaps, south to a tube station (in order to get to Paddington Station) or maybe north to get on an arterial road leading to the M4 motorway, but should you actually try to go direct by any means of travel, London to Cornwall, it will involve you in a most absurd journey, often through brick walls. It was just the same in Ancient Britain: irrespective of the direction of your ultimate destination the stone circle will give you the local leyline and your *initial* direction towards the Megalithic equivalent of a transport hub, after which The System will smoothly take over to ensure you arrive where you want to go.

One small but vital matter needs clarification at this stage and that is to identify who was responsible for placing the capstone. The Megalithic System operates on three principles:

1   no pre-literate society can afford to employ people in any great numbers on a day-to-day basis so everything must be arranged for the infrastructure to need only a minimum of maintenance

2   Megalithia *is* prepared to hurl vast numbers into the mix when it comes to constructing capital projects that will last more or less forever

3   to allow for all kinds of situations over the very long haul, Megalithia always builds in redundancies so the system remains functional even when, for whatever local or temporary reason, there is nobody around to service it.

Thus the stone circle can happily exist in complete isolation because each traveller can, if necessary, make his own dawn measurement of the rising sun or even just set off without further ado along the leyline. But either of these courses of action would not need a stone circle, just the heelstone. The fact that there *is* a stone circle is prima facie evidence that the measurement was done by somebody else on behalf of all travellers, somebody performing the sighting each morning (in practice it can be done on a weekly basis without losing accuracy) and shifting the capstone from one stone to the next as the sunrise moves round the eastern horizon. These Megalithic professionals are known as Hermits, i.e. servants of Hermes, and turn out to play an important part not only in the story of long distance transport but in British history generally. Notice though that, once the stone infrastructure is in place, no further maintenance is required and the 'software', the daily compass settings, can be updated by one person responsible for a great many circles over a large area. But the circles will continue to serve travellers even if for any reason there is no local 'hermit' to service the system. These are the essentials of the Megalithic Way.

So let us return to the Pentrithick Tin Mine Heritage Centre, swapping our white van for a packtrain of animals carrying tin ingots, and set off for Birmingham using only the Megalithic infra-structure. All you have to do is find a stone circle which, since you are next to a tin mine that has to export its product all over Britain, not to mention all over the known world, will surely be to hand. Stand in the centre of the circle (or the locus of the ovoid) and make your leather compass by drawing lines to the capstone and to the heelstone. Now face the heelstone and identify your first waymarker on the leyline. This is the sort of view that will greet you:

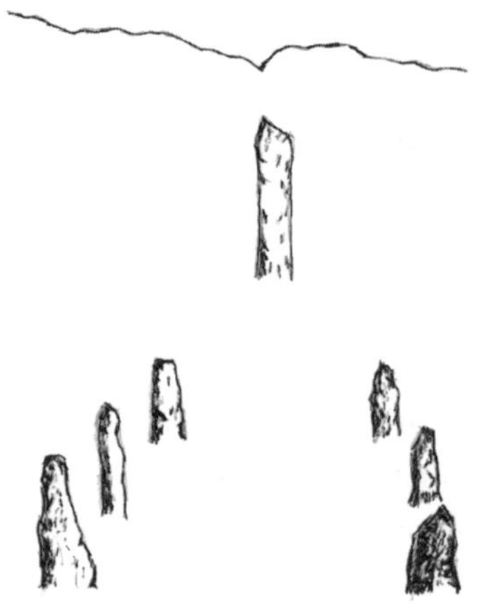

Are you really being told to march towards a very ordinary cleft in a very ordinary hillside? You might, in your time, have seen any number of clefts in any number of hillsides without taking much interest in them but from now on, as you take a more megalithic view of the landscape, you will notice that clefts are actually rather uncommon—it takes a peculiar local geology to form them naturally—and that therefore this cleft in this hillside might just be *un*-natural. This is where the power of leylines is revealed because if the cleft appears right on cue, above the heelstone when viewed from the centre of a stone circle, it can safely be assumed that it was specifically carved out. That is the general principle behind all Megalithic travel, what is ordinary becomes extraordinary when showing up in the hairsight of the leyline.

So the cleft is your first waymarker en route to Birmingham. But there are some snags in getting from here to the cleft: first, you and your train of eager pack animals stumble into a rather disgusting ditch; second, you spend an inordinate amount of time having to wend your way round a very substantial hedgebank; third, you are set on by a bunch of angry farmers wielding sharp implements because you are trampling their crops. Why not take the road instead? For some reason it comes as a surprise to discover that Ancient Britain was covered by a dense network of roads and yet we know from direct observation of everywhere else in the world with settled agriculture that roads are absolutely unavoidable. In fact there was not one but two different networks of roads, each with its own set of characteristics.

The first kind are the *organic* ones that come into existence quite naturally as agricultural communities go about their everyday business. Despite the impression you may have gained from your schooldays, *all* agricultural societies live in communities aka villages unless, like the Scottish highlands and islands, the land is so poor that people are obliged to live in isolated crofts. Ancient Britain was a country of villages, mostly the same ones that are there today, and the 'roads' are the footpaths that are mostly the ones that are there now. Of course many have not survived because, unlike our ancient forebears, we no longer walk from home to fields to mill to bake-house to pub to temple (though we do have roads linking us with all their equivalents) but that is precisely why people the world over live in villages as soon as agriculture permits them to do so. Doing certain things collectively makes sense, and as village transport modes did not change much between the Neolithic and the motor car, it follows that these paths just got more and more firmly ensconced onto the local landscape. And, just as you can get from your home to *anywhere* by road, irrespective of whether a road was specifically laid out for that purpose, so your Megalithic avatar could find his way from the stone circle to the cleft three and a half thousand years ago. Any path going in roughly the right direction will do.

The most important of these organic roads, the ones that come into existence simply by the repeated action of many people going the same way, is the one from the village to the local market. Being self-sufficient is not what sensible people are and anybody who has developed settled agriculture is sensible. Somebody who is good at raising sheep is advised not to make their own clothes with the fleece or they'll end up looking like the sheep. Much better to sell the sheep and buy the clothes which means regular trips to the local market, so there is a road in the making right there as everybody else in the village will need to get to the market. But even the making of clothes is quite a complex business and no matter how determinedly stay-at-home the average person might be, their simple demands, collectively and across the board, cannot help but set in train a pattern of economic activity sending tendrils out in all directions on their behalf. Specialisation of labour, and the transport requirements that go with it, tends to raise the standard of living and human beings are all in favour of raising the standard of living. More than that, the two sides of the equation have a ratcheting effect since demand will permit better transport links and cheaper transport increases supply. This has to be emphasised here because the overall view of prehistoric Britain seems to have arrived at a consensus that it was a self-sufficient steady-state where mere survival was the operative requirement.

On the contrary, as with human beings everywhere, it is the 'good life' that everybody was after.[1]

But this is to get into the *other* network, the non-organic one, the one that does not come about by the simple act of people carrying out repetitive journeys. Agriculture always results in an imbalance between cereal cultivation and stock-raising because no matter how much everybody goes in for 'mixed farming', local conditions will always favour one or the other, and hence there is always a potential long distance market for animals-on-the-hoof. Live animals are easily and cheaply shifted so long as there are passable routes so 'droving' becomes a matter of arranging that these routes exist, but do not unduly interfere with the settled agriculturalists. How this Great Divide between the settled and the unsettled started, developed and finally finished (and who won) is immensely significant for the Megalithic History of Britain.

The long distance transport system in Britain can be roughly linked to the three 'Ages' that academics assign to pre-history. During the Neolithic,[2] when life and transport were relatively rudimentary, nothing more than the leylines was possible and cross-country travel meant literally that, permitting only one man carrying what he could. But eventually, in the more heavily traversed areas, these purely navigational marks were increasingly augmented by *drovers roads* which permitted pack animals as well as meat-on-the-hoof to criss-cross Britain. Finally, by the time of the Roman invasions, we know there must have been real roads capable of taking wheeled vehicles because Iron Age Britain was a major corn exporter and cereals can only be transported economically by carts, giving us the overall picture:

---

1 Everybody fetishises past poverty, it makes us feel better. Apparently the general populace, apart from the unfeeling nobs, has always lived just above starvation subsistence. It will only take a few hundred years to discover that we are living just above starvation subsistence.

2 **Neo** = new **lithic** = stone i.e. New Stone Age. Used here to mean the period between the introduction of agriculture in Britain c.5,000 BC and the advent of metals, c. 3,000 BC.

Date	Era	Characteristic route type	Method of conveyance
5,000 BC	Neolithic	Leylines	Pedlar
3,000 BC	Bronze Age	Drovers' Roads	Packtrain
1,000 BC	Iron Age	Constructed Roads	Wheeled traffic

Though it must be borne firmly in mind that it is traffic density rather than technical advance that decides what transport is locally available. It is quite likely that even in the Roman period, leylines might still be operating in areas of the more distant countryside where not even Roman road-building enthusiasm reached and, contrariwise, continuous trackways are recorded from the Neolithic where presumably local conditions made it worth everybody's while to lay down and maintain these really quite expensive bits of infrastructure.

So, returning to Cornwall and looking once more at your distant hill cleft, it is virtually certain since you will be only one of a very great many people taking tin from here to *everywhere else*, that there will be a recognisable route going towards the cleft. Fortunately, since the cleft is halfway up a hillside, you will not have to arrive *at* the cleft itself. Leyline markers are designed to stand out in the landscape and that means they tend to be stuck up some place high, some place you'd rather not have to take a packtrain of animals, but by keeping the cleft in view and looking back at the previous marker, the stone circle, you will know the direction of the next marker. But what exactly are you looking for? Suppose there isn't a handy hillside in that direction, with or without a cleft. Not to worry, Megalithia Inc has been in this business since 4,500 BC. These are the top twenty Megalithic features to look out for.

Actual straight tracks All over the country you will come across these mysterious pathways, dead straight, running completely true for several miles but not apparently going anywhere. Often they will have been incorporated into roads by modern highway engineers but you will also catch sight of them taking off across country—sometimes as a footpath, sometimes just a crop mark—when the road you are driving along suddenly takes a sharp turn. Because they are straight, these tracks are almost always described as 'Roman'. More on this canard later.

Artificially constructed earthworks e.g. barrows, banks, ditches, mounds, tumuli They may be so small they do not make it onto the OS map, sometimes so large that geologists and archaeologists regard them as natural features.

Engineered natural features including rock formations such as 'logan' stones Making a cleft in a hillside seems to have been an early and unsophisticated example of what the Megalithics could do when they set their minds to it. Again, geologists and archaeologists constantly assume that because nature can sculpt things into unusual shapes, this is reason to assume that Man cannot do it better. The default position, in a Megalithic country like Britain, ought to be 'manmade unless shown to be natural'.

Individual standing stones Though many of these have been moved, destroyed or incorporated into walls, it is a delight to come across one "just where it should be" but unusual because the bigger the stone and the more isolated it is, the greater the chance that it is no longer *in situ*.

Church spires Obviously the church spires of today are not themselves the markers used by the Megalithics but the fact that so many spired churches are on prime megalithic routes indicates that equivalent structures used to be there.

Hilltop beacons This is a bit hit-and-miss because of the number of hilltop beacons used in Britain for more recent strategical purposes but names of hills that are etymologically linked to fires, dragons, worms and similar Megalithic keywords indicate a hilltop that marks the local leyline.

Hilltop copses Fire beacons are labour-intensive so Megalithia preferred to denote the hilltop that is the signpost by planting a circular copse round the summit. How so many of these have managed to survive into the present is an abiding question. One explanation might be that such specially planted trees themselves created the hill by virtue of preventing erosion, meaning that circular copses were the original marker.

Cairns Rather a neat system: since it is 'good luck' to add a stone to the pile, every traveller is deployed to maintain this signal on behalf of every other traveller.

'Sacred' wells, winterbournes, dewponds etc. The Ancient British were obsessed with water sources which is odd given that there are so many of them. However, transporting large numbers of animals about the countryside, especially chalk countryside, does require special attention be paid to how they are watered.

Pubs But only certain types of pubs. More on this later.

Hedges Hedges are extremely long-lived features of the British countryside. Even today, grubbing one up seems to tear at the psyche. Hedges last a long time for the same reason that roads do, they link up with so many other things that shifting them is something to be undertaken only once a millennium, when an Enclosure Movement or a Common Agricultural Policy comes along. Old hedges are not necessarily megalithically significant, but those that line sunken lanes, delimit ridgetop trackways or act as parish boundaries generally are.

Fords Bridges are technically difficult to build and expensive to maintain so Megalithia Inc preferred fords. We have on the whole lost touch with the science of ford construction but in any case our idea of what constitutes a ford would not necessarily be theirs. Megalithic animals were far more robust swimmers than today's pampered beasts; how many cows do you know would be able to swim the Menai Straits, as they routinely did in yesteryear? Fords are unlikely to be exactly on the leyline but they are normally in plain sight from somewhere that is.

Crossroads Crossroads occur everywhere and in themselves are not necessarily Megalithic. Those that are will have acquired special status and will be, for instance, places of execution or boundary markers and they will have legends and memorable names attached.

Castles Very little changes over the millennia in the countryside, so sites of strategic importance are a constant. If it was worth the Romans building a camp or the Normans a motte-and-bailey, something Megalithic in the vicinity can be expected.

Hillforts Not, as we shall see, necessarily the same as the previous entry.

Cursuses These currently unexplained (except in this book) linear features can stretch for several miles.

Devil's Dykes Also ditches, moats and other ancient linear features found lying across main roads that, unlike cursuses, are clearly designed to be impassable to animals i.e. to avoid paying tolls by going across country. Usually declared by historians to be 'defences to Anglo-Saxon incursions'. Rather unsuccessful apparently.

Pictograms and petroglyphs Certain types of markings, notably cup-and-ring and mazes, carved on prominent surfaces.

Chalk figures The turf is removed from a hillside to leave a Megalithically-significant figure: white horse, man with surveying rods, giant penis, etc. But beware, most chalk figures are modern.

Hermitages Forget everything you thought you knew about hermits. Hermits were employees of The Megalithic System, servants of Hermes, and distributed along routes as custodians and toll collectors at wells, fords, hillforts, etc. It is this enforced isolation that led to later religious types in search of solitude adopting the name. The reputation for wisdom comes from Megalithic hermits being trained in British geography in order to carry out their function as speaking signposts.

Even so you might get lost. One of the inherent weaknesses of a 'virtual' route-map, as the Megalithic System is over much of its network, is the constant danger of losing your way. When relying solely on the 'straight and narrow' there is no obvious way of getting back to the leyline once the line of sight is lost. You have your leather compass of course but, since this only gives the general direction, it will not get you back on your specific route. Megalithia addresses the problem with one of its trademark maintenance-light and idiot-proof solutions. When following a given straight line to a particular place there are three possibilities: veering off to one side, veering off to the other side and going beyond the destination.

All these eventualities are catered for. Here you are, for instance, with your load of tin, having passed the cleft in the hillside, crossed the river at the indicated ford, made your way along a straight track and found your way to a hilltop copse. You now look for your next marker but realise you have gone wrong somewhere or at any rate you cannot be certain as to the exact way ahead. All you have to do is look about you until you see this sign:

Cup-and-ring marks

You are unlikely to miss them because they are always to be found in high-visibility positions throughout a swathe of countryside parallel to one side of the leyline and may be carved on trees, dry stone walls, the turf of a hillside or on specially sited standing stones. At their simplest level, i.e. just being cup-and-ring marks, they are indicating you have wandered too far from the leyline and that you have to move back towards it in a particular direction; but from the complexities of some that have been found, we can be confident they give more specific information for more expert observers.

However, as usual with all things Megalithic, it does not really matter whether you are an expert or not; you do not need to be able to read the cup-and-ring marks in order to make use of them, all you need to know is that you are too far to one side of your intended line and that you need to shift over in the other direction. How far? It doesn't really matter because when you have shifted too far, in other words when you have crossed back over the invisible leyline, you will begin to see, not cup-and-ring marks, but mazes:

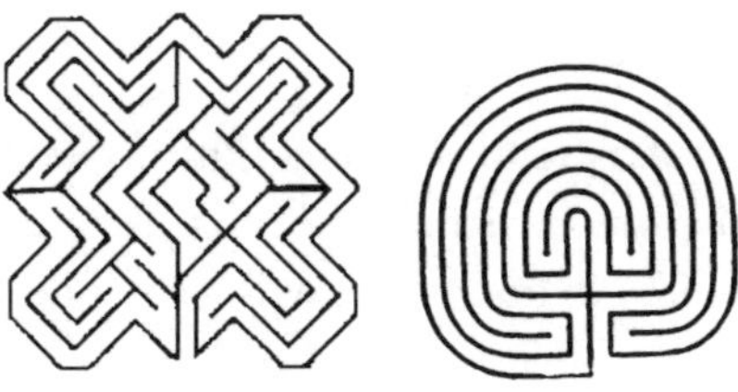

Mazes

Again, by reading the lines on the maze glyph, you will know precisely how far you need to shift back though, again, just veering back until you reach cup-and-ring territory will tell you where the leyline is.

The maze and cup-and-ring system is more or less foolproof except in one particular situation: should you be nearing your destination when going off course, by the time you have regained the correct route you might have gone past it and since the leyline cannot give you this information, the System itself must provide a failsafe. In fact, the System ensures that you *cannot* get past your destination by constructing a *cursus*.[1] This will be a ditch, a line of posts, a trackway—any linear feature that cannot be missed by the traveller—stretching at right angles to the leyline. Thus, were you to find yourself too far to the south of your destination, you will be certain to encounter the southern half of the cursus and be guided by it to where you wish to go, and likewise if you are too far to the north:

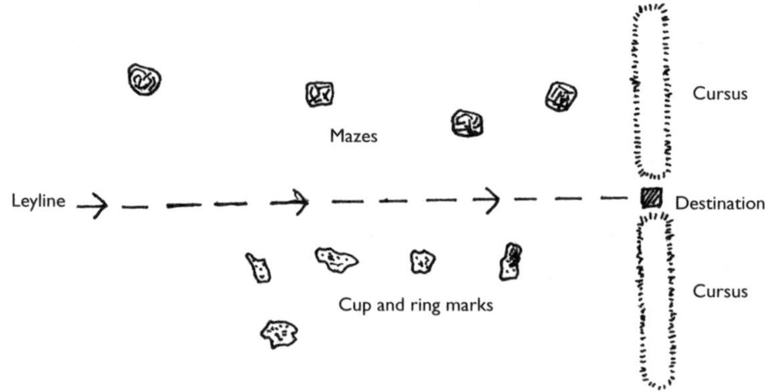

As a neophyte master of the Megalithic System you, your ponies and your tin will now have managed to trek into the interior of the Cornish peninsula. No doubt you will be wondering, since nobody has consulted you, how it is that Megalithia Inc can possibly know that you are headed for Birmingham, and why the Cornish interior is the best way to get there. But never fear, the true glory of the Megalithic System is now to be revealed to you!

---

1 This is the archaeologists' term for it deriving from the Latin for racecourse because they first thought Megalithic cursuses were Roman athletic tracks.

TWO

The Michael Line

The Megalithic System operates on the same principles as any road network, a few major routes and a vast number of feeders. Where major routes get built will always be decided by demand so, for instance, at the present time there are no motorways in Cornwall because in modern Britain Cornwall is an unconsidered appendage, not on the way to anywhere.[1] But in Megalithic times, Cornwall was at the heart of matters, full of tin and the natural terminus for ships from the Mediterranean so, unsurprisingly, Cornwall was well served by *megalithic* motorways. In fact the M1 of the entire Megalithic System not only runs the length of Cornwall but crosses the whole of Britain from Cornwall to the North Sea. Or, as the question would be posed by a Megalithic transport engineer: where is the longest possible straight line that can be surveyed over land in southern Britain? Answer: from the tip of Cornwall to the Norfolk coast.

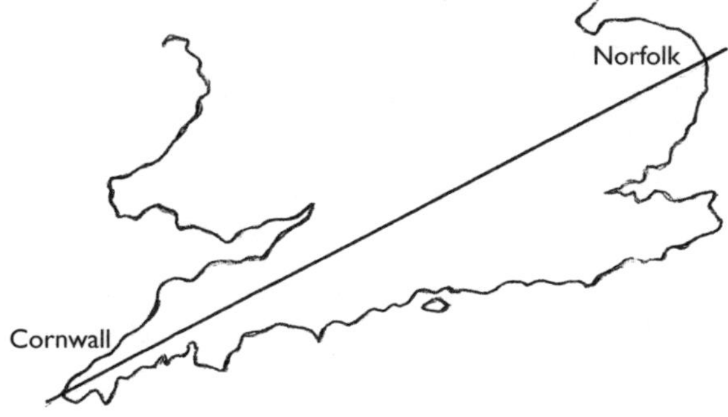

---

1 Except the Eden Centre whose visitors disapprove of motorways on principle.

It is to reach this line that the local leylines have directed you and your tin-laden pack animals and this is so for all Cornish travellers irrespective of their starting point and irrespective of their ultimate destination. Unfortunately for present purposes, demonstrating this line actually existed is difficult because … it never existed. Like the Equator, it is a notional geographical construct that is not laid out continuously on the ground but is nonetheless a critical navigational aid. Even so, the circumstantial evidence that such a line was used by the Megalithics is persuasive thanks to the coincidence of names and earthworks along the line, even though 'along the line' does not necessarily mean exactly 'on the line' because, like fords, local geography does not always precisely fall in with Megalithic needs but, like fords, what the Megalithics want you to see, the Megalithics make sure you will see. This principle is on show right at the start of the line at St Michael's Mount:

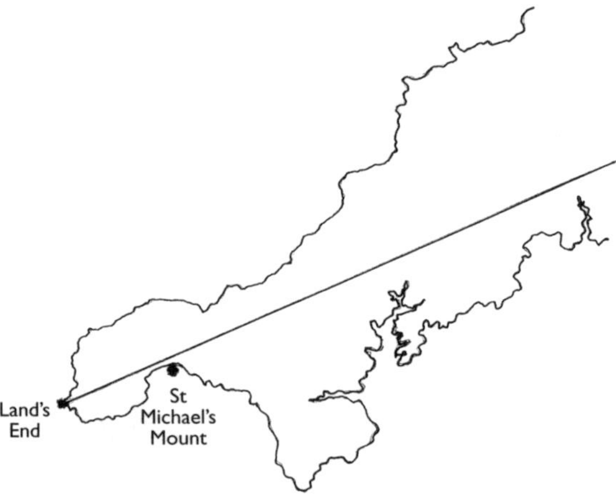

While strictly speaking this is not on the line, it can reasonably be inferred to be the start point because Mount's Bay in which St Michael's Mount is situated is an excellent place to bring ships in, especially Phoenician ships coming from the Mediterranean to acquire Cornish tin.[1] There is good local evidence to this effect:

---

1 Land's End on the other hand does have, along with its equivalent Finisterres (= 'End-land') in France and Spain, a Megalithic *maritime* significance.

1   The Mount is connected to the mainland by a causeway at Marazion, a Phoenician place-name

2   Offshore islets connected to the mainland with a causeway is a Phoenician speciality, their home city of Tyre was of this pattern

3   Marazion's chapel was dedicated to St Catherine, not only a Megalithic saint but one whose body, according to legend, was carried by angels to Mount Sinai, aka Sion[1]

4   The Benedictine priory of St Michael's Mount was later owned by Sion Abbey

5   'Cyan' is the colour associated with Hermes/Mercury.

6   There was a chapel-of-ease at Marazion dedicated to St Hermes according to a document of 1308

7   The *Michael* in St Michael's Mount is both a 'dragon' saint and the chief-of-angels; dragons and angels are constantly linked to Megalithia

St Michael's Mount is only the first of a whole string of 'Michaels' that appear along the western half of the line, hence its modern name of *The Michael Line*:

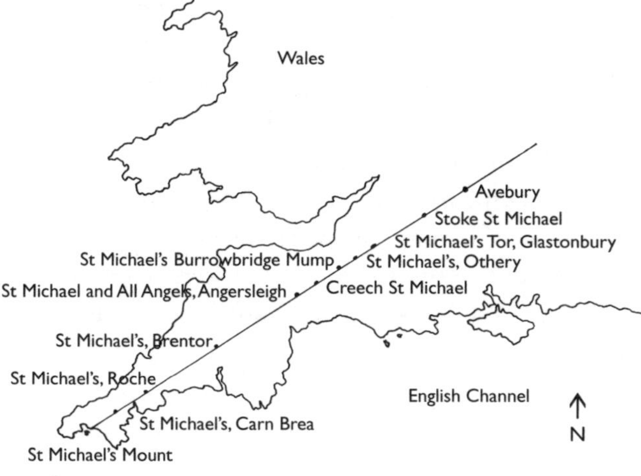

---

1   The link is that both are connected to *Sin*, the Sumerian moon god, though it is moon goddesses that come to dominate this story.

Because it bisects the peninsula, the Michael Line can be readily accessed from anywhere in Devon or Cornwall so, irrespective of your starting point, the local leyline will speedily deliver you to it. At this point the Michael Line will offer a choice between moving 'down' south-westwards in order to export the tin via the Phoenician ships waiting at Marazion, or 'up' the Michael Line north-eastwards in order ultimately to reach any destination in Britain. The changeover from leyline to Michael Line, that is from branch to trunk, as with all alterations of direction in the Megalithic System, will be signalled by a new stone circle and a fresh heelstone. The highly indented nature of the Cornish coastline means that a given start point may not always be in line of sight with the Michael Line and so an inter-mediate switching circle would then be required, which is why there are so many stone circles in Cornwall.

However, once on the Michael Line itself there will be little need for you to worry any more about stone circles or leather compasses or any of the other uncertainties of ordinary leylines because, this being a Megalithic Motorway, your route will now be clearly marked and, in any case, there will be any number of other travellers, coming from all over Cornwall making for various destinations in the rest of Britain. This is the way the Megalithic System in general and the Michael Line in particular works, the greater the traffic, the greater the investment. It does not matter where any particular individual is eventually going because, for the moment, everybody is going the same way and with so many people banded together, Megalithia Inc can afford to ensure the way is marked by unmistakable features on the landscape. No need now for hard-to-discern clefts in hillsides, the Megalithic traveller will henceforth be making his way by landmarks such as:

The Cheesewring

*This logan, or rocking, stone on Bodmin Moor is a pile of granite
slabs balanced on top of one another. In Cornish folklore the
Cheesewring was the work of giants; in the more rational era
of the eighteenth century it was attributed to Druids; in the
allegedly scientific twentieth century it was proposed that it was
completely natural! And still is in the twenty-first century by the
more credulous academics, i.e. all of them.*

The moors of Cornwall and Devon are marked by various 'tors'
which geologists and archaeologists also assume to be purely
natural physical features in the landscape. The etymology suggests
an element of artificiality since whether in Cornish *tor*, Welsh *tŵr*,
Scots Gaelic *tòrr*, or good old English *tower*, the inference is that
they are to some extent man-made.[1] One of the problems of identifying the Michael Line, and Megalithia in general, is that while
these navigational marks are designed to stand out in the landscape,
thousands of years of erosion have rendered things uncertain. It is
also the case that British geology and British antiquarianism are
of roughly the same age but unfortunately they have tended to
diverge, not always along scientific lines. So recognising Megalithic
features is often a matter of the 'eye of the beholder' and further
along the Michael Line there is another 'is it or isn't it?' signpost:

1　Tory Island off Donegal is the north-west navigational marker of Ireland and
　the counterpart of Skellig Michael, the south-west navigational point of Ireland.
　Tory Island also gave its name to the oldest extant political party in the world.

Burrow Mump

Burrow Mump is an isolated island of marl, a mixture of muddy clay and bits of chalk or limestone. The 'Mump' is about ten miles from the larger Glastonbury Tor, also exactly on the Michael Line, and the two cone-shaped hills are intervisible. The Mump's position, on the A361, at the confluence of two rivers, is extraordinarily strategic. There are traces of terraces further down and the summit is conspicuously level.

It can be argued as to whether The Mump is artificial or natural but what cannot be denied is the presence of a now ruined church on the summit, dedicated to St Michael, built on top of an earlier 'chapel' or hermitage. The Mump marks the southern edge of the Somerset Levels and from this striking vantage point you will be able to see Glastonbury Tor rising out of the flat terrain:

Glastonbury Tor

The Tor is unmissable in an otherwise flat landscape and can be seen miles away from any direction across the Levels. Despite the New Age takeover of Glastonbury, despite the Arthurian industry, despite the Arimathean claims of medieval Christianity, the tor is simply a Megalithic signpost.

It is evident from a Megalithic standpoint, if not from a modern academic one, that this vision has been placed there deliberately. Anyone with half an eye for the natural contours of the countryside will see that Glastonbury Tor is essentially man-made though whether shaped, augmented or built *de novo* is something that requires some fair-minded digging. If it is natural then Mother Nature must be thanked for providing a hill in the middle of a pan-flat plain smack dab on the longest landline across England. An even more statistical freak of nature arises from the fact that Glastonbury Abbey and Bury St Edmunds were the two most valuable abbeys in Medieval England and, as it happens, Bury St Edmunds is also on the Michael Line. One is therefore left wondering what is the overall probability that the two most valuable abbeys in a given country will be situated on the longest east-west landline in that country.

But from a purely Megalithic point of view Glastonbury is no more than a waystation. *Avebury* is where the Michael Line is headed. There are not many countries in the world that can boast that their longest landline passes directly through their largest megalithic site, which is what Avebury is, but such is the statistical state of Britain. The coincidence promptly vanishes if it is put in a different form: the longest landline of any given Megalithic country will be the main navigational route of that country and will therefore be certain to go via the main Megalithic site of that country. Of course *where* exactly on that line the main Megalithic site will be placed will be a matter of selection, taking account of the geography of that country. Specifically it will be placed so that the greater part of the country is in direct line of sight, i.e. not requiring intermediate switching circles, with that central clearing point. Avebury is situated with the geography of southern Britain in mind:

Shaded areas are not in line of sight with Avebury

It is placed precisely where the most westerly point is in line of sight with the largest area of land throughout southern Britain. So, irrespective of where a boat lands or a journey starts, Avebury will be easily accessible along straight lines, with no body of water needing to be crossed. Even areas of southern Wales that are cut off by the positioning of Avebury might be a modern artefact because the prehistoric extent of the Severn Estuary is not known. Similarly, on the east coast, the parts of Yorkshire and Lincolnshire presently not in line of sight may have been so when the Humber and the Wash were not so extensive. But in any case everybody on cross-Britain journeys will be able to make their way readily to Avebury and, just as the Michael Line concentrates traffic, so Avebury collects up everybody that requires despatching to other parts. Now the Megalithic Principle of applying resources where traffic is greatest can really take effect.

With Avebury acting as the Central Clearing House of the whole System, it means that everybody can be catered for individually. Your own journey taking tin from Cornwall to Birmingham is a solitary one and you may not know where Birmingham is, and certainly you won't know the precise means of getting there, but having made your way to Avebury all these decisions can be taken out of your hands. Anybody specifically taking tin from Avebury to Birmingham will be joined by everybody else making for Birmingham and, for nearly the whole way, by anybody making for the north of England. At worst this means whole groups being conducted by a professional guide but in practice it probably means there will be a continuous track heading north from Avebury. And along that track, now that there are large numbers travelling together, it is worth Megalithia Inc having someone to show people where to get *off* the track to Birmingham, and to all other parts. This is the essence of the Megalithic System, and it exactly mirrors your own experience, you have to find your own way from your own house at the start of every journey but help will need to be at hand to finish it. In navigational terms it means that everybody can complete journeys without knowing the route beforehand.

The scale of the assistance will always be proportional to demand. The importance of the traffic between Avebury and the east coast for onward transmission to northern and central Europe means that east of Avebury the Michael Line is largely replaced by a continuous path called (by us) The Ridgeway as far as the Thames and the Icknield Way thereafter. The Pilgrims' Way similarly serves the Kent ports (for northern France and the Low Countries):

Continuous line: Ridgeway and Icknield Way
Dotted line: Pilgrims' Way

Though it is only now being pieced together, there seems to have been another route laid out southward from Avebury to Southampton, Portsmouth and Central France. Of course this does require there to be people at Avebury with prodigious memories for the geography of Britain but that is where memory systems can operate quite acceptably since it is a practical proposition to train a very few individuals in these arts just as it is possible at a lower scale to have people with a knowledge only of the West Midlands operating *in* the West Midlands. Avebury's requirements were well within the compass of Ancient Britain, at least according to marvelling Classical accounts of the Druids and their reputed eighteen years of training. The particular West Midlands situation is precisely mirrored by our own 'taxi-trade' where each taxi-driver need only know their local area but, so long as there are taxis at every railway station, anybody in Britain can find any destination wherever they are going and wherever they started from. The 'Hermit System' ensures that relatively few individuals are required to operate the entire network and that the higher levels of expertise are only sparingly necessary.

This is at base how the Megalithic System operated in the Neolithic and early Bronze Age but it is clunky having to detour via Avebury for cross-country trips so no doubt over time more and more hermits were on hand once any trunk route was reached to redirect traffic where it was practical to cut out Avebury. Consider though just how swiftly and economically *you* made the trip from a Cornish tin mine to a bronze foundry in the Midlands, even though you did not know how to get there. The route was relatively direct, even granted that Avebury is a little out of the way (and that the route was selected to show The System off to advantage). You reached Avebury unaided, you required one guide at Avebury to send you north and one more guide to know when to leave the trunk road. It can be safely assumed that local assistance will take you to the foundry itself. One other point should be noted about The System. In so far as we can still identify the signposts today, several thousand years later, we may take it for granted that The Megalithic System required very little by way of day-to-day maintenance.

THREE

The International Dimension

It cannot be known for sure whether Hermes is Greek, Egyptian or ... British. Stone circles seem awfully British, but this may be an artefact arising from local interest and expertise and perhaps because the British are incurably nostalgic and tend to preserve these things better than other more go-ahead nations.[1] Certainly similar megaliths are to be found in other parts of the world and with just as early dates attached to them. Nor is it possible to tell whether the stone circle system started on a small, local scale and expanded out or is a long distance system whose gaps got filled in. It cannot even be claimed with any confidence whether it all began as a maritime or as a land-based method of navigation. The best guess arises from plotting out where early megaliths appeared and drawing preliminary conclusions from the distribution:

Megaliths 4800–1200 BC

---

1   The British passion for long walks in the countryside may have something to do with it too.

Given such a peculiar pattern—and allowing that the evidence is not exactly fulsome—it can reasonably be inferred that Megalithia was originally a sea-based system because the earliest megaliths (shown in black) are in coastal areas which can only be linked by sea. The later (striped) areas indicate that as the system developed, it spread out across the land. Circumstantial support for this notion is that the Megalithic System demands appreciable capital and maritime trade also requires, and for that matter generates, appreciable amounts of capital. The other noticeable feature is the contemporaneous appearance of early Megalithia in the Mediterranean and in Northern Europe. This is highly anomalous because voyaging between the two areas at such an early date is sufficiently fraught as to make the idea that the one gave rise to the other via maritime links highly unlikely *unless sailing between the two actually gave rise to the System.*

In the Mediterranean long distance maritime travel is straightforward because the Mediterranean is tideless. Each trip is the same on every occasion, every coastline is the same as the last time that particular coastline was visited, hence every individual route is learnable by trial-and-error within a single crew. Experience rather than information is the critical factor, data does not need to be stored because experience is sufficient to keep everybody safe, aside of course from the normal hazards of maritime travel. Furthermore, the Mediterranean being enclosed means that coastwise sailing, making landfall each night, can be supplemented by crosswise sailing, going direct from port-of-embarkation to destination using a known heading. None of this applies to the Atlantic. Voyagers travelling from, say, Carthage to Cornwall by hugging the Spanish and French coasts *might* make it there and back the first time but the experience would do them little good because the next time they sailed the whole thing would be different—the state of the tide renders everything new. Memory will not serve when, every time landfall is sought, which in coastwise sailing means every night, there is a thirty foot difference in what rocks are to be negotiated this time compared to last time. Ships simply cannot be sailed into Quiberon

Bay on a regular basis in the hope that *this time* the bottom won't be ripped out. Taking this gamble every night, there and back, is not a feasible career since every journey will be a completely new and potentially terminal experience.

But even this is not the worst feature of the voyage. For the entire journey, out and return, the coast is a 'lee shore', that is the prevailing winds, which are westerlies, are constantly blowing the ship onto the land. In the Age of Sail, mariners went to great lengths to avoid lee shores, so the idea they would develop a route that was *all* lee shore, there and back, is out of the question.

Western seaboard with prevailing winds

Before the Third Crusade (1189) there are scarcely any historical records of ship journeys between Britain and the Mediterranean, though afterwards they became relatively common.[1] What changed? The twelfth century is the time when portolans and other such (literate) aids to navigation were being introduced. Only literacy makes the direct journey feasible because only then is it possible to build up the requisite data and disseminate it. Sailing

---

1 For some reason, lost in the mists of history, 1189 (when Henry II died) was adopted as 'time immemorial' for legal purposes, except in Courts of Heraldry which used 1066.

into Quiberon Bay, *sheltering* in Quiberon Bay, is a practical proposition for anyone possessing a basic chart *of* Quiberon Bay. Yet we know from the copious archaeological evidence that prehistoric sailors travelled between the Mediterranean and Cornwall on a regular basis, and that they did so without charts, without literacy of any kind. So again, what had changed?

From an illiterate mariner's point of view the trip from the Mediterranean to the British Isles is quite safe so long as the boat is taken right out into the Atlantic, far beyond anything that might rip out the bottom, and by sailing northwards using the Pole Star[1] and dead reckoning.[2] Knowing roughly when the ship is as far north as Cornwall allows the mariner to start sailing eastwards until land is sighted. Sailing east is also something that early sailors can do with reasonable fidelity using sun and stars. But what land has been reached? This is the great weakness of the dead reckoning technique, it is simply not capable of delivering sailors where they want to go with the degree of accuracy required for routine trading purposes. When land is sighted it is not certain to be Cornwall, much less the place in Cornwall that is the intended destination. And, wherever it is, the sailor is approaching an unknown lee shore.

The Megalithic System solves these problems because it does not really matter precisely where travellers land so long as they can be confident that a) it is safe to do so and b) there is some way of getting from where they initially land to where they actually want to go. The Megalithics realised that making observations at sea is always a hit-and-miss business whereas a known site on land can be surveyed by experts with some assurance, so instead of concen-

---

1 Not necessarily Polaris. The star that happens to sit above our North Pole varies over time and it was mainly Draconis the Dragon that provided the Ancients with their northern guide. Which is presumably why dragons feature so prominently in the Megalithic System.

2 Judging speed through water is a familiar maritime skill: you tie knots in a rope, throw it into the water, count one-elephant, two-elephants … and that's how many *knots* (nautical miles per hour) you are sailing. Tying knots in rope is something pre-literates do—indeed if the Meso-American evidence of *quipos* is anything to go by, knotted string is the immediate precursor of literacy.

trating on maritime navigation (as we do), they concentrated on land navigation. Essentially, they applied the Avebury principle: it doesn't matter exactly where a traveller lands because The System will take over as soon as and wherever they do. Megalithia Inc will tell sailors where ships can land safely at all states of the tide and furthermore will guarantee to provide everything needed to reach the final destination. So the Ancient Mariner, having sailed as far north in the Atlantic as calculations suggest, sails east until land is sighted but now sails *along* the coast in either direction, safely out to sea, until a *menhir* (as the Bretons called them) or an *obelisk* (as the Egyptians called them) is spotted on a clifftop, or some other handy eminence:

Menhir by the sea

There are still hilltop sites looking out to sea that serve as 'lighthouses' and local names often make reference to these sites being 'beacon hills' or some other proto-Megalithic marker. They are generally described (by today's archaeologists) as Iron Age hillforts even when older artefacts are uncovered, and no evidence of military use is present. The site of a menhir-by-the-sea would often be occupied by a church or chapel, some of which escaped destruction during the Reformation as they were essential landmarks for sailors. Several clifftop churches are known to have fallen into the sea due to erosion and had to be relocated further inland.

The obelisk-on-the-clifftop represents safe haven. It may mean that the incoming ship should heave to and await pilots coming out, it may mean that there is a harbour nearby, it may mean there is a bay suitable for beaching, but the point is that Megalithia Inc in some form is at hand. To understand this side of things it is necessary to switch perspective from ship to shore. There must of course have been seaside communities in Megalithic times so the question is whether such communities would want to be part of international trade. This is entirely analogous to seaside communities today who have to make collective decisions about whether they wish to be holiday resorts, fishing ports, ferry terminals or to be content minding their own business as a community that just happens to be on the coast. Now, as in Megalithic times, the decision is not straightforward because on the one hand it is a nuisance having outsiders tramping around the place, on the other there is money to be made. Basically, says Megalithia Inc, it's up to you. If you do not want to take part, do nothing. No obelisk will be put up on your local headland so no ships will be putting in. But if you do want in, then Megalithia Inc provides you with your very own obelisk. Before listing the likely obligations and rewards it should be pointed out, as always with Megalithic solutions, how hard it is to buck The System. Any community that gets fed up with sailors descending on them at all hours just knocks down its local obelisk; but any community that decides to start robbing sailors (even by putting up the price of beer unduly) runs the risk they will find their obelisk mysteriously lying on the ground in pieces. They had been warned.

It is certainly not the case that building and erecting obelisks is an everyday business. Indeed it is sufficiently difficult that Megalithia Inc actually made coastal obelisks at one central depot, Carnac in Brittany. Conveniently placed halfway between the Orkneys and Morocco and where easily mined granite comes right down to the sea, the Carnac quarries churned them out. The ones that were awaiting collection when The System came to an end can still be inspected, all lined up in nice tidy rows so the ponies-and-carts (or oxen or people lugging sledges) could manoeuvre easily amongst them. But of course, if you prefer, you can believe the prehistorians' view of Carnac which is that its inhabitants carved menhirs with crazed profuseness, arranged them in not very straight rows, did not align them to anywhere in particular, and did all this for the usual 'ritual purposes'.

Stone rows at Carnac

Carnac is a famous megalithic site where more than three thousand stones stand in straight rows, in no obvious order of height or direction though admirably arranged for collection and delivery as befits a production line for megaliths. What we see now at Carnac is, like its British equivalent at Merrivale, the uncollected orders, still outstanding when this form of navigational indicator was superseded.

But back to the decision about whether to have an international gateway in one's backyard. Should a community choose to take part, it is entirely up to them how much they wish to be involved. This is highly characteristic of the Megalithic Method because, it being designed to last for millennia, every conceivable change in local politics has to be catered for, every level of participation allowed for. Including none, since even if the entire population departs, Megalithia Inc has provided the three vital things for incoming sailors: the beacon, the bonded warehouse and the route map to the hinterland. Having come ashore thanks to the first part of the Megalithic Trilogy, the clifftop obelisk beacon, the international trader needs only look for the local storage facility aka the *dolmen*.

Dolmen

Dolmens are in appearance large versions of altars and indeed the word dol-men *means 'stone table', illustrating once again the intimate link between ancient Megalithic and later Christian structures. In the open, dolmens are mainly found in association with stone circles and megalithic structures generally but are also to be found buried beneath churches, e.g. Chartres cathedral.*

A dolmen is a structure made of very large blocks of stone, ingeniously built so that not only is it water-proof but it is virtually air-tight too. Their constructors appear to have gone to very great trouble to make sure the stone slabs fitted exactly. A corollary of this seamless technique is that the dolmen is rendered practically immortal since interstitial weathering is prevented, a primary consideration in all Megalithic structures which are designed to last for aeons with the minimum of maintenance. One other important characteristic of a dolmen is the door, also a large slab of stone, which is exceedingly difficult (but possible) to remove. This last factor is what gives away its purpose since all other constructions are either easy to open, e.g. dwellings, or impossible to open, e.g. tombs. The dolmen is designed to be opened only when large groups of people are present, e.g. ships' crews, townsfolk etc., but not when passing individuals, e.g. thieves, are about. A dolmen is a very collective enterprise.

Looking after the dolmen and its contents, as well as looking after visiting ships and their crews, is what signing up with Megalithia is all about so far as coastal communities are concerned. It is a classic going-with-the-grain Megalithic arrangement, the coastal community joining in at any level it chooses. The minimum that is required of the locals is that they do not interfere, and hence Megalithia can come and go using the dolmen as a secure store, but equally it is perfectly possible for any coastal town to get into the international trading business on its own account by taking delivery of and responsibility for everything coming in or going out locally. Dolmens arise strictly from the economic facts of maritime life, which never vary, ancient or modern. The most capital-intensive part of long distance trade is always the ship, so the ship must maximise its earnings by a quick turnaround. It is ruinous waiting while the cargo is bought, sold, transferred, exchanged or whatever, so it pays to have secure warehousing at ports in order that ships can dump-and-run.

There is a further purely Megalithic factor that arises from the vagaries of dead reckoning, there being no guarantee that an oceanic ship has reached its intended port. Thanks to Megalithic readings on dry land, mariners will know their exact latitude on landing and therefore how far away their intended port is, giving them the choice of leaving the goods where they are for onward transmission by locals, or resuming their journey. But the dolmen arrangement accords with the compelling economics of pre-literate *sailing*—short onward journeys can be economically undertaken either by oared vessel, not subject to the restrictions of sail, or by land transport, leaving the ship to return to its proper function on the high seas. It may well have been this imperative that created the internal *British* megalithic system in the first place because it would certainly pay international shippers to maintain a land transport network of sorts for this kind of short haul work, which would in turn lead to the system spreading out across country as cheap local and international transport links come within range of more and more of the country. Archaeology is eloquent that Megalithia, at least in the form of stone circles, lasted for three thousand years and therefore these *system* demands are driving it onwards for all that time. We have the evidence from our own period that international trade is mainly responsible for cultural and economic advancement. The modern 'Western model' was built on Spanish, Portuguese, Dutch and English ships expanding into new markets and no doubt it was the same then.

What ties the whole system together, after the obelisk and the dolmen, is the third part of the Megalithic Portal triad, that ubiquitous local feature, the *stone circle*. The underlying principle is always to provide a relatively expert system for the use of relatively inexpert travellers, and the stone circle is another example of how this works. Dead reckoning might give a rough idea of a mariner's position in the world but a fixed stone circle, constructed and placed by professional surveyors/astronomers, will tell him *exactly* where he is and therefore whether it is worth putting out to sea again, proceeding by land or negotiating with the locals for onward conveyance. The land traveller does not need to be either a surveyor or an astronomer to use the stone circle for identifying the local leyline and nor does the newly landed mariner need to be an expert navigator because the stone circle has already done the necessary measurement. The professionals back at Megalithia Central[1] have been measuring latitude in order to set up the local stone circles correctly. The fact that there are strikingly similar instruments appearing at either end of the Megalithic world, from Egypt and from Ireland, and which in turn are strikingly similar to a pre-modern navigational instrument, gives us solid evidence as to how this was anciently done:

a) Egyptian ankh   b) Celtic cross   c) Medieval cross-staff

1   At Avebury, Stonehenge, Thornborough, the Orkneys, etc., wherever there are stone circles more sophisticated than those required for routine guidance of drovers and traders.

*The first two are only representational of the original instrument,
which has not come down to us, but the similarities are clear
enough. All points on the earth's surface have a unique relationship
to various heavenly bodies on a given day and Megalithia works out
that relationship and delivers it in a form which can be understood
by anyone with a minimum of training. Since both ankh and Celtic
cross are central to their respective religious faiths, this is further
evidence that Megalithia stands anterior to organised religion.*

When travelling between the Mediterranean and Northern
Europe, the calculation of latitude is all-important so it is not in
the least surprising that an instrument for this purpose should have
been developed at an early date. To travel safely between the two
requires that the sailor, once out of the tideless conditions of the
Mediterranean and sufficiently far out into the Atlantic Ocean to
avoid tangling with the Iberian peninsula, turns north and, using
an ankh, measures the height of the sun, moon or star (they all
work) until they are at their highest reading, i.e. at noon or at
midnight. The ankh will have been 'pre-notched' at the start of the
voyage so that the latitude of a particular destination corresponds
with a particular reading, whereupon the mariner turns east. But of
course this ease-of-use requires Megalithic professionals to make
all the necessary pre-computations and for this one other vital
ingredient is necessary: today's date.[1] After that everything is, as it
were, plain sailing, on land as well as at sea. The Megalithics knew
the one great thing about The Heavens is that for every known
place on earth there is a known place in Heaven[2] and it is different
every day. Once this is known it is possible to set up a system of
stone circles (or notched ankhs) each of which is a 'known place'
and all the traveller has to do is provide 'the known date', and
counting the days since he left port is something anybody can

---

1   The seven days of the week list the seven anciently known bodies of the solar
    system: Sunday (sun), Monday (moon), Tuesday (Tiw, Fr. *mardi* = Mars),
    Wednesday (Woden, Fr. *mercredi* = Mercury), Thursday (Thor, Fr. *jeudi* = Jupiter),
    Friday (Freya, Fr. *vendredi* = Venus), Saturday (Saturn). A seven-day week of
    course fits the 28-day moon cycle month though what humanity would have
    done if the solar system had not had seven visible bodies is anybody's guess.
2   The origin of the Hermetic phrase "As above so below".

manage. This is the real reason why the Ancients were so obsessed with calendars and date-keeping and it has nothing to do with the risible explanations offered by archaeologists such as

predicting eclipses people had spotted that eclipses didn't last very long and didn't do anybody any harm

the agricultural year the idea of farmers planting and reaping on a given calendar day is quite fantastical. Applying for subsidy cheques requires knowledge of the closing date but otherwise farmers operate by the temperature of the soil, whether the catkins are in bloom or whatsoever country lore

religious rituals counting up to 365 or observing the first full moon after the vernal equinox or whatever is quite sufficient for priestly functions. After all, who else is counting.

Why the system ended, when it did, is not at all clear. The introduction of charts (rather more than the magnetic compass) certainly ended the need to sail far out into the Atlantic, but the actual demise of Megalithic-style sea voyages seems to have happened much earlier than that. It would appear to be bound up with the struggle between Phoenician Carthage and Classical Greece and Rome since it is known that the Phoenicians favoured the sea route (terminating at Cádiz, at the western mouth of the Mediterranean) whereas the Romans used overland roads through Gaul originally terminating at the Greek city of Marseilles. The Greeks even put about a story that the Atlantic was un-navigable! But however it happened, it would seem that the memory of the Phoenician method was completely erased because medieval inclination was overwhelmingly to use the land routes even though these were manifestly more expensive. This would not be the first time that modern practice took aeons to catch up with the Megalithics.

FOUR

The Megalithics After Megalithia

Technically, Megalithia finished in 1500 BC, this being the last dateable alteration to Stonehenge or any other stone circle. It would seem that the era of 'Big Stones' was largely over by that date. As the stone circles (and the wood circles before them) go back to 4,500 BC and since the circles are found all over Britain, it can be reasonably inferred that Megalithia must have been a nationwide organisation that lasted for three thousand years. If this is the case it can also be safely assumed that such an organisation would continue, stones or no stones, after 1500 BC so long as the conditions that brought it into existence in the first place continued. The archaeological evidence from 1500 BC until the Roman era in 0 BC is clear enough: intensive agriculture virtually everywhere, no literacy, a rather advanced Bronze Age (and Iron Age) culture and considerable trade with the rest of Europe. In other words there is now a demand for the Megalithic System as never before but the stone circles were no longer being used. So what was?

The essential facts of British strategic transport *c* 1500 BC can be reconstructed by observing other non-literate but agriculturally advanced societies elsewhere in the world. There are two rather different user-groups, the drovers who shift live animals from traditional rearing areas to equally traditional centres of demand, and the pack-animal transporters who are conducting the carrying trade from anywhere to anywhere. The first group 'know the way' because they are using their own well-trodden drovers' ways whereas the second group do not necessarily know the way but can use the (by now, continuous) drovers' ways to get them there so long as they have access to basic directions. What neither group has is the collective ability to maintain these continuous tracks nor, even more crucially, do they have the political muscle to ensure rights of transit across the different political states (not to mention across farmers' lands).

Most of these problems are obviated by literacy because literacy permits bureaucracies and bureaucracies permit political organisations that can develop far enough and be strong enough to ensure strategic movement in the interest of all. And of course the provision of signposts and written travel instructions makes inland navigation open to all. But this raises the always unasked question of why Britain (and the rest of Megalithic north-west Europe) remained *non*-literate for the millennium-and-a-half from the end of formal Megalithia until the arrival of the Romans, writing being such a very useful facility. The British were certainly exposed to literacy, there were copious links with the Mediterranean via the tin and copper trade and the Mediterranean tin and copper trad*ers* were literate so it defies all common sense that literacy would not be introduced into Britain, which had not thus far shown a marked reluctance to import useful innovations like agriculture and indeed metallurgy itself. One explanation for this curious state of affairs would be that literacy was being *deliberately* kept out and this at least would be easily accomplished since both the tin and copper trades had their termini on the very western edge of Britain, at Cornwall and North Wales respectively, so the 'literates' could be conveniently isolated from the rest of the country. We know there was a powerful intelligentsia, based specifically on memory rather than writing, operating during this period, the Druids, and since it is hardly likely that Ancient Britain had *two* nationwide organisations it makes sense to assume that the Druids were the Megalithics.

But whatever they were called, their function is clear enough: what was required was a pragmatic, workaday method for shifting goods and animals around that was less cumbrous than the stone-circle and leyline way of doing things. Any kind of *continuous* trackway makes the cross-country stone circle system somewhat redundant, greatly simplifying navigation overall because there is little likelihood now of getting lost. Even Avebury itself is going to fall into decay once each individual traveller can tailor his journey specifically. Decisions about which road to take are reduced to a handful over a journey that might extend for hundreds of miles. For instance, the British leg of the well-established amber trade from Carthage to the Baltic is no more complicated than that the trader

1   lands on the Cornish coast at a recognised port
2   is directed to the Icknield Way[1] by port authorities
3   turns left at Royston[2] (Hertfordshire) onto Ermine Street
4   turns right for Hull
5   sails off to Scandinavia

with no more than two changes of direction required. But what makes the Druidic memory training so important is that while it may take only two 'Druids' to make sure that this trader on this route makes the necessary changes of direction, these two 'talking signposts', at Royston and the Hull cut-off respectively, must know the whereabouts of a vast number of places in order to assist *every* traveller coming along. In this book, these 'talking signposts' are called Hermits, the servants of Hermes, but the name Druid might be just as apposite.

Even this relatively humble provision of service requires a formidable organisation to be operating in the background. Going from Cornwall to Hull in the Bronze and Iron Age requires crossing

---

1   The Icknield Way replaced the Michael Line. We only use the term nowadays for its eastern parts but Henry of Huntingdon, when outlining the ancient trunk routes in the 1130's, took it as axiomatic that the Icknield Way "crossed the width of the country".
2   That is 'King's Stone'. Writing of the original cross at Royston, the 19th Century antiquarian, Dr Beldam, says, "It was certainly the practice of that people to set up a Hermes at crossways for the guidance and protection of travellers." A parallel etymology, *Rosy Cross*, would have even more hermetic ramifications.

anything up to a dozen separate political entities, none of whom have a particular vested interest in seeing that the traveller completes the journey speedily. There always has to be a nationwide organisation whenever the requirement for long distance travel outstrips the capabilities of the local governmental unit, and this is still the case today where it is recognised that local authorities cannot be given responsibility for through routes because they simply won't bestir themselves to help people that are literally here today and gone tomorrow. In an age when a bureaucracy was not technically possible, and therefore governmental units were limited to the fifty or so mile radius of the 'tribal unit', two things must happen to permit trade over distances of more than fifty miles: firstly, a supra-territorial organisation to maintain the physical network, collect the tolls and provide the 'speaking roadsign' services; and secondly, the formation of a 'Higher Authority' that is recognised by the individual states, to allow these activities to be carried on.

In Britain (and Ireland and Gaul) this supra-territorial entity is known as a High King, a *fainéant* king, a Bretwalda, but the overall political situation is always that the supra-territorials, the Druids and the High King, cannot possess direct political power—which remains at the tribal level—but must have some kind of 'moral' authority over the tribal units to ensure that the strategic infrastructure can continue to function. It is in the tribal units' interest to recognise this superior power since they benefit overall from long distance trade even though they may not directly benefit from the long distance trade that is passing through their territory. But it is also in their interest that this necessary national infrastructure does not become over-mighty and, significantly or not, a lack of literacy ensures this will always be the case because the 'national authority' itself cannot organise internally without a bureaucracy. All in all a very stable setup, at least the evidence from Britain would seem to confirm that something along these lines lasted from 4,500 BC until the Romans arrived. It was only now that the one great shortcoming of the system became suddenly, violently and terminally apparent.

The differences between the two systems, Megalithic and Roman, are clear enough quite apart from the military potential of either side:

1   The possession of writing meant that signposts, maps, gazetteers, written instructions took the place of the hermits, stone circles, leylines etc.
2   Roman administration was 'national' and hence no tribal-unit-plus-High-King type of organisation was necessary for law and order purposes
3   Roman roads seemed to have been free and hence no elaborate tolling system was required
4   International trade was now overland via Gaul and the south-east ports rather than maritime via the Atlantic and the western ports.

But this is all very technical. It does not explain why, according to Caesar, the chief reason he invaded Britain was because he was concerned that independent British Druids would encourage Gaulish Druids to undermine his own recent conquests. Apparently the danger continued long after Caesar's time, despite Gaul being thoroughly pacified, because Claudius decided that Britain required complete occupation. Extirpating British Druidry seems still to have been quite high on the Roman list of things to do when in Britain which is odd because the general pattern of Roman occupation policy in newly conquered territory was to work *with* the local grain, and the Druids had always operated *with* the local temporal power. Surely an accommodation was possible? After all, both archaeology and the literary sources agree that the British religious apparatus was able to reconstitute itself under Roman auspices, in the standard fashion of virtually every country the Romans conquered.[1] But no, the Druids were forced to retreat

---

1   The other notable exception being Judea. The fact that Vespasian was used to put down both Jewish and British rebels has given rise to various conspiracy theories, going back to the (at the time) very influential British Israelite Movement.

to Anglesey where they were thoroughly beaten and never heard from again. Under that name.

To understand what is really happening it is necessary to re-evaluate events without the blinkers of a Classical education. It is taken as axiomatic that the Romans did things 'the normal way' in terms of empire-building but actually the Roman way was rather revolutionary in contemporary Mediterranean terms. For example, the accounts that have come down to us portray the struggle between Rome and Carthage as apparently a straight-forward political battle between rival empires and yet, for some reason, although Rome keeps beating Carthage, keeps sowing salt in the ruins to make sure it never rises again, Carthage always does! It is still there, hugely significant, in the fifth century AD of St Augustine's time when Rome itself is but a provincial capital. What is really in question here is which of two very different economic models is superior: the Roman method of physical occupation with mostly land trade between cities, or the Phoenician method of indirect political influence gained by mostly maritime trade between trading partners. The first way is undoubtedly superior so long as the 'occupying power' has the requisite muscle but history is eloquent, right down to our own day, that this method is constantly at the mercy of fissiparous forces at home and exponentially increasing resistance from abroad.

With this in mind let us revisit the Roman accounts of the Battle of Britain. Why for instance did the 'last great battle' occur in Anglesey? The impression given by the Roman version is that Anglesey was Druid GHQ and Paulinus was just doing a Scipio Africanus on the last redoubt of the enemy. But given that the Druids had been operating a sea-borne trading empire covering the Western Approaches of the British Isles for the preceding centuries (if not millennia) it makes a lot better sense to regard Anglesey as simply a stage in a fighting retreat, and that the Druids were in the process of withdrawing to Ireland in just the way that they had already retreated from Gaul to Britain. Since the Romans never invaded Ireland it can be taken as read that Druidic influence continued in Ireland throughout the Roman period. Nothing changed in the internal trading and governing arrangements within Ireland and the Romans themselves took little interest in international trade around the outer swathe of the British Isles and Scandinavia. On the other hand the importance of Roman Chester would seem to be evidence that trade *between* Britain and Ireland continued to be significant, so Ireland was definitely still on the international map. Irish history, insofar as it is possible to reconstitute it during this period, seems to be that Ireland was governed in the traditional Megalithic way of tribal units of roughly equal area[1] with a High King in Tara claiming a vague suzerainty.

To understand modern European history it is necessary to appreciate that there is always a world just beyond the *historical* one. By definition, history consists of the internal events of literate states and what is happening in 'barbarian-land' is essentially irrelevant except insofar as these 'others' trade with or invade or prevent the expansion of the 'civilised' area. Of course we know intuitively that this cannot be the case because the people on the other side of the border are the same as those on this side but *sans literacy*, literally uncivilised, without cities. So whenever the 'civilised' bit goes awry, these others step in to fill the vacuum. With highly alarming results, say the historical sources (rather naturally). But from a wider perspective this is no bad thing. We tend to favour civilisation over barbarity because we are ourselves civilised but actually we really mean 'we are developed' rather than 'we are civilised' and we equate development exclusively with civilisation. This is by no means an automatic association. Development does occur in civilised conditions but stasis is the more usual condition of civilisation since large, civilised states rapidly come to the realisation that threats to their longevity come rather from within than without. The Roman Empire itself is an excellent example of this since, despite being the last word in modernity, it actually became the last word in modernity for several hundreds of years. As we

---

1   It has been argued that the four provinces of Ireland—Ulster, Munster, Leinster and Connaught—are 'Megalithically-shaped'.

shall see, it was the areas just beyond the Empire that provided the sparks that led to the modern world, first from Ireland and then from Scandinavia. So while reading the account that follows, always bear in mind that while the Romans are busy organising Britain, the Megalithics are busy organising Ireland; and while the 'Roman' Church is busy Christianising Dark Age Europe, the Megalithics are evangelising Scandinavia.

In Britain the Roman period lasted for four hundred years so it can be reasonably inferred that the Megalithic System proper was more or less finished. In place of hermits there were mileposts, in place of drovers' routes there were Roman roads, in place of Druids there was a Roman (or co-opted Romano-British) bureaucracy. Of course the old system must have survived to some extent cheek-by-jowl since there is the same requirement for droving as before and it is more than likely that droving tracks were used whether or not a Roman road duplicated the route, but the larger point is that the drovers' *political* significance was eliminated. The Roman villa system was geared to the commercial production of food, for sale to the Roman cities or for export to other parts of the Empire, and this presumably included meat as well as corn. The advantages of moving meat on the hoof is just as applicable to the Romans as it is to anyone else who lives before refrigerated transport but whether the Romans allowed their precious roads to be used for this purpose is not known. It may be that the droving routes continued to operate but if so Roman unitary power would have ensured their upkeep without any need of Megalithic toll-and-control operations.

Even so, there is more to political power than national supremacy. A degree of native British counter-culture must have continued underneath the Roman veneer because of the nature of Roman rule everywhere, even in Italy. Roman civilisation was based on the cities and, in that miniature duplication of city life, the villa. It did not extend very far into the countryside which is where the 'pagans' (*paganus,* country-dweller) lived. Orthodox history, because it is overwhelmingly based on Roman sources, gives the impression that the local population lived on the villa estates but this is quite wrong. The kind of 'senatorial latifundia' based on slave labour was not a widespread model, any more than *coloniae* of veterans were. The British were living where they had always lived, in the villages that are still there now and which were for the most part founded in the late Neolithic when agriculture was first established in Britain. The Roman *villae* were little different from that which came after under the Anglo-Saxons, the Normans and the English gentry simply because it is the only practical means of control anywhere before the hyper-modern era. The only way to pay for the upkeep of collective needs is for everybody to contribute between a third and a half of their income to the government and that government is normally living in the Big House that dominates the village. It has to be that way in all eras before the wholly cash economy because the third-to-a-half contribution has to be made mostly in perishable goods or locally supervised obligatory labour. These 'taxes' are also largely expended locally but a proportion gets passed on to defray regional and national (or in Roman times, supra-national) requirements, but that is of limited concern to the country folk who take roughly the same interest in whoever is contemporaneously forming the national regime as that regime takes an interest in them (so long as they contribute their share of communal tasks with a minimum of fuss). *Today* we still work between a third and a half of the time for the government, that is we pay taxes in that proportion, just as peasants worked two or three days on manorial estates during feudal times and doubtless Romano-British peasants worked two or three days on or for Roman villa estates. One difference though is that today we identify with the state, and in turn the state enters all our lives to a remarkable extent. But this is a very modern phenomenon, it is unlikely that Roman Britain entered very deeply into the skein of the countryside.

What happened when the Romans were obliged to leave? The archaeology is decisive in showing that the superstructure collapsed rather promptly. This is surprising since, although the legions and perhaps the top brass were called home, it might be supposed that several centuries of settled administration under the blessings of civilisation might have put down stronger roots. But, as things turned out, the Roman Empire was a carefully crafted machine that could not survive the removal of any of its component parts, either in Britain or in Western Europe generally. The cities were soon bereft, the villa economy in ruins, the roads no longer maintained. Government returned to the pre-literate (or at any rate pre-bureaucratic) world of 'tribal units', the old order of statelets fifty to a hundred miles across, what one man carrying one message can convey, the whole being held together very loosely by some kind of High King. This at any rate is the world described by the dubious effusions of Gildas and the Arthurian industry.

The entire country was ostensibly Christian. Apart from unofficial Christian evangelising during the period 50 – 300 AD, Britain became technically Christian along with the rest of the Empire under Constantine in the fourth century.[1] How much this new religion permeated the countryside is as doubtful as the effects of Roman rule itself, it being impossible to judge how much Christianity was seen as a foreign, Roman ideology. What can be said with greater confidence is that Christianity had sufficient power—it was after all the monopoly provider of literacy—to be used eventually by all the *post*-Roman regimes. What is at first sight baffling though is why, in the former heartlands of Megalithia in the British Isles and northern Gaul, these 'native' Christians should so rapidly and so radically adopt a 'Megalithic' version of Christianity. Today we take for granted that this 'Celtic' Christianity might be at variance with the Catholic version belatedly arriving with St Augustine two hundred years later but it is seldom wondered just why Britain, Ireland and northern Gaul should feature a Christianity of such extreme deviance to the mainstream. How can it possibly be, even if it is granted that these outposts might be naturally heterodox, that these 'Christians' would adopt practices so uncannily redolent of a

---

1 Constantine actually launched his imperial career from Britain.

system that had apparently passed away so many centuries before? Even if we accept that early Christians were using sound business sense when siting their places of worship on previously sanctified ground, it is decidedly odd that those responsible for selecting a saint's name (from hundreds of 'orthodox' ones available) should so often choose to commemorate ones with, say, dragon associations. And it is all very well siting a new church on the foundations of an old temple but not, surely, if the site is so far out of the way that its only obvious function is as a navigational marker rather than a convenient place of worship.

The simplest way of resolving these anomalies is to assume that a Megalithic structure of some kind survived beneath (or beyond) the Roman one and that Megalithia re-emerged once the Romans had left and taken with them their ability to organise a functioning bureaucracy. Dark Age Britain was very close to *pre*-Roman Britain both in the demand for and in the supplying of long distance trading routes so it makes sense to assume that Megalithia was responsible both before and after Rome for servicing these networks. Nor is it surprising that the Roman system itself would seek eventually to make a come-back, suitably recast for the new conditions. The conflict between Megalithia and Catholicism, between the Phoenician Model and the Roman Model, would now take on a new form and, fortunately, since both sides had access to a literacy of sorts, the early days of this epic conflict can just about be followed from literary Dark Age sources.

While the *bishops*, the city-based successors of the Roman Empire, were busy taking over the reins of power in concert with various unlettered barbarians in the south of Europe, there were stirrings from a much more traditional source in the north. It can be assumed from the physical Megalithic evidence still surviving that Ireland had always been firmly part of the original Megalithic Empire and, given that the Romans had made no attempt to interfere with the island, it can be reasonably supposed that Ireland was still Megalithic in *c* 400 AD when formal Roman rule over neighbouring Britain ended. More than this, since the Romans were known not to favour maritime trade in the north, that trade was almost certainly in the hands of the Megalithics including routes via Scotland, into the North Sea and beyond.[1] Ireland was at this time ruled quite normally for pre-literate times by tribal states under a High King so we can infer that these routes were subject to Druidic control, as was the maintenance of internal but inter-state trade within Ireland. Of course Ireland was small beer compared to the pre-Roman Megalithic Empire but in the conditions prevailing *after* the Romans had left, Irish Megalithia must have been at least a medium-sized fish in the small pool of international traders.

With Rome gone from the whole of the British Isles and western Gaul, a great vacuum loomed in territories that the Megalithics knew well so naturally things started moving with some speed. The first event of note in the post-Roman era was that literacy suddenly arrived in Ireland. In orthodox terms, this is baffling. For several centuries, between 50 AD and 450 AD, a literate Latin culture had been flourishing next door in Britain but had had no effect on Ireland and yet the very moment this literate Latin culture departed, Ireland adopted literacy! Or to put this sequence in the correct Megalithic perspective:

1   the Megalithics had a long record of keeping literacy out
    to make sure their own memory-system was the sole way
    of controlling intra-tribal society, so Ireland was kept
    non-literate right up to *c* 400 AD but
2   with the Romans gone it was safe to introduce literacy
    under strict Megalithic control until
3   the Romans (aka the Catholic Church) finally re-imposed
    control whereupon
4   the Megalithics broke the Latin literary monopoly by
    inventing the world's first *alphabetic demotic*, written
    Irish, the first easy-to-learn alphabetised version of a
    language ordinary people actually spoke.

---

1 Not to mention westwards if St Brendan's voyages are to be believed.

Unsurprisingly, the long-delayed but radical marriage between Megalithia and literacy resulted in some revolutionary progeny, the first of which was the *scriptorium-monastery*, an institution designed for a very particular set of circumstances where the civilised state has collapsed but the civilised arts are still available. It was designed to control the whole of literate society: educating chosen youths, employing the scribes, writing and reproducing manuscripts, stocking the libraries, providing the state with a rudimentary bureaucracy. Such a useful innovation was swiftly taken up by the Catholics since they were faced with a very similar set of local circumstances but there was an obvious snag for both sides: literacy is a wondrously dynamic tool and left to its own devices would soon burst out of the control of the monasteries and of the people controlling the monasteries. So both the Catholic Church and the Megalithics came to an understanding with their respective temporal 'overlords': they would retain control over all aspects of literacy in exchange for assistance with state-building, and hence the barbaric tribal units operated by the Anglo-Saxons, the Franks, the Visigoths et al. were able to begin building larger-scale political units with the help of monkish bureaucracies. This is the true explanation for the 'Dark Ages' which orthodoxy insists on regarding as a perfectly normal five hundred year gap when everybody forgot the civilised arts and was incapable of reviving them. It is the sheerest nonsense to suppose that a complete swathe of the world can spend several centuries *with* civilisation and then another several centuries *without* it unless this entire swathe of the world is being *prevented* from becoming entirely normal. The proof of this particular pudding is what happened *after* these regimes were overthrown, *c* 1000 AD, and Western Europe was at last permitted to resume its normal development.

The Dark Ages were essentially a conflict between two highly restrictive regimes, the Catholic bishops in the south and the Irish-based Megalithic 'saints' in the north. The Catholic bishops were completing their control over Italy, southern France and northern Spain and re-establishing the old Roman land routes while the

Irish 'missionaries' were re-occupying all the old Megalithic haunts in Britain and Gaul and re-establishing the Atlantic trade routes including north-about Scotland. The eventual resolution of the conflict between the two forces has always been recorded as a decisive victory for the forces of Catholicism, ending with the Synod of Whitby, but this is entirely to misunderstand the difference between the Megalithic and the Catholic agendas. The Megalithics had always eschewed temporal power. Not, it should be hastily pointed out, because of any Cincinnatian modesty on their part but because they had acquired several thousand years' experience of how to operate effectively and indefinitely in any given contemporaneous military-political sphere. Essentially this meant following what one might say is the maxim "Never raise your head above the parapet without making sure you are the only people around who know how to build and maintain parapets." The Catholics, as heirs of Rome, knew no other way than the direct exercise of temporal power even though ostensibly they had to share it with their barbarian political 'masters'. In the best Hegelian manner, each side was preparing the way for the other. The Catholics were ensuring that the barbarian political governments would be ripe for some Megalithic-style policy innovations when the 'monastery-scriptorium' system had reached its full flowering, while the Megalithics were converting the locals to Christianity and it was but a small step, since the Megalithics cared nothing for Christian ideology, for the locals to switch from the Megalithics' date-for-Easter, how to tonsure one's hair and suchlike fripperies to the Catholic version—and to accept Catholic bishops to enforce the notional changes.

All this was no more than shadow boxing because when the adherents of the two related-but-different religious outfits *did* care about ideology, meaningless changes would be resisted *sine die* and if necessary to the stake. It is all a matter of what constitutes political control, for instance in the disputes with the Arians or Greek Orthodoxy or the various manifestations of what eventually was called Protestantism, the Catholics understood that heresy-hunting is at the beating heart of temporal power (as did their opponents in each case). The Megalithics held to a very different recipe for influential longevity: ignore temporal control but retain the commanding heights of whatever was the *intellectual* fulcrum of contemporary society. Hence at the Synod of Whitby and at all the other local interfaces between northern Celtic Christians and southern Catholic ones, the Megalithic strategy was always the same: complete surrender of temporal matters to the territorial control of the bishops except, oh by the way, would it be possible for the monasteries to be kept separate under their own regime of abbots since the monastic orders operate in more than one bishopric? And look, since the bishops will have their hands full running the existing set-up, why don't we take missionary work off your hands as well and go over and convert Scandinavia, Prussia and the rest, and then these new territories can be handed over to bishop-rule as soon as local conditions make that possible?

The Catholics were naturally quick to accept this arrangement, unconditional surrender as they saw it, while the Megalithics for their part were confident that temporal power is always limited, in scope and in time, so long as the intellectual firmament is kept bubbling—something that had never happened under the Roman Empire but that they were confident they could engineer under the much less formidable *Holy* Roman Empire. The confidence of both sides seemed entirely justified as each extended its particular speciality throughout the territory of the other, hence monastery-scriptoria were soon sprouting all over southern Europe while the British Isles rapidly acquired the formal trappings of bishoprics. Armed now with a functioning bureaucracy the Anglo-Saxon statelets in Britain were able to cohere more and more into country-wide states (as did Frankish Gaul) while in the Christian south (Spain had become Moslem) the rise of the new-style monastery chains proved unstoppable. But now another very peculiar thing happened, if the orthodox interpretation of history is to be relied on: just as these new Catholic model states were reaching their apogee of power in Charlemagne's Empire and Anglo-Saxon

England the entire map of Christendom was put in jeopardy by tiny bands of Vikings who were able to place the whole of this new, civilised, unified Europe in desperate peril.

Historians regard this very remarkable development as 'just one of those things' but the explanation is readily to hand in that the Megalithics had transferred their power base to Scandinavia, an area of the world, like Ireland before it, where 'Rome' (in either the old form or the new) never quite reached. In other words the Megalithics were able to hold untrammelled sway. As soon as the Catholic Bishops—the enemy, as the Megalithics saw things—had very conveniently brought Western Europe into a manageable but not very coherent whole, some mysteriously talented Vikings pitched up in Normandy, right at the strategic join between the former Megalithic and Catholic areas. The Normans were not at all shy about advertising their Megalithic sympathies. For instance, when invading England they waited until the feast of *Michaelmas*[1] before sailing for Hastings, which has *St Michael* as its patron saint (there used to be a St Michael church at *White Rock* close to the pier east of *Maze Hill*) and even today *All Saints* Church organises an annual *Blessing of the Sea* ceremony each *Rogationtide*. The 'Norman Conquest'[2] is suffused with Megalithic lore. So the story of Harold being blinded in his left eye has echoes of Odin who sacrificed his left eye in return for wisdom; the Megalithically named Edith Swan-neck, Harold's concubine, was supposed to have identified his body on the battlefield, although a long-held belief claimed Harold later became a hermit and was buried in Waltham Abbey, on the prime meridian. But whatever the mechanisms of the takeover, now that the Megalithic heartland of England and northern Gaul was in safe hands, the Normans

---

1 Italicised words have Megalithic significance as will become clear in the next two chapters.
2 It is not difficult for revisionist historians to doubt the most important event in English history, the Battle of Hastings, since no physical evidence has ever been found despite the precise site being contemporaneously 'recorded' by the building of Battle Abbey. All the written (and indeed embroidered) sources attesting to the battle ever having taken place were in secure Norman hands.

promptly set about reconstituting the Megalithic territories and sea routes in Scotland, Ireland, Sicily, Greece and Tyrian Palestine. Fancy that.

It goes without saying that while enjoying a monopoly of power, the literate classes of both sides made sure that the language used in writing (in this case Latin) was not the same as the one everybody spoke on a daily basis. This simple device ensured anybody who wanted to become literate had first to learn a foreign language but just to make sure that nobody would bother unless they had a professional need to do so, the entire corpus of literature consisted of the most tedious of reading matter in the form of unbelievable saints' lives, textural commentaries and purely bureaucratic material. But, when it was time to break with the Catholic bishops, the Megalithics were not satisfied with introducing the notion of learning to read in one's own language, they made sure there was something worth reading by launching the Troubadour Movement, the Grail Cycle and modern literature generally. The Megalithics' invention of written demotics and literature started naturally enough with Irish but, as Megalithic methods and influence gradually spread, the new dispensation appeared in northern France (*langue d'oïl* French), southern France (Occitan) and thereafter suffused through Europe. It is to get way ahead of ourselves but once language-speakers had their own literature the way was at last open to the emergence of the nation-state and an end to the cumbersome need for alternating periods of secure empires with no developmental potential with periods of city-states that had lots of developmental potential but no security. Competing nation-states squared this circle and have taken care of the rest of history.

But meanwhile back in the eleventh century, something had to be done to get the economy going. It was all very well refounding the old trade routes but there had to be something to trade. So the next extraordinary set of characters to pop up on cue were the Cistercians who started expanding through the mainly rural parts of Western Europe bringing their revolutionary brand of those old Megalithic specialities—hydraulic engineering, wool and pack trains—to create vast new agricultural estates and the economic development that went with them. Nor were the cities ignored because at the same time the Knights Templar started spreading through Western Europe introducing mercantile principles, banking and long distance sea-trading. Finally came the introduction of universities to take over from the monasteries in supplying state functionaries and especially those very curious creatures, canon lawyers.

Is this all conspiracy theory? Yes, but the problem is that 'conspiracy theories' have attained such pejorative status in these days of wholesale disclosure that they are equated with 'untrue, never happened, products of disordered minds'. This may be a reasonable stance regarding modern conspiracy theories but is not necessarily so when literacy is a monopoly of the governing interest. Such a situation always results in a dearth of written material anyway so from our modern vantage point things might look esoteric when in truth they are merely unrecorded. One of the great differences between written-systems and memory-systems is that the latter has always to be face-to-face, or as we would say in our internet age, one-to-one rather than one-to-many. The difference between the two systems is sociological, even logical. This is nicely illustrated by looking at that great constituent of both the twelfth century renaissance and modern conspiracy theories, the Gothic Cathedral. Something that appears to have eluded their admirers is that the Gothic Cathedrals were a complete dead end. They flourished, they were impressive, they led to nothing. The architectural and constructional techniques that were developed to build them were never used for anything else beyond perhaps somewhat higher castle walls and slightly loftier palace dining rooms. The next time anybody had a practical use for such large interior spaces were the railway termini of the nineteenth century and they owed nothing to lessons learned in the Middle Ages. So what were the Gothic cathedrals for? It is normal to say that they were for reducing the ordinary folk to religious awe but this was simply not required since the Church held an easy monopoly, and in any case most ordinary folk would never get to see a Gothic cathedral even once in their lives.

It can be said with some confidence that these cathedrals were not the product of orthodox 'Catholicism'. There seems to have been no impetus from Rome or the hierarchy in general to build them. On the contrary they seem to be the product of a combination of particularly messianic bishops and local moneyed interests. It cannot be said with any certainty that these 'local forces' were Megalithic but it is certainly true, because the evidence is set in stone, that the cathedrals were platforms for 'Megalithic art'. How else can one describe the riot of Green Men, gargoyles, grotesques and anti-Christian characters of every description that stare down at the faithful from all sides? We are asked to believe, once again, that these are set there as warnings for the unlettered laity. Ooh, scary. And then there is the mathematical formulations built into the various internal fittings and overall dimensions of the cathedrals. Since these are truly esoteric, revealed only via quite sophisticated later analysis, nobody could argue they were for the benefit of either parishioners or clergy. Yet they would seem to be the whole point.

If one had to guess, it seems that the cathedrals are the product of a tacit agreement: "We'll build you truly stunning buildings, the like of which have never been seen on earth before, to the glory of God, but you must accept our control over ... well, that's our business." This truly is a Megalithic-style agreement between the temporal power and a group of people who were, if not opposed to the temporal power, certainly not its creatures either. The Gothic cathedrals have certainly proved every bit as immortal as the stone monuments of Ancient Megalithia. But what purpose did the Gothic cathedrals serve for the Megalithics? Aside from demonstrating that 'Big Stone' was back in fashion, one way of looking at the cathedrals was as a means of concentrating—if not creating—armies of that other staple of conspiracy theories, masons. But this can be put rather less conspiratorially by asking exactly how, in an age when even highly skilled workers were often illiterate, is it possible to concentrate these highly sought after operatives in the kind of numbers required when constructing Gothic cathedrals? And at the individual level how can technical qualifications be conveyed other than by possession of written documents? The answer is that a particularly Megalithic-style 'organisation' could do both jobs nicely. Pubs! All that is needed is a network of pubs 'in the Megalithic know' that can reveal their function to their potential patrons by a sign that indicates a Megalithic/Masonic/Templar theme: The Turk's Head, The Seven Sisters, The Green Man, The Trip to Jerusalem.

When formal written qualifications are unavailable, anyone can turn up and claim they know how to carve a pillar but if anyone who has been specifically trained to carve a pillar has also been taught the legend of Boaz and Joachim, then the reciting of the legend is sufficient proof of qualification. In fact, knowledge of the legend is a *better* credential than actually carving a pillar because just doing a bit of pillar-carving is something that anybody can pick up in a few weeks but knowledge of the legend is eloquent testimony that a qualified expert thought the applicant was now a qualified expert. So much for *operative masons* but since all trades are going to have to be catered for, there needs to be another group who know all the legends rather than all the techniques because there is no guarantee what trade is going to be in local demand, nor what particular specialist is going to show up. Hence the rise of what are now called *speculative masons*, people who are expert in the lore but have probably never picked up a hammer in anger. Likely they owned the pub. So you turn up at The Saracen's Arms with a simple handshake and a pregnant phrase and you are swiftly on your way to help out with the local flying buttresses.

But why esoteric? Why in the twelfth century is there any need for secrecy? This is the aspect that always leads conspiracy theorists astray: the secrecy is not to keep the orthodox ruling elite from interfering (they are paying for most of it) but to keep the lower orders out. The contemporaneous guild movement used the exact same techniques; they too were in the local protection racket keeping their own prices high by keeping the less qualified from competing.[1] The guilds were equally reliant on personal contact, gesture and ritual rather than the written word. It is secret, yes, but only for functional reasons because in a sub-literate economy everything has to be done by word of mouth, by handshake, by pub sign, by tacit understanding, and for that secrecy becomes not an end in itself (however enjoyable) but because it enjoins a certain confidence in the person who is 'in on the secret'. None of this enters the historical record and so long as historians decline to get involved, the subsequent gaps in our knowledge will continue to be filled by fantasists, conspiracists and novelists. However, just to keep the tradition going, it is noticeable in the Rise of British Capitalism to world domination how often families prominent in brewing turn out to be the new captains of industry. The English even have a term for it, *the beerage*. But do even *they* know?

---

1 Perhaps the chief difference between city guilds and Knights Templar is that fishmongers are not the stuff of best-sellers.

FIVE

The Megalithic Saints

The six centuries between 410 AD and the Norman Conquest are called the Dark Ages due to the paucity of historical evidence which means tracing the Megalithic story after the Romans becomes largely a matter of piecing together the *circumstantial* evidence. It is not surprising that Megalithic methods were used in the Dark Ages because it was a system specifically designed for a non-literate world, the question is whether it was the Megalithics themselves that returned or whether it was only their techniques that were being re-invented and re-applied. As things turned out, not only was it for the most part the Megalithics who were taking charge but, fortunately, they forsook their previous aversion to literacy to leave posterity just enough 'history' to follow their operations.

What is surprising is how openly the Megalithics signalled their esoteric presence in the officially Christian Dark and Middle Ages, and even more surprising is the degree of complacency with which the Christians regarded these blatantly pagan efflorescences. It suggests an uneasy co-existence. Since virtually all the surviving written accounts of this period are by or about 'saints' these somewhat neglected hagiographies and legendary accounts have to be treated as key to understanding the period, though not always necessarily in the way that conventional history does. The other and equally overlooked source is the particular saint's name attached to a particular church in a particular place. This is definitely not a matter of happenstance.

The easiest way of telling Megalithic Christians apart from Catholic ones is by the saints they chose to honour. The orthodox canon is familiar enough, headed by Jesus, the Virgin Mary, the twelve Disciples and St Paul. The Megalithics chose an *anti*-canon. For instance John the Baptist is a Megalithic figure because he is a sometime rival of Jesus;[1] Mary Magdalen is the Megalithic equivalent of—reputedly the moral opposite of—the Virgin Mary; Martha is Megalithic because she is supposedly the Magdalen's sister; John the Apostle is Megalithic because he is a 'Son of Thunder' along with his twin brother James [Jesus gave John and James "the name of Boanerges, which means the Sons of Thunder" (Mark 3,17)] and hence the pair take on the mantle of Castor and Pollux (the sons of Zeus, the god of thunder) who are critical figures in the pagan pantheon with important functions in navigation. Both sides supplemented their stock characters with various lesser figures so, for instance, the Christians favoured martyrs, popes, kings who promoted the cause and worthies of various kinds, but the Megalithics chose people with very specific associations—dragons, angels, travel, rocks, metallurgy—as well as creating their own special *local* saints, usually scions of Irish, Welsh or Breton royal houses, but who included the familiar cast of 'missionaries' from the Western British Isles who were ostensibly spreading Christianity to other parts of Europe. They were doing no such thing of course.

In Britain it is generally possible to decide whether a saint is Megalithic or Catholic by considering the situation of any given sacred place and its relationship to its saint's name. Churches dedicated to St Michael, the most popular of the Megalithic saints, are often associated with prominences (Mont Saint Michel, St Michael's Mount, etc.) visible from the coast, in other words they are strategic landmarks. So, a cone-shaped hill like Brentor in Devon, with its St Michael's Church on the summit, can be recognised as Megalithic rather than Catholic by using a catechism such as:

---

1   In calendrical terms they are complementary opposites, being born respectively a few days after the winter and summer solstices.

Q: Would Christians build a church on the top of an isolated crag on Dartmoor?

A: Probably not but Christians were wont to build on formerly sacred sites so it cannot be ruled out.

Q: Would Megalithics build a 'church' on the top of an isolated crag on Dartmoor?

A: Yes, crags make excellent sighting posts and Brentor is on a major Megalithic route.

Q: Would Christians name the church after St Michael?

A: Probably not since Michael is fairly obscure (four brief mentions in the Bible) but it cannot be ruled out.

Q: Would Megalithics name their 'church' after St Michael?

A: Yes, almost all the churches at the western end of this Megalithic route are named for him. Michael has twin Megalithic associations, he is both a dragon-slayer and the head of the angels.

It is not possible to identify for certain whether any particular religious building (not just churches but chapels, oratories, hermitages, monasteries etc.) is either Megalithic or Catholic but, given the unusual number of those with specifically Megalithic names that are in specifically Megalithic places, there can only be one of two possibilities:

1 The Christians of the fifth, sixth and subsequent centuries had an odd habit of siting many of their buildings in places of considerable inaccessibility and then choosing names closely associated with a culture that had ceased to operate at least five hundred years before and which was wholly at odds with the fundamentals of the Christian faith or

2 A non-Christian organisation was building and naming these churches, chapels, hermitages etc.

Michael is a good starting point for investigating British saints because his name appears, as per the Michael Line, in a series of places at the western end of a line that constitutes the longest land route across Britain and they are peculiarly distinctive landmarks:

St Michael's Mount
St Michael's, Carn Brea
St Michael's, Roche Rock
St Michael's, Brentor
St Michael and All Angels, Angersleigh
St Michael's, Creech St Michael
St Michael's, Burrowbridge Mump
St Michael's, Othery
St Michael's Tor, Glastonbury
Stoke St Michael, Tower Hill

But why 'Michael'? Michael is the *angelos*, meaning messenger in Greek. Their messenger god was Hermes, known as Thoth to the Egyptians, Mercury to the Romans, and Michael in his Christian guise. The identification is clear enough in Catholic iconography where St Michael is shown carrying scales because he is undertaking Thoth's task of weighing souls against the feather of Ma'at. Michael also has Hermes' task of conducting the souls of the dead (to Heaven rather than the Underworld) and had swans' feathers for his wings. Hermes invented letters from the 'flight of cranes' and Thoth, the Egyptian inventor of the alphabet, was an ibis-headed god, ibises and cranes being interchangeable. In Britain, where neither cranes nor ibises abound, the swan is Hermes' symbol and in Celtic mythology swans feature as the escort to the Otherworld. Writing, a speciality of Celtic monks, was done with goose or swan quills; a master poet such as Virgil or Shakespeare could be likened to a swan, a simile that is surely not fortuitous since Hermes is celebrated for eloquence. The link between swans and Hermes, the god of roads, is why so many strategically-sited pubs are called The Swan (or, for that matter, The Angel), for instance the Swan Hotel by the Goring-Streatley Bridge is where the Michael Line crosses the Thames. The monks, taking over from the bards' recitals of noble ancestry, were responsible for written genealogies or 'pedigrees', i.e. *pied de grue*, crane's foot, which physically resembles a family tree. The concept of the pedigree is at the heart of domestic animal breeding, the original Megalithic claim to fame.

It is not even possible to say whether Michael was a Christian figure at all. Michael is a Hebrew name meaning 'Who is like God?' but he seems to have originally been a deity of the Chaldeans who feature significantly in the Megalithic story. Michael's Christian status derives from the Book of Revelation ("*And there was war in heaven: Michael and his angels fought against the dragon*") but who wrote the Book of Revelation and who decided it would be included in the final Biblical canon are all topics of controversy. If the authors of The Revelation were Gnostic, which is proposed even by some orthodox Biblical scholars, and Gnostics were latter day Megalithics, which is not proposed by any orthodox scholar, then a Megalithic saint gets intruded painlessly into the 'Catholic' Bible.

Michael is the chief dragon-slaying saint. Dragons are as mysterious as they are ubiquitous in Megalithia. Their origin would seem to stem from a problem faced by early navigators: they did not have a Pole Star! We take it for granted today because we have Polaris which is not only a very bright star but is readily identified by following the line of bright stars that make up the very recognisable Plough. Since the earth wobbles the star that happens to sit over the top of our North Pole changes over time and several thousand years ago the 'Pole Star' was just a patch of empty space dotted with faint stars. Nor was this empty space easily identifiable by following a path of nearby bright stars so the Ancients came up with an *aide mémoire* in the form of a sinuous animal that allowed them to trace the requisite path across the heavens. The animal they chose varied, the Ancient Egyptians for instance thought a crocodile appropriate, but the Megalithics opted for a worm or a snake or ... a dragon, which seems to be a grander version of these (in Britain) rather ordinary animals.

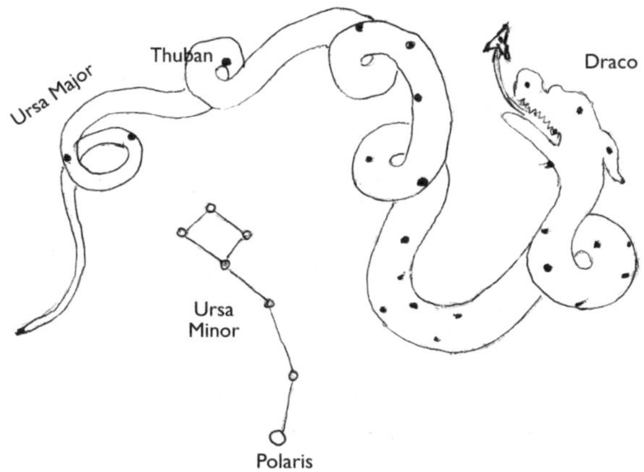

In any event the Megalithics' pole star (or rather 'pole constellation') was named Draconis, the Dragon, and dragon 'beacon' hills crop up frequently on ancient routes. But for reasons which really do appear unfathomable, this purely navigational aid started to be applied to other Megalithic interests and soon dragon, worm and orm (all essentially the same term) are turning up in mining contexts[1] and dragons seem also to be deeply involved with smelting processes, presumably accounting for their fiery attributes. The names of smiths in mythology are typically fiery, cf. Hephaestus 'the shining one', Vulcan i.e. volcano, and St Brigit, the patron saint of blacksmiths, whose name is a synonym of 'bright'. These themes are often combined in saints' legends: the fifth-century Welsh St Cynog defended the locals against 'ormests', giants ravaging the countryside, at the cost of losing a large piece of flesh from his thigh (an inescapable fate of heroes). He then died fighting over access to the 'miracle spring' that he owned, mineral water playing a key role in ancient metallurgy as part of the metal hardening process. *Cyn* in Welsh means chisel or wedge, an essential tool in mining, and this formidable hermit appears

---

1 The Great Orme at Llandudno is claimed to be the ancient world's largest copper mine.

to have been a servant of the moon goddess Artemis, Cynthia being one of her names. Moon goddesses play a central role in this not-very-Christian Christian milieu.

St George is another prominent 'dragon-slayer', apparently a later and more acceptably Christian version of Michael. George, meaning 'earth-worker', is etymologically linked to gore—dirt, dried blood, the gouging horn-tip of a bull[1]—which places him as a metallurgical saint, but his name is also cognate with *gorge*, a narrow valley, mirroring Michael's long distance travel associations. For instance, the Goring Gap marks the halfway point between Avebury and Ivinghoe Beacon on the Ridgeway (aka the Michael Line) where Ogbourne St George, the only village actually on the Ridgeway, acts as a waymarker. The *Via Iceniana* in Dorchester crosses the River Frome at Fordington, overlooked by a St George's church on a beacon hill. Nowadays St George's name is more likely to be associated with pubs. A coaching inn called The George might just be commemorating the monarch but a 'George and Dragon' is always of megalithic interest. The patron saint of innkeepers is St Goar of Aquitaine, a sixth century monk famous for his hospitality, after whom St Goar, a town in the Rhine gorge at the river's narrowest point, is named. He is represented as a hermit being given milk by a hind, alternatively as a hermit with the devil at his feet, or most curiously of all with a devil on his shoulder, reminiscent of Odin and his ravens, not to mention pirates, that is pilots, with parrots on *their* shoulders. Medieval travellers' tales claimed that parrots "of their own nature speak and call out to men who are crossing the desert, speaking as clearly as if they were men."

St Margaret is a female 'dragon saint'. She was swallowed by a dragon but the cross she was holding irritated its throat (its gorge!), since it was really the Devil, and she was safely vomited out none the worse for the experience. Her name appears at the very end of the Michael Line where it reaches the Norfolk coast at Ormesby St Margaret, opposite Ormesby St Michael (*orm* also

---

1 Bulls' horns as well as deer antlers were used as mining picks.

meaning dragon). This habit of twinning as 'gate-keepers' is characteristic of Megalithia,[1] and Michael and Margaret are themselves paired as guardians of church doors. Similar pairs of villages with different saints' names oversee important routes, for instance Barford St John and Barford St Michael at the river Swere. As a virgin-saint and patron saint of childbirth, it can be assumed that Margaret was originally a moon goddess, whose key attributes are always chastity and childbirth. The recurring association of Megalithic saints and childbirth points to the once elevated status of midwives and there is little doubt that the Megalithics' attitude to women was rather different from the pronounced misogyny of the Roman Empire and the Pauline Church. Margaret also acts as a navigational 'menhir-saint': St Margaret's at Cliffe, between Deal and Dover, at the narrowest part of the Channel, is situated high on the cliff top. As the parish council website remarks "*it has always been a puzzle to understand why such a small village should have such a large church ...*". According to popular lore, the cliff above St Margaret's Bay is where the sun first reaches Britain every morning.

In British churches St Margaret was often twinned with St Catherine, another 'moon goddess' saint, the two being perhaps the most popular saints of the High Middle Ages. Both of them are pictured with books which is highly unusual for either sex in Christian iconography and seems to reflect the new (or as may be, old) and more enlightened view of women's role in society. The neo-Megalithic Normans who appear to have introduced the Catherine cult into Britain were similarly unusual in having no qualms about leaving their women in charge. Equally relaxed about gender were the Cathars, the Normans' contemporaries in southern France, who take their name from *katharos* meaning 'pure' in Greek, which is the same root as *cathedral*, the late medieval flowering of the menhir. Another derivation is the

---

1　The same pattern occurs on drovers' routes up and down the country, entrances/toll-gates to towns passing between towers, usually marked by a church and a castle or manor house.

kithara, the Greek lyre, which takes us full circle back to Hermes, inventor of the lyre.[1]

Known to Catholics as St Catherine of *Alexandria*, she is actually the Christian version of the Egyptian Heqet, who in turn is Hecate, the Greco-Roman goddess of magic, witchcraft and crossroads, protector of shepherds and sailors, and guardian of the underworld. In other words Hecate is the female version of Hermes, she was referred to as 'the triple Hecat',[2] in the same way that Hermes is Thrice-Great Hermes, Hermes Trismegistus. Catherine is the patron saint of philosophers, in particular of the University of Paris, and both Oxford and Cambridge have colleges named for her. She was seen as an all-purpose 'intellectual saint' and her familiar symbol, the 'Catherine wheel', would appear to be a modified cross-staff, a navigational device for measuring latitude. Her intellectual, navigational and Norman associations explain why so many prominent landmarks near the English Channel bear her name. For instance a series of beacon hills with the remains of chapels/hermitages on their summits are named for St Catherine and dominate the chalk ridge connecting the south coast and the Isle of Wight. At the southernmost end of the island is St Catherine's Down with a former lighthouse, St Catherine's Oratory, on the site of a disused chapel; its counterpoint, at the northernmost tip, is *Egypt* Point, also with a non-operational lighthouse/obelisk.

St Catherine's Hill, Winchester, topped by a chapel and a maze, the Mizmaze, overlooks the weir on the River Itchen next to the crossing-place of the Pilgrims' Way that links Winchester with Canterbury and the ports of Dover and Margate. It is not often wondered why Canterbury and Winchester are consistently England's richest dioceses. The Pilgrims' Way is usually dismissed as a mere pilgrimage route but for most of history Canterbury and Winchester have stood at either end of Britain's most important economic artery.

---

1 Cecilia, another Norman favourite, was the patron saint of music, and also of Albi, the eponymous home of the Albigensians aka the Cathars, and a key departure point for the Troubadour Movement.
2 That is the Triple Goddess of maiden, mother and crone (traditionally represented as the Three Sisters or Fates), though moon goddesses were revered as a single entity i.e. three-in-one, a similar ambiguity to that employed by the Christians.

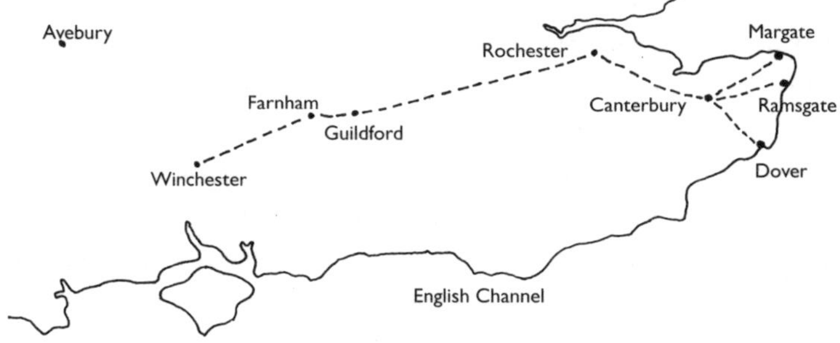

The Pilgrims' Way

Notice it is laid out to serve also the lowest crossing point of the Thames, later known as London. The very earliest track went to Avebury.

The Mizmaze is said to have been built by a student of the nearby boys' school where 'tolling the labyrinth' was a popular game. The older English public schools have a habit of appearing in somewhat antique surroundings which is not surprising given that they are a cross between two Megalithic institutions, the monastery and the university. Essentially they are Megalithic extensions into the modern era carrying forth the message of administering the Empire *sotto voce*. For instance, Marlborough, i.e. 'marl-barrow', is on the A4, aligned with Silbury Hill and various other Sites of Special Megalithic Interest. But we can leave these esoteric connections for elderly house masters to pursue. St Catherine's Hill looks across to Magdalen Hill just as another Catherine Hill, at Guildford, is paired with a St Martha's Hill, both with 'chapels of ease' on their summits, and both on the Pilgrims' Way. They are referring to the same thing, Martha being traditionally Mary Magdalene's sister.

St Catherine's Hill at Guildford is beside the River Wey and, as at Winchester, above the point where a river is forded by the Pilgrims' Way. It directly overlooks the Artington springs[1] whose waters were

---

1 As does the nearby Masonic lodge today. The *art* in Artington is probably a reference to Artemisia or 'magic art', since drugs from the Artemisia plant genus are powerful hallucinogens, rather than directly to the moon-goddess.

believed to have healing properties, particularly effective for eye complaints, as is usual for 'holy wells'. The Guildford Catherine's Hill was formerly called Drake (= Dragon) Hill and according to legend a dragon guarded the springs. Drake Hill was almost certainly renamed for St Catherine by the Normans, her cult being particularly strong in Rouen, the capital of Normandy. Rouen itself has a dragon saint, St Romanus, who reputedly tamed a dragon called La Gargouille, i.e. gargoyle or waterspout, that lived on the left (the 'wrong') side of the Seine. St Catherine's Hill used to be the site of a fair known as Tap-up Sunday due to the amount of beer sold, which took place on the Sunday preceding the Feast of Guardian Angels on 2nd October, the first available feast day after Michaelmas.

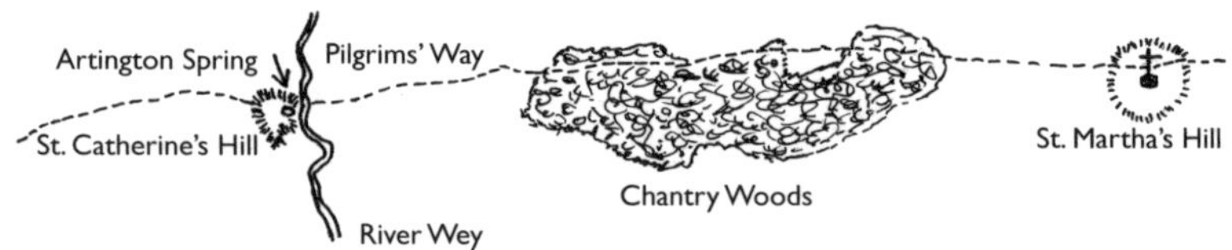

St Catherine's and St Martha's Hills, Guildford

The name Guildford or Geldeford is claimed to mean 'golden ford', from the colour of the sand on the slopes to the south of the town centre. A less poetic and more likely reading is 'geld ford', the geld or tax paid to the custodian of the river crossing where the Pilgrims' Way descends via Ferry Lane to the ford. St Martha's Hill is a markedly solitary feature but festivities still take place there with the local Morris dancers appearing at Mayday sunrise.[1] Martha is traditionally a Provençal saint and as such is unusual in England. Her presence here points to the influence of Eleanor of Aquitaine who laid out Guildford's castle gardens and is credited with introducing the culture of courtly love, troubadours and the chivalric code into England.

---

1 Mazes were also known as 'morysies' which suggests that Morris dancing is connected to the older custom of 'dancing the maze'. St Martha's Hill is reputed to have had a turf maze on the site of the earthworks.

Notwithstanding their Christian backgrounds, Catherine and Martha have gone down in folklore as giantesses who built the two chapels by tossing a hammer to and fro across the valley, a familiar Megalithic motif. Sites that are imposing and supposed to be unimaginably old are often ascribed to giants, just as huge dykes are thought to have been built by the Devil. The legend suggests the two hills are to some extent man-made. At any rate, these hills, as with many holy springs and wells, have been only unconvincingly incorporated into Christianity. The main function is clearly navigational and St Martha's Hill is almost certainly to some extent artificially conspicuous, so much so that it had to be camouflaged to avoid aiding Luftwaffe pilots.

A little way along the Pilgrims' Way from Guildford is Chaldon whose church has a 'Ladder of Salvation' wall-painting more characteristic of a monastery on Mount Athos than a church in the Surrey hills. Celestial ladders were adopted by Megalithic esoterica as symbols of a higher plane, cf. the Kabbalistic Tree of Knowledge. A more homely variant is commemorated in Jack and the Beanstalk in which Jack (= Everyman) uses beans (= the Pythagorean seat of the soul) to reach the giant (= his apotheosis).[1] As is usual with ex-Megalithic routes, there are significant names along the way, e.g. Rook Lane and Tollsworth Manor, but no sign of a village. Despite this lack of local parishioners, Chaldon church has a disproportionately high roof and contains a St Catherine's chapel.

Catherine is just as vigilant at the other end of the country. A headland called St Catherine's Tor in north Devon had a chapel on top which fell into the sea, as has much of the tor itself, due to coastal erosion. Catherine is often associated with such 'menhirs-by-the-sea', as in Dorset where a St Catherine's Hill stands sentinel over Chesil Beach and the Abbotsbury swannery, two unique but very Megalithic constructions. St Catherine's chapel, built over an earlier pagan shrine, is on a platform and closely resembles St Michael's hilltop chapel on the island-like Glastonbury Tor.

---

1   To "spill the beans" is to reveal a secret.

St Catherine's Chapel, Abbotsbury

*This chapel-on-a-hill presumably replaced a menhir erected to
assist sailors looking for a landing-place (of which Chesil Beach
is a magnificent example, irrespective of whether it is natural or
artificial or a bit of both). In any event the chapel's usefulness as
a landmark saved it when the Reformation was demolishing so
much other church architecture.*

The abbey at Abbotsbury was founded by Orc, either a Norman
or a Scandinavian, married to a native of Rouen where Catherine
shrines turn up in interesting places, such as a pool in nearby Lyons-la-
Forêt, formerly known as Saint-Denis-en-Lyons (St Denis = Dionysus).
Lyon, France's traditional second-city, is named after Lugus or Lugh, a
multi-skilled god, the patron saint of travellers and traders, who had
a crow as his messenger—in other words Lugh, who is sometimes
shown with three faces, is Hermes.[1] London was originally Lugdunum.
The relationship between Lyon and Lyonesse (Lyon-Ys) is a matter of
speculation but a straight line running from Lyon to London passes
through Paris, i.e. Par-Is, 'by Ys'. 'Lion' place-names crop up at 'the end
of the world', places of extreme interest to navigators who have to sail
round them. Finistère (world's end), the western tip of France, has Leon
close by; the western tip of Spain, Cape Finisterre, has León close by
and the western tip of Britain, Land's End, has, allegedly, Lyonesse close

---

1 Luke is reputedly the Christian Lugh, being a physician with the symbol of
a winged ox which is both hermetic and Megalithic, ox bones being used in
divination. However, it may be that *all* the apostles lead a 'double life'. Peter, for
instance, is clearly a 'rock saint', the importance of which will be demonstrated
later in this chapter. Jesus himself is becoming more and more 'Megalithic' as
successive Dead Sea Scroll revelations out him as an Essene.

by (under the sea). The most westerly point of the Channel Islands is Lihou (pronounced 'Leo') Island. Cádiz, the major Phoenician terminal for the British metals trade, and the end of the south-west European world, was built on an island called Leon which according to Strabo had a shrine dedicated to Cronos, the crow-god, i.e. the local Lugh.

Catherine goes through various transformations, as is appropriate with a Triple Goddess or a female Hermes. Her earlier British manifestation is as the *sheela-na-gig*, a grotesque stone female with engorged vulva, carved in church walls usually over windows and doors. These female phallic symbols were intended to be in full view, like Hermes-pillars. Newly-wed brides would file past a sheela-na-gig at St Michael's at the Northgate, Oxford, which has a chapel dedicated to St Catherine. St Michael's tower is a landmark of Oxford, north being the cardinal direction associated with moon goddesses and navigation generally.[1] Sheela-na-gigs are almost always associated with churches dedicated to Megalithic saints built on or near important routes, e.g. Buckland's *All Saints* church close to the Lower Icknield Way and the Royston cave, which is actually at the crossroads of the Icknield Way and Ermine Street. The favourite hunting lodge of James I, a noted Rosicrucian, was sited a short distance from Royston crossroads. It may not be entirely coincidental that so many churches close to Ermine Street, as well as the church at Avebury, are dedicated to St James. One of the very few sheela-na-gigs outside the British Isles can be found at St Radegunde's (q.v.) at Poitiers on the Santiago (St James) de Compostela route.

In between the very ancient sheela-na-gig and the Norman Catherine comes *Elen*, the Druid goddess of crossroads, aka Ellen of the Ways, who is equated with road building in Welsh folklore. *Sarn Helen* is an ancient road that runs the length of west Wales starting opposite Anglesey.[2] This Elen is reputed to have introduced

---

1 The Megalithically named Minehead in Somerset was the chief embarkation port for Santiago de Compostela. The highest hill here is North Hill with a St Michael's church acting as the landmark for incoming sailors.
2 *Elin* in Welsh means elbow, or angle, and Lundy Island, off the south coast of Wales, is *Ynys Ellen*. Lundy Island is the right-angle in the Pythagorean 5, 12, 13 triangle formed with Stonehenge to the east and the Preseli Mountains (where the Stonehenge blue stones come from) to the north.

monasticism into England, and monasteries played a pivotal role in ensuring that Megalithia flourished into the Christian era. Elen thus performs the same mythological role as St Martin of Tours who is said to have introduced monasteries into France. *Tour* meaning 'tower' is the equivalent of *tor* pointing to Tours being a Megalithic site[1] and Geoffrey of Monmouth claims that Tours was established by the Trojan, Brutus, the eponymous founder of Britain and who is said to be buried on Tower Hill in London. The cloak of St Martin, one of the most famous relics of the Middle Ages,[2] was in the care of the monks of Saint-Denis and, inevitably, St Martin's shrine at Tours became a major stopover on the Compostela pilgrimage.[3] In the thirteenth century Tours cathedral was rebuilt and dedicated to Saint Gatien who is commemorated by Sangatte in the Pas-de-Calais still so handy for cross-Channel traffic that both the Channel Tunnel terminal and illegal immigrants congregate there. But the link is rather more ancient, Sangatte's twin on the English side being Sandgate, one of the Megalithic '–gate' cities of the Kent coast along with Ramsgate and Margate.

Helen herself rides the cusp between Megalithia and Christianity. In classical mythology Helen is associated with Troy but the Christians presented a British Helen as the mother of Constantine the Great and as the discoverer of the True Cross. Helen, or Selene, is a moon goddess like Artemis and Hecate and, since Constantine as it were founded Christianity i.e. is a latter day Jesus, Helen becomes, in a manner of thinking, the mother-of-God. Helen's father, (Good King) Cole, was the legendary founder of a British kingdom

---

1 The tallest tower in Oxford is St Martin's church, now called The Carfax (= *Carrefour* = crossroads). It is reputedly at the dead centre of the city which in turn is held to be the Megalithic centre of England. For some unexplained reason the (modern) French government decided to name the Tours region "Centre" (even though it isn't).

2 St Martin divided his cloak in two after encountering a beggar and the following night the 'beggar' made himself known to Martin as Christ. The theme of tearing a veil (or cloak) is familiar to Gnostics, both pagan and Christian, as symbolising initiation into knowledge or entering from darkness into light (cf. the description of the rending of the Temple veil at the death of Jesus on the cross).

3 Purportedly, the British church in longest continuous use is St Martin's, Canterbury, i.e. at the end of the Pilgrims' Way, Britain's equivalent of the Compostela route.

called Elmet, roughly today's Yorkshire, which makes Cole the grandfather of Constantine. But since Cole (or Cole Hen, i.e. Old King Cole) seems to be a version of Coelus, a sky-god associated with the cult of Mithras, Constantine becomes descended from another line of Gods. Constantine was declared to be Roman Emperor, and hence a third type of God, at York in Elmet. It was Constantine who managed successfully to unify the somewhat elitist Mithraism, with its wealth of Megalithic associations, and the much more plebeian Christianity.[1] Constantine re-establishes the Trojan link by moving the Roman capital to his great city on the Bosphorus, at the other end from Troy, but this is only one of a series of significant historical links between Yorkshire and Troy. The most prominent connection is via the *Parisii*, the sometime inhabitants of this part of Yorkshire, whose eponym, Paris, was the husband/abductor of Helen of Troy. Troyes is just down the road from Paris (France) but the true relationship of the British and *French* Parisians is a matter of continuing speculation.

Elen/Helen place names are plentiful in Elmet/Yorkshire. St Helen's holy well in the village of Goodmanham is close to a prehistoric temple allegedly dedicated to Woden,[2] now the site of All Hallows Church (All Hallows = Hallowe'en = Samhain). On the other side of the ancient trackway to York is Market Weighton's church of All Saints (All Saints = All Hallows = Samhain). Another All Saints Church is to be found at Barwick-in-Elmet, the site of the tallest maypole in the country.[3] Market Weighton was made famous by the conversion of King Edwin of Deira whose severed

---

1 Constantine was allegedly baptised by Sylvester I, an interesting (woodland) name to be added to the Megalithic canon since Pope Sylvester was, rather unexpectedly, a dragon-slayer. Sylvester II was the first French pope (999–1003) installed for the much-dreaded Millennium and whose activities were spectacularly Megalithic. Popes always choose their throne-names with great care.
2 Woden is equated with Hermes, as in Wednesday i.e. Woden's Day which is also Mercury's day (*mercredi*, *miércoles*, etc.).
3 *Barwick Green* is the theme tune of *The Archers*, the world's longest-running soap opera. The tune was originally a 'maypole dance'. The BBC is a congeries of Megalithics, at least that is one explanation for why this central pillar of Britain's heritage industry is still playing in the twenty-first century. The Archers that is, not the BBC. And the BBC.

head was enshrined at York Minster, built on top of a Roman temple of Diana, their moon goddess. Legendary severed heads are always Megalithic so the decapitated saints of Christian lore whose heads (or heels) create wells, springs, hilltop chapels and the rest are thoroughly immersed in the old tradition. A St Helen's well at Chapel Hill, Pocklington is further north on the same route. To the south is Welton with its St Helen's church and an effigy of a Knight Templar. From this church it is possible to sight an array of spires—York, Lincoln, Beverley and Howden—a characteristic Megalithic pattern. The road from York ends at Brough just south of Elloughton and is overlooked by Elloughton Hill.[1]

Brough, or Petuaria[2] as it was known, is the terminus of Ermine Street (= Hermes straight) and therefore a suitable place to honour the patron goddess of roads. Petuaria was the historic capital of the Parisii and lies almost exactly on the meridian. Officially Ermine Street started from London, Bishopsgate (more precisely, St Helen's Church, Bishopsgate[3]) and ended at York but in fact the road leads not to York but to Winteringham, on the south bank of the Humber facing Brough/Petuaria. A good reason to head for Winteringham is the nearby 'chalybeate springs', chalybeate meaning ferruginous, related to the Latin *chalybs* for tempered iron or steel. Chalybs refers to the Chalybes, aka the Chaldeans, people credited with the invention of commercial iron working and the rise of the Hittites of Anatolia, making yet another link between the Yorkshire Parisii and Old Troy in northern Anatolia. But the link is also with London at the other end of Ermine Street because London's ancient name was Trinovantum (*Tri* = Troy, *nova* = new, New Troy). Troyes in France is where 'Troy weight' for weighing precious metals supposedly originates but Troy weight is 'London weight', according to the English. The kind

---

1   The pub in Elloughton is called 'The Half Moon', not surprisingly since Ellen is a moon-goddess. The pub at Welton is The Green Dragon.

2   Petuaria from *pedwar* means 'fourth' or 'quarter' as with the French *quartier*, i.e. a borough or Brough.

3   Facing St. Helen's is Gresham College, first home of the Royal Society (the 'Invisible College'). These founding fathers of the Scientific Revolution later moved from this highly significant Megalithic address to another one, Crane Court opposite the Inner Temple.

of meticulous measuring process required for the commercial trade in precious metals involved two specific ingredients, 'pure' (distilled) water and mercury, both features of the thoroughly Megalithic pursuit of alchemy. Troyes was the native town of Chrétien de Troyes, the originator of the Grail romances, 'grail' being interpreted in a dozen different ways in a thousand different books, but rarely being awarded its correct meaning as a chemist's flask.

The Chaldeans were also the great mathematicians of antiquity, credited with the concept of the 360 degree world circle.[1] This presupposes a prime meridian. The present prime meridian leaves the North Pole and never touches land until it reaches Holderness in east Yorkshire, the area settled by the Parisii. A historic rivalry between London and Paris attaches to the apparently very modern selection of the Greenwich meridian—London winning out over Paris—but meridians in general must have been of some importance to long distance navigators such as the Megalithics. Longitude was officially discovered by the French astronomer Picard using a triangulation method in the seventeenth century (A.D.) but certainly Eratosthenes was using lines of longitude in the third century (B.C). There is the suggestion that Ermine Street itself acted as the ancient Prime Meridian ultimately linking the 'Paris' of Yorkshire and the Paris of France. A local saint points up this link. Winestead Church in Holderness is dedicated to St Germain, a patron saint of Paris, as is Selby, one of the great Yorkshire abbeys, which in true Megalithic style is where 'three swans gathered on the Ouse'. Today, Selby's premier visitors' attraction is its medieval 'Washington Window' portraying the coat of arms of the local family whose most famous son, George, was steeped in Freemasonry.

St Germain is remembered as a bishop of Paris but first he was a hunter, Germain/Germanus being cognate with Cernunnos, the stag-headed god particularly associated with the Parisii of Gaul.

---

1 The Chaldeans appear to be linked to the mysterious Culdees, small groups of hermits and monks mainly in Scotland and Ireland who colonised remote islands. The Celtic Renaissance was the work of 'small groups of hermits and monks mainly in Scotland and Ireland who colonised remote islands'.

Cernunnos features in south-east Britain as Herne the Hunter, notably at Herne Bay where two of the chief gateways to France, Margate and Ramsgate, are situated. Herne was branded a thief (cf. Hermes) and hung from a tree (cf. Woden). The 'horned god' appears on the Atlantic trade routes too. In Spain he is known as St Cermanos, the patron saint of Cádiz, the 'gateway' of south-west Spain, and has his counterpart in Navarre where he is known as Cernin or Fermin who are the same person or at least both suffered the same fate of being martyred by a bull. San Fermín or San Cernin is certainly Saturninus, the Christian version has the latter baptising the former. As San Fermin he is commemorated at the famous bull-running festival because Pamplona (made up of villages one of which was called St Cernin) was on a main drovers' route. He also turns up as far away as Fermain Bay in Guernsey in the Channel Islands, opposite the island of Herm. St Fermin completes his round trip on Ermine Street, at Thorney, on the meridian, whose abbey is dedicated to Saint Fermin and again further north at St Firmin's Well in Bowes[1] (the Roman Lavatrae), an important watering stop and toll point for cattle on a prehistoric trans-Pennine route.

Little wonder then that St Fermín is a patron saint of bootmakers. There is a close association between leather, bulls and Megalithia, and Fermín himself is in reality the ever-booted Hermes. Leather is a typical high-value, much-in-demand trade good so dear to the Megalithics, their pack-train animals supplied the raw product as well as distributing it. Leather production itself is an evil smelly business that in many cultures is carried out by special castes, in special places, and therefore gives special profits, i.e. it was of prime interest to the Megalithics. Some of the so-called hillforts near the coast were in fact abattoirs where butchering and tanning took place. In early sea voyages hide was needed for the bodies of leather coracles, plus the leather sails *and* the ropes

---

1　The Bowes-Lyons are an illustrious Megalithic family who, alas, had to dilute the bloodline when Elizabeth Bowes-Lyons married George VI of the arriviste Saxe-Coburgs. The Lords Lyon are the Scottish heraldry authorities.

before the whole industry switched over to specialised timber and hemp, which themselves promptly became Megalithic plantation crops.[1] 'Bull saints' seem to be very ancient, harking back to the bull cults of the Eastern Mediterranean, notably in Crete and Egypt, as well as various Manichean traditions culminating in Mithraism (or in its later incarnation, post-Constantine Christianity, with its heavy emphasis on Heaven or Hell, God or the Devil, salvation or damnation). It is reasonable to think of them as being the ancient progenitors of the metallurgical routes of the Trojans, the Minoans and the Phoenicians, which were in their turn superseded by the 'Irish saints' and Knights Templar of later Megalithia.

In the fifth and sixth centuries large numbers of these 'Irish saints' land and set up their 'churches' in all the old Megalithic places—beacon hills, 'gates', springs, standing stones and so forth—accompanied by legends laden with megalithic inferences, so for instance the saints would arrive floating on millstones or barrels or a stone altar, and once ashore would win stone-throwing contests with indigenous giants, subdue dragons, create holy wells and the rest. These newer networks can be traced by the regular appearance of various individual Celtic saints, as exemplified by St Sampson, apparently so busy in his lifetime (though naturally not so busy as to omit a dragon-slaying episode) that he has one of the Scilly islands, the chief commercial port of Guernsey and various churches in Brittany, Normandy, Cornwall, Wales and finally at York named for him. It is possible that some kind of franchising system was being operated. The best known, perhaps always the chief, of these Western saints is St Patrick, who in Cornwall is known as Petroc or Perran or Piran, the variation in names cannot disguise they all refer to rock. The legend of Piran, or Perran, claims that in Ireland he was chained to a millstone and thrown into the raging sea like one of Patrick's snakes[2] but as soon as he rolled off the cliff the sea grew calm and he floated on

---

1 Bridport, the outlet for the Megalithic Chesil Beach, was still enjoying a hemp monopoly under the Tudors.
2 The Megalithics, as part of their animal domestication programmes, routinely got rid of snakes and other predators that ate ground-nesting birds' eggs.

the millstone to Perranzabuloe on the Cornish coast, the site of a St Piran's church now buried in sand near Perran beach.[1]

Padstow is the Anglicised form of Petroc(k), who is not only the patron saint of Cornwall but, as St Piran, is also the patron saint of tin miners. Petroc is predictably a dragon-saint who expelled the last Cornish dragon by throwing his girdle round its neck and leading it into the sea, after which he retired to live as a hermit. But this gentleness—Petroc also removed a splinter from a dragon's eye—is new and something of a western motif linking these Atlantic seaboard routes with the later flowering of courtly love and the underlying air of civility emanating from southern France, which in turn percolated out into the rest of Europe via the troubadours, the Arthurian Cycle and chivalric principles in general. The event itself is commemorated in Padstow by the May Day processions of the Hobby Horse[2] during which the townspeople, playing the part of hostages, have to pay a penny to be released, as per the usual reference to Megalithic tolls, from a creature which once resembled a dragon but is now more like a pantomime horse. Exactly the same sequence has been followed in faraway China where the dragons associated with their form of geomancy are now similarly affable adjuncts to festivals.

An important route linking Padstow in the north to Fowey on the south coast is the 'Saints Way' footpath, a better proposition than sailing round the perilous Cornish peninsula. The church at Golant next to an ancient ford on the River Fowey is dedicated to St Sampson, and has a well that never dries up near the entrance. St Sampson is depicted in a window with St Anthony,

---

1 Millstones seem to represent the *omphalos*, the navel of the earth around which the cosmos turns as if on its axle. Underneath the crossroads of Ermine Street and the Icknield Way lies a millstone inside a bell-shaped shaft cut into the rock with symbolic carvings on the walls.
2 Hobby means 'hobbled', a technique in domestication. Hobby horses are sometimes called 'hodening' or 'hooden', i.e. blinkered, for taming purposes. A hooding method is also used to train hunting birds. The *hobby* is the smallest and fastest of the falcons.

the archetypal hermit.[1] Inland from Fowey is the village of St Neot, the patron saint of (salt) fish. There is a holy well here where the saint kept three fish, only one of which was to be eaten, i.e. the other two are stock fish ultimately for trading purposes. This St Neot is linked by Christian lore to St Neots near Huntingdon in Cambridgeshire because the latter's monastery allegedly purloined some of the former's saint's relics. However, this is only a piece of Christian window-dressing to explain the duplication of a very obscure saint. The actual connection is rather more interesting. A good starting point is the well-known riddle "*As I was going to St Ives I met a man with seven wives*" because both St Neots are in the vicinity of a St Ives and whatever circumstance underlies this double connection it is unlikely to be a bone-heist.

Both the St Neots are on fords (the Huntingdon one over the Ouse) and both have major metal connections, tin at the Cornish St Neot and iron in Huntingdon. A suburb of St Neots is Wintringham, a name elsewhere linked to chalybeate springs. The Huntingdon St Neots was clearly important to the Normans who built a castle here between the church and the river. It was owned by Payne (Paganus) de Beauchamp, the husband of Rohese de Vere after whom is named Rohesia's Cross, the Rosicrucian marker at Ancient Britain's most important crossroads where Ermine Street meets the Icknield Way. The De Veres became earls of Oxford, the Megalithic centre of Britain, and crop up with disconcerting frequency throughout British history in connection with Templars and beer.[2] The manor of St Neots was granted to a priory (now a brewery) by the De Clares, another leading Anglo-Norman family up to their boots in the Merovingian and Templar past. On the opposite side of the river from the manor is St Mary's church, built in the Gothic style, which is

---

1 In Catholic tradition St Anthony is portrayed as a desert anchorite, making him an odd choice as the patron saint of domestic animals, but the connection of course is entirely natural in the Megalithic view of things where hermits and animal domesticators are cut from the same cloth.
2 The seventeenth Earl of Oxford was Shakespeare, say some. A claim which, though presumably not literally true, demonstrates that the Megalithic and esoteric principles underlying the Elizabethan and Jacobean courts are even now not very well understood.

visible for miles around and is known as 'the cathedral of Hunting-donshire', as befits a Megalithic river crossing on a main route.

The Cornish St Neot is at the edge of Bodmin Moor (Bodmin = Abode of Mines), on the River Loveny (previously the Loysan)[1] which is noticeably straight, suggesting it has been canalised at some stage to increase flow and power the town's several mills, though originally probably to facilitate tin streaming. St Eloy or St Loy or Eligius is the patron saint of metalworkers.[2] St Eloy's birth was announced three times by an eagle and to add to the Megalithic *mélange* his cult in France is associated with May offerings. He once removed a horse's leg "to shoe it more easily", a piece of leg-pulling that obscures the pagan connotations of the severed leg. The Egyptian Book of the Dead, for instance, illustrates a three-legged calf whose severed leg is being offered to the gods. The Isle of Man has a flag with three (severed) legs joined at the thigh, a symbol known as a *trefot* (three feet) and which closely resembles the strange glyph of three hares running in a circle linked together by one of their ears, thought to be an alchemical sign somehow connected to tin mining, probably because most three-hare carvings are on churches in tin-rich Dartmoor.[3] The three-hare motif is also found in China as well as Europe and the Middle East so if there is a metallurgical link it will be much wider than tinning. It almost certainly goes back to Hephaestus, the original smith, working at his three-legged table. Three-legged icons generally have Megalithic resonances because three-into-one ('Thrice-great') is an alchemical principle, the three prime ingredients being sulphur, mercury and salt[4] and the three initial stages are represented by those very Megalithic birds the raven, the swan and the peacock.

The three-legged motif has a peculiar role in the saga of Oxford

---

1 Also Lausanne in Switzerland which, with Geneva across the lake, is one of the great Megalithic hotspots, best remembered today for the reversed Rosicrucian flag of Switzerland and the distilling of gin. (Gin = juniper = Geneva).
2 And of REME, the British army's successors to the miners-and-sappers.
3 Thoth, the Egyptian moon-god of wisdom, was called the 'hearing ear' by the Greeks. The hares' three ears form a triangle and knowledge is received through the ears (cf. the Gnostic saying "He who has ears, let him hear").
4 It has been suggested that *neot* = nitre, alchemical salt.

where a sixteenth-century Oxford scholar, Richard Hooker, is said to have invented the three-legged stool! According to Hooker the three legs represented the Anglican tenets of reason, scripture and tradition. This pious claim should be viewed in the light of Hooker's Megalithic background: he was the rector of St Mary's Drayton Beauchamp on the Icknield Way, his mentor was Edwin Sandys (= St Denis), and he later became Master of the Temple Church in London. His philosophy was very influential, notably via John Locke, in the remarkable rise at that time of British philosophy to world status. Two sources confidently state that St Neot founded Oxford University, something of an anachronism since Neot was a contemporary of King Alfred in the ninth century and Oxford was founded in the twelfth century, but Megalithically it makes complete sense because the universities were the direct successors of the monastic scriptoria. According to the Welsh authors of the *Mabinogion* King Lud measured Britain to find the centre which turned out to be Oxford, making it from a Megalithic point of view an ideal site for the country's premier seat-of-learning.[1]

But trying to pin down when these 'legends' first appeared is tricky because precedence is often a *political* matter. One of the main thrusts of the Tudor regime, to confound enemies both domestic and foreign, was to give an English (even a Welsh) under-pinning to British history with an English rather than a Roman Church and with English intellectual pretensions being at least on a par with Continental and Catholic claims. The Tudor and Stuart monarchs were engaged in an ideological Cold War with the European great powers which, from Henry VIII's divorce onwards, required the wholesale forging of useful documents, some of which are now accepted by historians as genuine! It was urgently required in the sixteenth century to show that England was not just another papal province but a Christian foundation in

---

1 The *Mabinogion* is most likely a modern invention but Oxford's links with the Classical world seem to be anciently rooted. Oxford = Bosphorus i.e. Ox = Bos, *cow*; ford = phorus, *passage of*. It is located on a stretch of the Thames called the Isis. However it should not be automatically assumed that the British places are named for the Classical ones rather than the other way round.

her own right. Given this contemporaneous demand, it becomes entirely understandable that Asser's *Life of King Alfred* is a Tudor concoction, and this is really the sole source of the whole cherished theory of a great Alfredian Renaissance in Anglo-Saxon England. All those 'English' savants bringing the light of learning to Europe becomes somewhat tendentious. On this reading, Alfred is no longer the only English king worthy to be called 'the Great' and takes his place as just another provincial Anglo-Saxon kinglet. Academics themselves half acknowledge this uncertainty, viz.

> *"The authenticity of Asser's book has been much disputed. The unique MS. survives only in charred and illegible fragments, but it is clear from external evidence that Parker's edition (1574) contains large editorial alterations and interpolations from the Lives of St Neots"*.[1]

It is not surprising that St Neots, alongside the unusually intellectual Alfred, gets a mention in this context because the struggle for hearts and minds was being decided largely by English, French and Italian universities so claims, however tenuous, for Oxford's foundation and hence seniority over her Continental rivals was always useful.

It is a relief to return, as it were, to real mythology. The British centre of the three-legged symbol is located appropriately at the geographic centre of the British Isles, the Isle of Man, whose flag as we have seen consists of three (severed) legs, or *trefot* (three feet).[2] The island's

---

1 Another source of national pride is *Beowulf*, the sole Anglo-Saxon epic. This is a familiar story of a priceless manuscript that somehow got completely lost for hundreds and hundreds of years then reappeared in the nick of time in a Tudor library, only to disappear conveniently some time later. Without patriotic overtones this would immediately be recognised as a classic example of a chain of forged provenance. The poem is ostensibly written in the eleventh, tenth, ninth or eighth century (the 'experts' naturally cannot agree), and after its fabulous voyage through obscurity, fire and dubious cataloguing, it has ended up in the British Library where it would be more than anybody's job's worth to impugn England's founding saga by a few simple scientific dating techniques.

2 The trefot is also the symbol of that other island at the centre of things, Sicily. The patron saint of this strategically and Megalithically important island between Carthage and the toe of Italy is Lucy, whose name means 'light'. According to the medieval Golden Legend account, Lucy resisted defilement by becoming 'as heavy as a mountain', in other words a menhir.

patron saint is St Maughold or Mac Cuil, pronounced Mc'cool, a near-homonym of Michael.[1] Maughold's Hermetic associations are evident from his curious combination of being both a member of the Irish Royal Family and a pirate, literally a Prince of Thieves. Armed with a miracle-working staff, his caduceus, he arrives on the island in his unoared coracle, a method pioneered by Aphrodite/Venus in her cockle shell, to begin his true métier as a hermit monk (and one of the Culdees no less). St Maughold's church was built on an earlier Bronze Age site and just north of the churchyard is the horseshoe-shaped St Maughold's Wishing Well, containing chalybeate water. Barren women wishing to conceive sat on a rock called St Maughold's Chair, above the stone trough which can be guessed to be a Megalithic watering point because the women have to pay the usual 'toll'. The well is duly tended in a flower dressing ceremony every 12th August, the start of the grouse-shooting season which, if not accidental, neatly combines fertility and hunting in the best moon-goddess tradition. The church overlooks Maughold Head, the easternmost point of the island. A pair of peregrine falcons, traditionally presented to kings at their coronation on behalf of the island, came from this site. Successfully reintroduced falcons still nest there but nowadays the kings have to go to them.

If the patron saint of the Isle of Man is suitably Megalithic, so too are the other national patron saints, the familiar dragon-slaying St George of England and the entirely Megalithic Patrick/Piran in Ireland and Cornwall. St David of Wales has his own multi-stranded Megalithic associations and, in keeping with the other western Megalithic saints, his background is royal, from the House of Ceredigion. His mother, St Non, gave birth to him on a *cliff top*, the site of which is marked by the ruins of St Non's *chapel*, just south of the town of St David's and overlooking *St. George's* Channel at its most Megalithic point, the *south-westernmost tip* of Wales. The chapel-on-a-cliff swiftly became a popular destination for pilgrims who on cue throw coins into the

---

1   Mc'Cool is 'Son of hazel', *coull* in Manx, *coll* in Irish, means hazel, traditionally a symbol of wisdom. Hazels are often found in burials and claimed to be symbols of rebirth by rather over-Christianised archaeologists.

nearby St Non's holy well renowned for its healing powers. St David's, which could easily be mistaken for a market town in Gloucestershire rather than some more typical Welsh settlement, is the terminus of another Ermin Street, this one running westwards from London, and it is also the southern terminus of a Pilgrims' Way, from Holy Well in North Wales. Historians have noted that "his cult seems to have spread eastwards along what remained of the Roman road system of Wales" but even a cursory examination of these routes reveals significant Megalithic details. Ermin Street in only a few miles goes via Pen Troydin, a reference to the maze motif known as the 'Troy game', then St Clears (i.e. St. Clair's, a Megalithic family)[1] at the confluence of two rivers, the Taf which flows down from the Preseli mountains, source of the Stonehenge bluestones, and the Cynin, meaning 'chief'.

David is a characteristically pragmatic Megalithic 'travel saint' but for the most part Welsh saints are seen as more 'mystical'. St Melangell is a good example though true to type she was an 'Irish princess'. St Melangell's church, overlooking the Tanat valley in Powys, occupies a circular Bronze Age site marked by yew trees, a recognisable scenario of a church on an ancient droving route with control over access to water and presumably hunting rights. Melangell is the patron saint of hares in Wales and the hare is connected with Easter and Eostre[2], a Celtic goddess. March hares denote lunacy, i.e. the moon, and the time of the vernal equinox. The legend of Melangell states that while she was praying inside a thicket of thorns a hare being pursued by a prince and his huntsmen took refuge under her cloak after which the prince's dogs refused to attack either her or the hare. The hare in this story symbolises underground knowledge[3] and the breaching of Melangell's cloak is her 'awakening'. The references to chastity and hunting clearly point to St Melangell being a moon goddess, *Mel*

---

1 The Norman invasion of Ireland under the Clares was launched from this part of Wales.
2 Thus completing the Christian takeover of both Christmas (Yule) and Easter. It is thus rather ironic that Christians are forever complaining that these festivals are losing their traditional religious significance.
3 Even though hares do not burrow and therefore are not 'underground' animals. However, as is made clear later, the relationship of hares to rabbits (who do burrow) is a very Megalithic one.

means dark in Welsh so Melangell is the 'dark angel', the crone aspect of the moon. The similarity between 'rabid' and rabbit suggests the Easter bunny too has more than a hint of madness. Reciting 'hares' and 'rabbits' on the first and last days of every month is a folksy reminder of their link with the moon. Hares serve as messengers of the moon goddess and their attributes are trickery, promiscuity and speed, all characteristics of Hermes.

Scottish saints are different again since Scotland is tied in to the North Sea trade routes rather than the Western Approaches. The patron saint is officially St Andrew but nobody takes much notice of this non-Megalithic personage. The new Scottish Parliament has been futilely promoting St Andrew's Day (November 30th) as being on a par with St Patrick's Day or St David's Day but the true Scottish National Day remains Burns Night, Burns himself being a suitably Megalithic bard, kitted out in his Masonic regalia. The original patron saint was the canonised Queen Margaret, named 'Pearl of Scotland' after Scotland's famous pearl-bearing mussels (*Margaritifera margaritifera*!), pearls being an ideal trading item for long distance exchange. However, Margaret's personal Megalithic contributions to Scotland are her chapel built on the very highest point of Edinburgh Castle, her introduction of monastic orders to Scotland, the rebuilding of the monastery at Iona and the free ferry (Queensferry) across the Forth for pilgrims. The port of Edinburgh is Leith, a town largely in the hands of the Templars in the twelfth and thirteenth centuries until the order merged with the Hospitallers to form the Order of St Anthony, named for the famous hermit, and patron saint of the guild that had been awarded the Scottish wine monopoly. A ruined chapel and hermitage dedicated to St Anthony is situated on Arthur's Seat, Edinburgh's most prominent hill, and is clearly visible from the Firth of Forth. Guarding the approaches to Edinburgh and Leith, in the middle of the Firth of Forth, is the Isle of May, honouring Maia, the mother of Hermes, and fittingly the site of Scotland's first lighthouse.

In England it is more a case of 'dip your bucket, pull up a Megalithic saint' and not only because they are clustered around wells. Even an almost unknown saint such as St Radegund turns out to be significant, having several English churches dedicated to her besides being the patron saint of Jesus College, Cambridge. She started out as a Thuringian princess, *Rad* in German being 'wheel', *gund* or 'gard' meaning world, so *Radegund* seems to be somewhat cosmic, probably a reference to a cross-staff as per the Catherine Wheel. Thuringia is a region noted for megalithic monuments, including the Goseck 'sun observatory', a wooden henge that has striking parallels with Stonehenge. In France Radegunde is celebrated as the chaste wife of the Merovingian King Clothair and the founder of a convent at Poitiers on the main Compostela route. A dolmen at Poitiers is known as St Radegonde's 'lifted stone'. The enormous capstone was said to have been transported on her head, the uprights being stones that fell out of her apron, these astonishingly un-Christian feats being routine for Megalithic saints. Radegund was known as a dragon-slayer, rather oddly since there are no dragon-slaying episodes in her legend, but she does feature as a female knight in Edmund Spenser's epic *The Faerie Queene*.[1] Her name appears in all the right Megalithic places. St Radegund church in the Nottinghamshire village of Maplebeck is on the main road to Doncaster and is linked by Robin Hood's Way to Rufford Abbey, a Cistercian monastery. She also has churches dedicated to her at Scruton on the A1 between York and Middlesbrough, at Whitwell on the Isle of Wight and at Postling near Folkestone, the junction of Stone Street connecting the Saxon Shore Way to Canterbury, where there is a St. Radigund's Street at Northgate. The very grand Radigund's Abbey, now derelict, is on a hilltop a mere two miles or so west of Dover and, inexplicably, has a large pond in an otherwise dry chalk area. At Usk in Wales a priory dedicated to St Mary Magdalene and St Radegund was founded by Richard de Clare, Strongbow, the Norman conqueror of Ireland, who died of 'an injured foot'.

A similarly obscure saint with a Continental reach is St Rombald whose name is connected to holy wells at Astrop in

---

1 The neo-Platonist Spenser is a prime candidate for the authorship of Beowulf.

Northamptonshire and another one nearby at Brackley.[1] His Christian legend is, even by Dark Age standards, a marvellous account of a seventh-century infant prodigy, born into the Northumbrian royal family, who lived for only three days but still managed to insist on being baptised with water from a hollow stone "too heavy to move", aka a megalith. The mother of this miraculous infant, Cuneburga,[2] was a Mercian princess and the patron saint of Castor, a major Roman industrial site adjacent to Ermine Street. Her son's three-day life was deemed sufficiently important to merit a complete Anglo-Saxon biography and to have a church dedicated to him at Romaldkirk village, north of Bowes Castle on the river Tees in County Durham. Not any church either since St Romald's church was known as 'the Cathedral of the Dales', a very imposing building for a small village. A St Rainbold, i.e. Rombold, was the first recorded priest at Avebury and there is a St Rombold's church in Buckingham (where he is supposed to have died, and where repentant Lollards made offerings). Another St Rombold's church is at Pentridge in Dorset next to Cranbourne Chase, where the longest cursus still extant in Britain is to be found and, according to John Michell, there is a leyline terminating at Stonehenge on Salisbury Plain.

Rombald's *Moor* is a high plateau between Bradford and Leeds[3] in Yorkshire and seems to be the northern equivalent of Salisbury Plain judging by its flatness and the unusual number of cup-and-ring stones located there. This Rombald was a giant fleeing from his angry wife who dropped stones held in her skirt, which sounds familiar. There may be a connection between Rombald and rhombus, an equal-sided parallelogram, since rhumb lines are mathematical projections

---

1 Brackley High Street has a Magdalen College Chapel, originally the Hospital of St. James and St. John (i.e. Castor and Pollux) and a sister of Magdalen College, Oxford, itself on the site of an earlier Hospital of St. John the Baptist. Magdalen College's bell tower at the east gate is the highest tower in Oxford, just topping St. Michael's at the north gate.
2 Cuneburga refers to 'coney burrow', coney meaning rabbit. Rabbit warrens tend to be situated near prehistoric industrial sites, even in apparently unsuitable areas like Dartmoor where artificial burrows called 'buries' or pillow mounds had to be constructed. All this to feed the miners in areas where food is otherwise scarce.
3 Where there is a local Pentridge too.

which help in direction finding when using a two-dimensional map to draw lines on the three-dimensional earth. In pre-literate times, before maps, a large flat plain and an unobstructed rhomboid plateau might have overcome these problems of perspective. But whatever the local case may be, Rombald is certainly of Europe-wide significance. His British influence reached all the way south to the Channel crossing at Folkestone (next door to Radegund at Dover) where he is the patron saint of the local fishermen. His birthday unsurprisingly is the 1st November, Samhain. On the other side of the Channel, St Rombald or Rombaut has a more credible pedigree as an Irish-born missionary bringing Christianity to pagan Europe in the sixth century. St Rombald's cathedral in Mechlin, Belgium, the town where this version of the saint died, is noteworthy for its flat-topped tower as well as a painting and a glass window of a Black Madonna. Mechlin is a version of Michael but its many varied spellings such as *Maglinia, Magliniensis* and *Meglinia* are significant because in Hebrew *migdal* means tower, as in Armageddon or Har Megiddo which translates into English as 'Tower Hill'. This apparent elision between Michael and Magdalen shows, paradoxically, one of the disparities between British and Continental Megalithia. In Britain, where the Celtic church reigned supreme, Michael with his angels and local saints seemed to have served most purposes. On the Continent, where the Catholic church was able to establish a fair measure of continuity from the days of the Roman Empire onward without any 'Celtic interregnum', Megalithic saints were, outwardly at least, more Catholic. Hence this St Rombald has the same saint's day as John the Baptist, displaying his Megalithic credentials to the cognoscenti while meeting Catholic sensibilities.

John the Baptist churches are always worth a detour.[1] He is the patron saint of Gozo, Malta, where the Mediterranean's most important Megalithic complex is sited. Ggantija, one of the oldest

---

1 The Baptist, the 'Voice crying in the Wilderness', is the leader of a water cult. He has some of the trappings of John Barleycorn, a corn deity, because his beheading took place at the time of the summer solstice i.e. the ears of the wheat stalk were flayed off.

temples at Gozo, is said to have exactly the same orientation as Stonehenge and would have been due south of Stonehenge on the old prime meridian.[1] St John the Baptist churches in Britain tend to be in strategic locations, as for example in Royston at the cross-roads of Ermine Street and the Michael Line. The Pilgrims' Way and its western extension, the Fosse Way, are top-and-tailed by John the Baptist churches. There is one at Margate, the eastern terminus of the Pilgrims' Way, on a knoll overlooking the sea-gate;[2] they crop up serially on the Fosse Way in south Gloucestershire; and at Weston-super-Mare, there is one on Worlebury Hill, overlooked by a curious and probably man-made promontory sticking out into the Bristol Channel. John the Baptist churches are also found at major sites of ancient activity, for example at Findon near Arundel in Sussex, where the church is beside major prehistoric flint mines on an east-west route passing between the church and *Tolmare* Farm, next to *Tolmere* Pond, a mile away from the Cissbury Rings, a flint mine where it is claimed there is an underground tunnel with the usual pot of gold guarded by two serpents.

The essence of the Megalithic System is that it is international and everybody had to be able to recognise common motifs in whichever country they found themselves. Leith at one end of a North Sea route linking Britain with the Continent, for instance, had a Black Madonna connection. The port's coat of arms displays a black virgin and child in a ship, a highly unusual 'Star of the Sea' icon in Britain and which has been traced to Ferrières in Normandy but may have spread from another Ferrières in Provence. The name Ferrières indicates iron-working *and* ferrying, both of which are organised around Megalithic long distance transport. Black Madonnas are equated with Mary Magdalen, hilltop locations being the pertinent link. Magdalen's presence in southern France is explained by a legend that states she

---

1   The newer Prime Meridian passed through Giza. Since vowel sounds are mainly a matter of modern convention when transcribing Semitic languages, perhaps it is time to start talking of the Great Pyramid of Gozo.
2   The church is the burial-place of John Dandelion (*Daunedeleon*, the yard-arm of Leon) who in local legend brought over the church bell on a mill-cog.

landed at Baume in Provence[1] and journeyed to Ferrières, just off the aptly named Route de Draguignan, the town of Draguignan having a local dragon-slayer called St *Hermentaire*.[2] This rather implausible tale is in fact a reminder of the Megalithic significance of the Gulf of Lion at the Mediterranean end of the major north-south Continental land route. Halfway along this route northwards is Ferrières Abbey in Burgundy, an important literary centre in the ninth century under Loup[3] de Ferrières, said to be the first humanist. This abbey in the middle of France claims to have been founded by St Columba which, while presumably untrue, is interesting in that the Burgundians, who themselves claimed Scandinavian origins, were creating links to a faraway Irish saint who had pioneered some of the North Sea routes.

A fair amount has been written about Black Madonnas in France and beyond but far less attention is paid to Mary Magdalen's sister, Martha, who according to tradition accompanied her from the Holy Land to Provence. Martha achieved independent cult status in Tarascon where she is celebrated as a tamer (rather than a slayer) of a she-dragon named La Tarasque that legendarily terrorised those crossing the river Rhone, an obvious gloss on extortionate toll collecting. La Tarasque was led away by Martha's girdle, a reference to Aphrodite's girdle since Martha, like Aphrodite on her clamshell, came ashore on a boat 'without oars or sails'. Martha is a 'goddess of the hearth' and her true connection with Tarascon and La Tarasque is tarragon (*Artemisia dracunculus sativa*), closely related to wormwood and mugwort and one of the four *fines herbes* that French cooking so prizes. The reference to Martha in the Bible highlights her role of preparing food

---

1   The body of Mary Magdalen was 'discovered' at the hilltop church of Vézelay in Burgundy having somehow been transported there from the mountain grotto at Baume. The need for this dramatic removal is presumably because Vézelay, on the Santiago de Compostela route, was where Bernard de Clairvaux launched the Second Crusade and Richard the Lion-heart and King Philip assembled their armies for the Third Crusade.

2   The earliest known Magdalen church in France is in the north-east at Verdun, built under the auspices of *Ermenfroi*. Verdun is known for producing *dragées* (sugared almonds).

3   'Wolf' names often turn up in Megalithic circumstances. One of the better known Loup namesakes is Saint Loup bishop of Troyes, who like St Denis of Paris protects against demonic possession, the malady that afflicted Mary Magdalen (freed from seven demons according to the New Testament).

for Jesus and therefore she is a suitable figurehead for the Megalithics' constant search for profitable spices. Tarragon is grown as a specialist crop in southern France, a characteristically high value/low bulk staple of Megalithic trade and 'Martha' governs the trade in *fines herbes*, not just the growing of them in plantations and their transport via dedicated toll-free routes, but their wider consumption throughout the new more genteel Provençal culture introduced into Europe by the troubadours. If the Megalithics are behaving in their normal fashion, even the growing of this crop was a Megalithic monopoly once 'Martha' has dealt with the local growers. Controlling the trade in these apparently minor culinary additions to the diet continued to shake the world for the next thousand years, launching a succession of trading empires from the Venetian to the British.[1]

The south of France was the Megalithic mirror image of the Celtic Renaissance developing at the same time in the seas around the British Isles. But here in the south, where the state forces of both Catholics and Muslims were far stronger than the tribal agglomerations of the north, the Megalithics' political policies were necessarily different. In the rude circumstances of, say, Anglo-Saxon Britain, the Megalithics could present themselves as a useful institution providing services otherwise unavailable, but in the relatively sophisticated south the Megalithics needed their own political institutions, even their own independent states, identifiable by religious *un*orthodoxy. Once Catholicism had demolished rival Christian sects such as Arians, the 'Jewish' state of Septimania took up the cudgels—not that the ruling elite in Languedoc were particularly strict followers of Judaism *per se* but it made them distinct from either Catholics or Muslims. Later, the same area opted for another non-Catholic, non-Muslim religion in the form of Catharism, which harked back to the dualism of Mithras

---

1 How far Columbus, Cabot, Vasco da Gama, Magellan and so on were 'Megalithic' is a matter of conjecture (red crosses on white sails, secret sailing instructions, links with Genoa = Genova = Geneva = Juniper, etc.). It has been plausibly argued that the independent countries of Portugal and Switzerland are of Templar foundation. Similar claims can also be made for more transitory territorial units such as the Aragonese empire, the Prussia of the Teutonic Knights, Burgundy and Savoy. This 'alternative' political history of Europe awaits its modern chronicler.

and Zoroaster. But these local attempts at counter-orthodoxy only broke out into the rest of Western Europe when *both* Megalithic strands, north and south, popularly represented by the troubadours of Provence and the Arthurian cycle from Britain, met in the middle, under the aegis of the Parisian St Denis (= Dionysus) to launch the Gothic Cathedrals and everything that went with them. One thing that did go with them was the Green Man symbol strewn with some abandon among the corbels and roof bosses. The wonder is how the conservative masters of Catholicism accepted so readily this riotous and blatant re-emergence of Dionysus.

Carving of St Denis, Church of St Dionysius in Kelmarsh, Northamptonshire

Traditionally Dionysus is associated with the vine and more generally is an all-purpose vegetation deity. These Green Men, also known as Wild Men, with their grimacing faces enveloped in foliage are obviously pagan. This is a typical treatment of it in an otherwise impeccably orthodox setting, the head of the martyr (he died by the normal method of sacral kings, decapitation) forming a waterspout. Dionysus is a pivotal figure in the transition between Old Megalithia and the new sources of Megalithic influence, the Gothic cathedrals and the universities.

Dionysus, as god of the vine, is linked to a secretive cult in underground caves, the connection presumably being grapes to wine to cellars to secret knowledge, but Dionysus is strongly associated with *all* kinds of intellectual stimulus, or perhaps stimulants. His later reincarnation, St Denis, is conflated with the so-called Pseudo-Dionysius the Areopagite, a pioneer of Neoplatonism and one of the links between Classical philosophy and the European Renaissance. The Gothic cathedrals are by definition a Christian milieu but they emphasised their pagan underpinnings by putting Dionysian Green Man symbols everywhere for all to see. At any rate for those with eyes to see. Being visible and invisible is always the mark of Megalithia.

The Age of Saints ended when literacy finally ceased to be in the hands of the monasteries and became available to other organs of the state and to the laity generally. As aids-to-prayer saints survived and even flourished as the Catholic Church regressed more and more into polytheism, but they swiftly disappeared wherever the dour ideology of the monotheistic Protestants took root. For a thousand years the forging of documents was, like the manufacture of saints' relics, a matter of supply and demand, but while it is taken for granted that most religious relics are by definition fake,[1] the same level of scepticism is never applied to documentation. It is worth noting that all written texts were recorded (or, as may be, invented) by people in monasteries, and monasteries were staffed either by Megalithics or their orthodox rivals. From Classical times right up to the Age of Mass Literacy the entire 'historical record' has been in the hands of people who had motive, method and opportunity to arrange their own historical past. It is unconscionable that modern historians, because they have elevated documentation to being their chief (and all too often, only) methodology, now absolutely refuse to question the documentation itself because that would be to question their own monopolistic expertise. Since the internet, Wiki and the advent of lay discussion groups, the barbarians have long been within the walls. Not that historians, safe in their ivory towers, have noticed.

---

1 The technical term for discovering a holy relic is 'invention'.

SIX

Festivals and Folk Beliefs

One of the great potential sources of Megalithic knowledge is what might be called The Folk Tradition. Folk beliefs appear embedded in the deep countryside and the countryside itself changed little from the beginnings of agriculture until the enclosures of the nineteenth century. That unvarying backdrop lends credence to the antiquity and authenticity of folk 'lore' but it takes a deal of disinterested analysis to sort out the actual meaning from the sometimes starry-eyed interpretations that can be offered by the folk enthusiasts of our own time. Even so, as a window into the past, especially the non-literate past, there's now't like folk.

Traditionally May Day is the most widely celebrated day of the year, at any rate of the annual festivals that are not linked to the astronomical calendar like Christmas, Easter and Midsummer. May Day would seem to be an entirely arbitrarily chosen date which has somehow got implanted in the folk-calendars of many nations. Mostly it is described—perhaps dismissed—as a standard Fertility Rite of Spring/Coming of Summer celebration, but just under the surface the hand of Megalithia can be observed. For instance, in Greece 1st May is *Protomagia*, a national holiday ostensibly given over to all things floral, but the details are revealing. A bouquet is nailed to the front door from May 1st to June 24th, John the Baptist's Day, that is from Megalithia's National Day to Megalithia's Chief Saint's day. The Ancient Greeks particularly prized apple-bearing sage which had to be collected on 1st May before sunrise which parallels pagan May Day customs such as washing one's face in dew. It is common to find references in folklore to specific moments such as sunrise and sunset or changes in the moon's cycle being crucial for the efficacy of remedies and spells. This is either an old wives' tale or farmers have lost touch with a whole science of maximising the potency of plants by time of planting and/or harvesting. Their re-education is presently being addressed not very successfully by the Steiner Movement.

The only known significance of May 1st (and even this is contested) is that it happens to be the day when the sunrise shines down the length of the Michael Line, which in turn is the longest landline surveyable across Britain. If this is the case then it would appear that the Michael Line has a wider significance than being merely a useful trunk route in southern England. The celebration of this day *in Britain* would perhaps be understandable but as this day is special throughout Europe, two possibilities would seem to arise: either Megalithia is essentially a British invention and its chief festival was exported to other parts of Europe along with the Megalithic System itself or southern Britain was a convenient location for making large-scale Megalithic navigational computations using the Michael Line to act as the 'base date' for everybody else's measurements. The difference between local sunrise and the base sunrise would then provide every locality with a common measurement. Megalithia as a whole is too far north to use the Tropic of Cancer as a base line for making large-scale astronomical calculations in the way Eratosthenes did later in Egypt. The fact that there are beacon hills along the Michael Line reinforces the notion of linear measurements, suggesting elapsed time was being relayed from observer to observer. The tradition of burning bonfires on May Day Eve would therefore hark back to when the May Day measurements were being calibrated the night before.

The whole month of May is of central interest in folkloric terms. May itself is named for the nymph Maia, Hermes' mother, the 'May Queen'. Hawthorn, known as the May-tree, is the only British tree specifically equated with a month, and its branches and flowers are collected early on May Day morning, woven together and placed on windows and doors or decorated with ribbons as 'gifts to the fairies'. Hawthorn was important for Megalithic purposes because it is the best hedging plant for keeping animals in (or out), preventing uncontrolled access to strategic water sources or avoiding toll points. The somewhat mystical custom of 'bringing in the may' has a very practical purpose of maintaining hawthorn hedging along trackways as well as discouraging the plants from seeding in all directions. The notion of keeping things apart is presumably why May is considered an unlucky month for marriage. There are injunctions against removing hawthorn bushes enforced by various taboos. *Haw* is the same as *hag*, both words meaning 'hedge', and Maia is a hag, at any rate one third of the time, being a Triple Goddess—maiden, mother and crone—better known in folklore as Queen *Mab*, a female *magus*. All these beliefs come together in the folk custom of putting hawthorn around windows to keep witches out but hawthorn was also placed on babies' cradles for protection, recalling the princess/saint who was protected by a thicket from pursuing animals, alluding to moon goddesses' formidable responsibilities as patrons of childbirth *and* of chastity *and* of the guardianship of wisdom *and* of the hunt. It may seem odd that moon goddesses oversee the apparently contradictory spheres of childbirth and chastity but the link is the monthly cycle of both Moon and ovulation.

In Welsh folklore hawthorn is the tree sacred to Olwen, a name which translates as 'white track' (*ôl* = 'track' and *wen* = 'white, fair'), hawthorn itself also being called whitethorn. White is a significant Megalithic colour presumably because it is used as a navigational marker; 'white hills' are a frequent occurrence along strategic routes though of course many of them are now white in name only, the Megalithic chalk and limestone flashings being long overgrown. Olwen is the Welsh Maia—in the *Mabinogion* her footprints make a path of white trefoil flowers, the trefoil symbol being widely used in heraldry[1] as the *fleur de lys*, the lily or flower of the Ys (isle).[2] Hawthorn was the emblem of Cardea,

---

1 Heraldry is shot through with Megalithic lore. Hermes with his wings and staff of office was the original herald.
2 The heart of Paris or *par-Ys* (by-Ys) is the Ile de France, the kernel of the country. The fleur-de-lys is a symbol of the French monarchy but it may all go back to a different kind of lily, the blue lotus of Isis (y-Ys) a flower with mysterious narcotic properties that was sacred to the Ancient Egyptians.

the Roman goddess of thresholds and hinges, whose name no doubt gave rise to the popular belief that hawthorn cures cardiac problems though it must be said that the heart is the 'hinge' of the blood circulation system, but perhaps this presumes too much about Megalithics' knowledge of animal biology. The *cardus* was the main north-south axis used by Roman surveyors when laying out towns, that is the 'hinge' on which everything else depended. In Italian and Spanish *cardo* means thistle and this heraldic symbol was adopted by the Stuarts, a premier Megalithic family, leading subsequently to the thistle becoming Scotland's national emblem. In Irish folklore thistles are associated with fertile land, indicating a presumably intentional link between the Stuarts or stewards of Scotland and the Irish High Kings as well as the Fisher King of Grail lore. But all this high-falutin' talk of Cardean Thistles may just be hiding the fact that most things Megalithic were built on the backs of lowly sheep and thistles were used for *carding* wool.

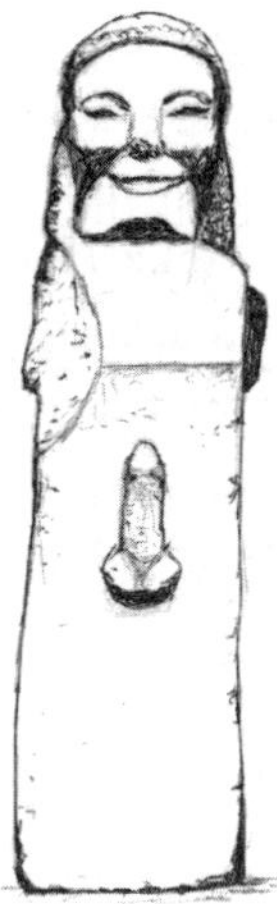

Hermes-pillar

Hermai are four-sided menhirs or stone pillars with the bust of Hermes at the top and often with a heap of small stones at the base. Offerings of food were placed by the stone markers,

The maypole is literally at the heart of May Day festivities. The most likely origin would seem to be the *Irminsûl*, loosely translated as 'world pillar' or 'pillar of all people', an Indo-European version of the world-tree. Early Irmin-pillars were made from tree trunks, with a shaped top sometimes described as the head of a deity but more likely a sun disc. There is no mistaking their relationship with *hermai* or Hermes-pillars. People dancing around the pole/herm may evoke the early stone circles, certainly there are plenty of folk customs referring to people dancing around stone circles, not to mention the stones coming alive and dancing around the people. The upright maypole on the village green is the temporary local version of the herm-pillar and the maypole wreathed in its traditional ribbons represents the serpents twined round Hermes' caduceus.

The custom of garlanding maypoles was also applied to church crosses, themselves the descendants of herms. The dressing of crosses in churches tends to take place on specific dates such as May 1st or Midsummer Day and the geographical location of these church crosses is very relevant when considering likely pre-Christian origins. The rood screen, traditionally used to separate the laity from the priest, was dominated by a rood cross which seems to be a Megalithic survival, originally a navigational cross-staff. The rood is the rod in 'rod, pole or perch' that generations of British schoolchildren would chant as a linear measure. 'Roodstones' were to be found all over Britain before the Puritan destruction of pagan idols, but one that has survived, apparently too big to be destroyed, is in the East Riding of Yorkshire at a highly significant meeting point of roads and cursuses connecting Beacon Hill and Rudstone Beacon, on the meridian. This Rudstone, at twenty-six feet, required an entire church to itself, All Saints' church (All Saints

= All Hallows = Hallowe'en = Samhain). It occupies the north side, the 'devil's side', where people were normally not buried but in this case the Rudstone is surrounded by graves. Certainly the locals seemed to have cherished their pagan monument as they provided it with a lead 'hat' in 1773. Purists decry this modern desecration but impurists regard it as perhaps better accentuating its phallic origins.

The Rudstone

Rudston's megalith, the largest in Britain, is in the centre of the Great Wolds Valley, where the Gypsey Race, the only river in this chalk downland to flow all year round, abruptly turns east and runs parallel to an ancient trade route, the Woldgate, that leads to the coast at Bridlington. The alignment of cursuses (four!) and the straightness of its course indicate the Race, as in mill race, is an artificial leat, possibly the longest in the country.

In their zeal to break down barriers the Puritans successfully undermined the leading Megalithics, especially their figurehead Charles Stuart, though banning all things Megalithic seemed to intensify passionate devotion to the old ways. Rood stones and crosses were just as much the object of Puritan ire as the better known rood screens and, for that matter, maypoles themselves. The only other rood cross surviving today is to be found, covered in greenery, in St Mary's Church, Charlton-on-Otmoor, in Oxfordshire, a notable landmark on a knoll at the northern edge of the fenland.[1] Memories of its Megalithic origins seem to have persisted through the ages, the cross being dressed twice a year with a rope-like flower garland (i.e. the snakes wound round the caduceus) on the saint's day, 19th September, and on May 1st , 'Garland Dressing Day'.

Abbotsbury in Dorset, a significant Megalithic site because of its swannery and its strategic position behind Chesil Beach, has an annual May Day festival, the Garland-Day Procession, when children collect money for a flower garland. Two garlands would be made, one of wild flowers and the other of garden flowers, that is a wild and a domesticated form, which were placed upon a pole and paraded around the village, then blessed and thrown into the sea. May 1st garlands are also paraded through Winteringham, the northern terminus of Ermine Street, where milk pail lugs ('ears') were decorated presumably in homage to Hermes, god of eloquence as well as flocks, after whom Ermine Street is named. The milk pail acts as a collection box, an emblem of commerce associated with Hermes, who always carries a purse.

The annual flower or 'Furry' Dance is celebrated in Helston, Cornwall, on 8th May, the feast day of The Apparition of St Michael, the town's patron saint. Schoolboys traditionally wear white buttonholes of lily-of-the-valley or *lys* and the dancing takes place at the aptly named Coinagehall Street, a steep hill above the east-west trunk road. A black stone was once situated at the rear of The Angel pub before it was removed in the eighteenth century.[2] It may be this 'heelstone', supposedly dropped into the Angel's yard by a fiery dragon, that gave its name to the village but perhaps the *Tolvan*, or 'Holed Stone', which stands east of Helston is the more likely origin of the name. Helston marks the spot where Michael fought the dragon, though the

---

1 With a tradition of radical dissent—in the nineteenth century against enclosures, and in the twentieth against the M40.
2 The Angel formerly belonged to the Godolphin family who made their fortune in Cornish tin mining. The Godolphin Arabian is one of three horses from which all British thoroughbreds are officially descended. The Godolphin stud was at Babraham, Cambridgeshire, down the road from the Gog Magog Hills on the Icknield Way.

original Apparition of St Michael is supposed to have taken place at Monte Gargano in Italy, one of the Michael sites on the reputed trans-European Michael-Apollo leyline from Skellig Michael to Jerusalem.

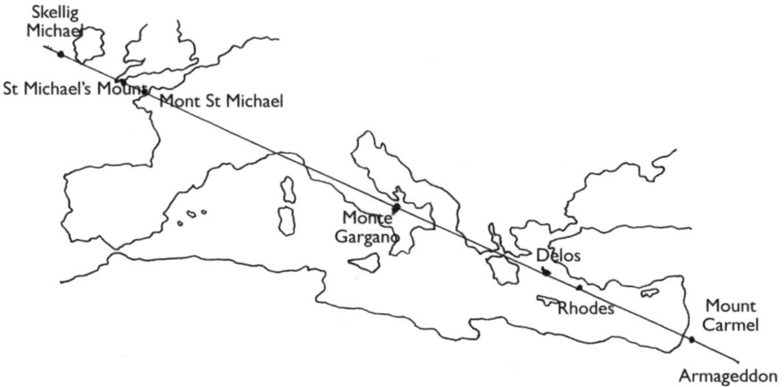

Apollo–St Michael Line

Like its counterpart, Mont Saint-Michel in Normandy, Michael's Mount is on a trans-European leyline that extends from Skellig Michael, off the southwestern extremity of Ireland, to Mount Carmel in Israel, via some of the most renowned sites in antiquity. The sites include the island-shrine of Delos, birthplace of Apollo and his twin-sister Artemis, and Monte Gargano in Italy. Mount Carmel, 'the Evergreen Mountain', means God's vineyard, an appropriately Dionysian reference.

All folk dance should be suspected of Megalithic influence. Maypole dancing has affinities with Morris dancing, the origins of which have long been a matter of intense speculation, theories veering between medieval Crusading import and twentieth-century pub-craze. In reality The Morris goes all the way back to Megalithia, at least if 'dancing the maze' is to be believed, mazes being known as 'morysies' and mazes themselves being firmly rooted in the Megalithic system. Each Morris dancer brandishes his own personal caduceus and the bells strapped round the Morris dancers' ankles are designed to draw attention to folklore's Achilles heel. A vulnerable heel or ankle is a recurring motif in the mythology of god-sacrifice and is a reference to the hobbling of animals, the alternative method of control being castration which is of course the other Divine Wound of Heroes. By extension, the protection of the heel and ankle itself becomes a sacred duty as exemplified by Hermes in his *buskins*, the leather boots that are one of his trademarks.

Hermes on an Early Classic Greek vase

Buskins, leather shoes generally, are frequently used as amulets when laying down the foundations of buildings. They were also placed above doorways and chimney-pieces and no doubt are the origin of the Christmas stocking as well as the genesis of magic footwear in folk tales such as the *Elves and the Shoemaker* and *The Seven League Boots*. It is not surprising that the makers of leather shoes required ritual protection and cobblers had two patron saints, Crispin and Crispianus, linked both by name and the legend of their deaths—after two attempted executions (drowning and burning), they were saved by an angel so they could be beheaded, thereby completing the necessary Triple Death, though even by Christian standards this seems scant reward for gaining divine intercession. Crispin and his near-homonymic brother are reincarnations of the heavenly twins Castor and Pollux, with whom they share a feast day (25th October).[1]

---

1 In England, St. Crispin seems to have been the *de facto* patron saint of all workers not just shoe-makers, entering popular lore as 'St. Monday', a centuries-old tradition of a day off before the concept of a two-day weekend took legal hold. Which is surprisingly modern, even as late as the 1960's it was usually the case that employees worked half-day Saturday.

Achilles was a disciple of Chiron the Centaur whose own heel was his undoing because, though a master-healer, he died of a poisoned arrow in the hoof. Fortunately the secret knowledge acquired by Chiron was passed on to someone who managed not to die young, Dionysus, the Master of the Revels. Though contrary to prurient imaginings, these orgiastic dances seemed mainly to consist of a hobbling 'partridge dance' in which the dance steps re-enact the capture of a cock partridge attracted by a lamed hen into the centre of a maze, acting as a bird trap.[1] The association of threads, usually called *clews* i.e. 'clues', and mazes (cf. Ariadne and the Labyrinth) suggests nets were used, though modern bird snarers, i.e. ornithologists, use nets without mazes. Nets themselves have Megalithic resonances on account of the 'shrouds' of sailing ships, a term that extends to the covering of dead bodies for whom Hermes was the escort. All this is harking back to Megalithic methods of capturing live animals and birds in order to domesticate them.[2]

Mazes continued to be popular in England until the seventeenth century when the fashion for garden mazes, love-knots and Celtic roses was so unacceptable to the Puritans that they were banned along with maypoles. One festival that survived in out of the way Cornwall is Penzance's Mazey Day, a celebration of John the Baptist in which the ubiquitous hobby horse is de-shoed, i.e. hobbled. Penzance itself is of Megalithic interest because it is on the other side of Mount's Bay from Marazion and St Michael's Mount. Padstow in north Cornwall has maintained not one but two rival hobby horses and Minehead

---

1 “And a partridge in a pear tree”, the refrain of The Twelve Days of Christmas, points to an end of the year celebration of Artemis, one of whose sacred birds was the partridge. Pear tree is a pun on perdrix, pronounced pear-dree, the French for partridge, derived from the Latin *et aperuit in aperto* (= “and she [the Virgin] gave birth in the open”). The gifts mostly refer to birds, the 'gold rings' being golden ring-necked pheasants or quail, said to be the birds most loved by Artemis (her birthplace was Ortygia, the 'isle of quail').

2 The connection between bird snaring and Megalithic principles is the subject of *The Magic Flute* by Mozart, a prominent Mason. Another of his operas, *Don Giovanni*, is actually a celebration of Hermes. Don Giovanni is based on the Don Juan legend popularised in Spain as the *Trickster* of Seville and the Guest of *Stone*. The modern play *Don Juan Tenorio* is performed in Spain every year on November 1st, Samhain.

goes one better with three 'horses' who, before the 'battle' can begin, bow three times to the May 1st sunrise. The town's hobby horse used to go in and out of houses 'for luck' i.e. to collect rent and anyone who refused to pay was bound and struck with an old boot.

Members of the Order of the Garter, a chivalric order apparently based on the Arthurian code, wear the garter around the top of the left (the 'sinister' or 'bad') leg. Discounting the reported tomfoolery between Edward III and the Countess of Salisbury, the actual origin is the wounded thigh of the sacred hero. At the other end of the social scale, Leggin'-Down Day was when boys and girls tried to catch each other's ankles to 'leg them down' on April Fool's Day, the Fool/Jester/Knave/Jack all being versions of Hermes the trickster.[1] The wider Megalithic significance of all this is well illustrated in Hungerford's festival of Hocktide, or Hock Day, which explicitly links hobbling with toll paying. Those local Megalithic characters, the innkeeper and the blacksmith, are in charge of 'Shoeing the Colts' which involves hobbling the legs of newcomers and driving nails into the soles of their shoes until they buy drinks. The festival days are Binding Monday when men and women tie each other up to collect 'head pennies' and Tutti Day Tuesday when two Tuttimen toll collectors, armed with poles decked out in contrasting red and blue flowers, visit every house to demand rent of a penny, finishing up naturally at the Three Swans pub. Hungerford is at a crossroads (and ford) strategically sited on the A4, the main east-west route that links Bath, Avebury, Silbury Hill and London, or in Megalithic terms links Aquae Sulis (the waters of Sul), Silbury Hill and St Paul's Cathedral (Paul = Saul). John of Gaunt, chief protector of the subversive Lollards and the patron of Hungerford, knew all this and built his main palace (now the Savoy Hotel) where the A4 enters London. John of Gaunt was buried, unusually for royalty, in St Paul's.

---

1   In Tarot cards *Le Mat* means both The Fool and Madman, a raggedly colourful joker, i.e. the motley herald Hermes, who typically stands on one leg. The term is thought to be related to 'check*mate*' and perhaps derives from *Ma'at* (truth and final judgement), a reminder of the underworld significance of Hermes/Thoth.

The building blocks of classical Megalithia are standing stones, whose folk name is *grey wethers*, wether meaning sheep which stones in a field are said to resemble. But the actual link is that a wether specifically refers to a castrated ram and a further etymological link is that *withy* means a tough fibrous plant, the chief method of binding testicles.[1] Turning a screw or tap in a counter-clockwise direction, or *widder*shins, has a tightening effect. The esoteric version is that the snakes wound round Hermes' caduceus represent withies tied round a penis, from which the religious symbology emerges since the castrator of the herd is all-powerful. Standing stones are also known as *sarsens*, a word that repays closer scrutiny. The Oxford English Dictionary claims *sarsen* is a "variation of Saracen" implying that the local yokels believed that some Muslim knights popped over and erected their ancient monuments when nobody was looking, but perhaps it is only the OED that believes in these kinds of unlikely explanation, as it so often does because its entire etymological paradigm is frankly hopeless. On the other hand, if 'Saracen' refers to a different set of Phoenicians, the ones of the Bronze Age who might have set up the original system, then that would make rather more sense. To Cornish tinners the term 'Saracen' just meant 'foreigner', someone prohibited by law from advancing inland.

The tendency to view May Day festivities, indeed all folk festivities, as essentially fertility rites is seriously flawed. Anybody who thinks that lads and lasses habitually cavorted under hedges on May Day knows little of the British climate. Megalithia shared the Christian attitude that nature could look after itself so long as ritual obeisance of a limited kind was rendered. Folk customs relate to the everyday economy and are earth- rather than heaven-bound. In a pre-literate era, with no recourse to permanent records or maps, people had to physically check, or 'beat', boundaries at frequent intervals, the three days leading up to Whitsun, Rogationtide, normally being the signal

---

1   The Semitic rite of circumcision has a close parallel with Megalithic herding practices. Both Jews and Arabs, as animal herders originally, have religious systems that are suffused with Megalithic lore.

for these very necessary local proceedings. In other words the villagers are carrying out land surveys, the local equivalent of what Megalithia Inc is doing on a larger scale. The techniques are sufficiently similar to assume that one gave rise to the other but which is chicken and which is egg cannot be known at this distance. The connection can be seen in the use, by both villagers and Megalithic surveyors, of hedges, walls, standing stones and specific species of trees as physical markers. Annual boundary beating involved literally beating knowledge into village children (!) whilst blessing various landmarks along the way, but such methods were necessary before literacy, when everything of consequence had to be seared in memory by communal repetition. Boundaries do not merely apply to individual villagers' property rights but to the village as a whole vis-à-vis the next village because one of the chief benefits of marking the common boundary is the opportunity presented for exacting tolls. But tolls themselves are inextricably linked to water rights so the modern versions of these proceedings normally feature the local well-custodians, usually the pub landlord and the parish vicar, receiving a small symbolic payment.

It is not surprising then that the maintenance of boundaries is something of a solemn duty. For example, the annual building of the Penny Hedge at Whitby in Yorkshire reportedly originated in the dying request of the local hermit who was attacked and killed by huntsmen, though the 'hedge' is now a willow-gate indicating an earlier toll point. Whitby is an intensely Megalithic place. Hilda, the founder of its monastery, was a 'dragon-slayer' who *herded* the local *snakes* sending them over the *cliff-tops* and turning them into *stone*. She was the patroness of *Caedmon*, reputedly the earliest English poet, which is something of a coincidence because *Cadmus* of Thebes was the man who allegedly invented writing. Inland from Whitby is the aforementioned Rombald's Moor which was the site of an annual perambulation, i.e. a boundary-marking walk, which took place on Rogation Monday at the Grubstones, a stone circle formerly known as Roms or Rums Law. The ceremony always ended with the chant "This is Rumbles Law". The Masonic Grand Lodge of All England is rumoured to have met at the Grubstones.

Modern celebrants are unlikely to appreciate the origins of their various boundary-marking rituals because these ceremonies arose from earlier requirements no longer relevant, but they survive because the whole experience remains enjoyable and usefully bonding. Readers of this book however will immediately recognise the proper historical significance of, to use one example from many, the *Hare Pie Scramble* at Hallaton in Leicestershire. The hare pie commemorates a local legend of two ladies saved by a hare from a charging bull; the parade from the Fox Inn next to the village pond, the highest point around, proceeds to St Michael and All Angels located at Churchgate on the main road. The hare pie is taken to Hare Pie Bank, thought to be the site of an ancient temple dedicated to a St Mawrel (i.e. St Melangell, the patron saint of hares), and broken up before the start of the Hallaton Bottle Kicking contest. At a stone cross on the village green, the Butter Cross, three barrels are decorated with ribbons, the start of a no-holds barred fight between opposing villages to get the 'bottles' across one of the two local streams, a mile apart. The licence for violence comes to an end when both teams drink the beer from the final barrel around the Butter Cross. All this is entirely 'functional' as understood by pre-literate communities. Water in the village is obtained from wells or pumps on the green so clearly water rights have to be asserted. But what 'asserted' actually means might vary over time. No doubt most villages preferred the simpler version of warfare-in-miniature, the annual football match, to reinforce territorial delimitations. It is noticeable that the coming of mass literacy and the widespread introduction of land registries coincides with the demise of many of these proto-Megalithic practices but it is a mistake to suppose that folk festivals only disappeared 'just the other day'. In truth, they have been disappearing (or if you prefer, evolving) for the whole of their existence.

Summer festivals are all about fecundity, the exuberance of life generally. It is now, rather than during the relative scarcity of springtime, that fruitfulness is celebrated. During the Oyster Festival in Whitstable, near the Megalithically-named Herne Bay on the Kent coast, pennies are collected by children for 'the Grotters', grottoes on the seashore covered in oyster shells. The best surviving example of a shell grotto is to be found at nearby Margate,[1] a terminus of the Pilgrims' Way from Avebury.

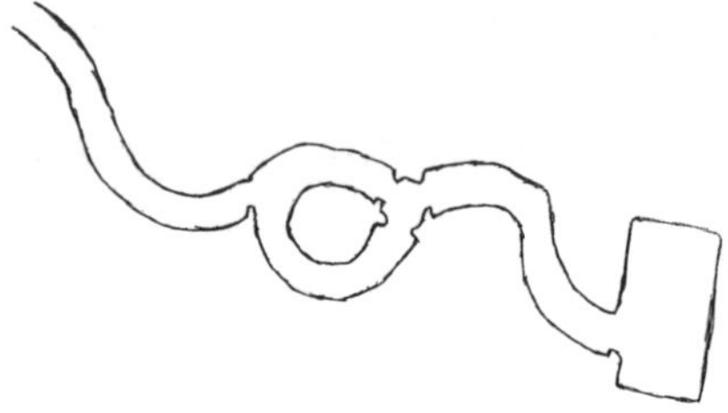

Plan of Margate Shell Grotto

This is not the only link with Avebury because Stukeley, the eighteenth century antiquarian, provided a diagram of the general layout of Avebury and its surrounding avenues:

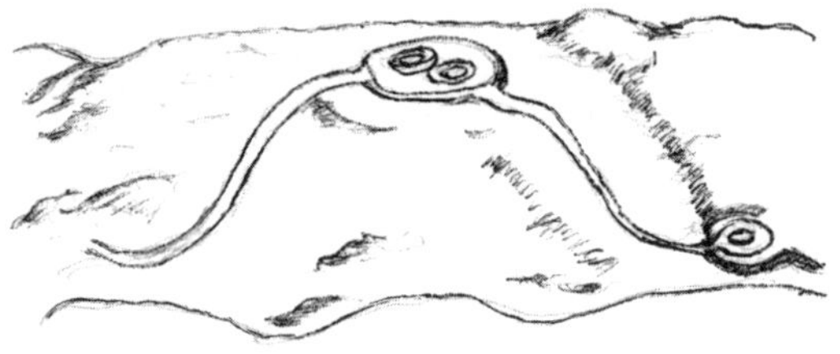

Stukeley's diagram of Avebury

The two layouts become more striking when compared to modern depictions of the uterus and fallopian tubes. The similarity may be accidental but reluctance to investigate human anatomy is a peculiarly Christian-era taboo and such prudery is very unlikely to have affected those animal fertility specialists, the Megalithics.

---

1 Modern commentators assume this is just a Victorian folly but then these same experts think that Margate is just a Victorian seaside resort. The Megalithics constructed it as the most easterly point of the Kentish peninsula and, reputedly, on a straight line between the British and German (Goseck) Stonehenges.

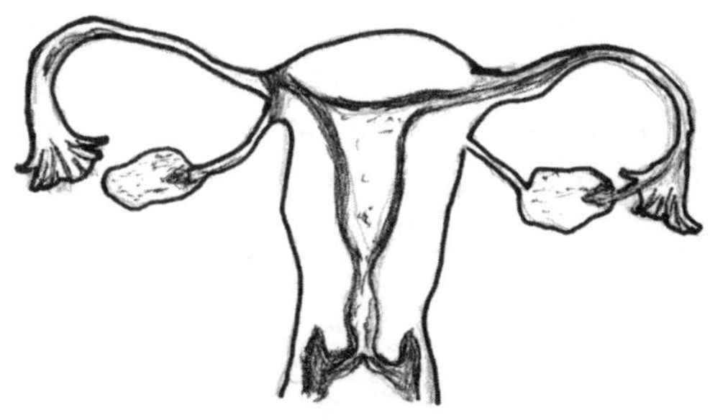

**A GCSE diagram of the female
reproduction system**

Reproduction is the business of the moon goddess, who rules over childbirth, but some Christian overlay has to be stripped away before she is revealed. The link between oysters and Avebury is St James, the presiding saint of the grotters as well as the patron saint of Avebury where he has a church dedicated to him. The Megalithic link is the cockle shell which is both St James' symbol, worn by all pilgrims to Santiago [Sant-Iago = St James] de Compostela and, as the scallop shell, is the 'boat' bringing ashore Aphrodite, the chief deity of childbirth. The association with Aphrodite gives oysters their reputation as aphrodisiacs—in Ancient Greek 'kteis' means both scallop shell and vagina. It is always amusing listening to modern-day nutritionists telling us solemnly that it is all due to the protein content.

In the Middle Ages cockle shells were mass-produced for Compostela pilgrims to allow the devotees to register their progress at river crossings and holy wells, somewhat like the Stations of the Cross but even more redolent of their Megalithic predecessors offering up tolls at the exact same places.[1] St James is the patron saint of Spain and also the patron saint of blacksmiths and so linked to metallurgy and horses. As St James the Moor-slayer he manifested himself in the

---

1   In these wayside shrines *now*, the scallop shell is on the petrol stations though whether the Shell Oil Company knows of its own Megalithic roots is unclear.

sky on a white horse above the Battle of Clavijo. *Clavo* in Spanish means hammer and Clavijo suggests 'Son (hijo) of hammer' which would make him Spain's Thor, the hammer throwing god of thunder.[1] In the Bible St James and his twin are the Sons of Thunder but in Spain his 'twin' is San Millán, from whose monastery written Spanish is supposed to have sprung.

Pilgrim Monument (Navarre, Spain)

A medieval pilgrim's garb of broad-brimmed hat, cloak, satchel and long staff mirrors that worn by Hermes. Hermes was usually portrayed wearing a traveller's cap and cloak and carrying a purse and staff, the purse being a direct reminder that the Megalithic System needed to be paid for.

With summer over, the year darkens and Megalithia's great autumnal festival arrives, Samhain. Better known today as Hallowe'en i.e. the evening before All Hallows aka All Saints, November 1st, Samhain is the reverse of Beltane or May 1st, and emphasises the death aspect of the natural cycle. Not surprisingly, and in contrast to May celebrations, the focus is on the sombre, the underground and the disagreeable—though

---

1   In dragon lore the only effective weapons against dragons are iron and thunderbolts.

naturally everything is lightened as always with folk festivities. November 1st is traditionally the date when debts have to be repaid, the origin of 'trick or treat'. It is the chief fire festival, though nowadays the bonfire events take place a few days later on Guy Fawkes Night when the populace is urged to "Remember, remember". The relationship is made explicit because *guising*, which means disguising, is the folk term for trick-or-treat, children in disguise going from house to house at Hallowe'en. Guisers or guysers, like mummers, wore masks or blackened their faces. The penalties imposed on people who 'do not pay the toll', i.e. did not give sweets to children, is a familiar Megalithic theme. Children collect these tolls in the 'Penny for the Guy' tradition.[1] 'Penny for the Guy' is a version of 'Penny for the Guide', the guide being the ferryman who rowed souls to the other side, and the ultimate guide is Hermes, who led souls into the underworld. When coins are placed on the eyes of the deceased tribute is being paid to Megalithia.

'Guy' in colloquial English denotes 'Everyman' and the even more idiomatic 'geezer' (i.e. *guiser*) is used in the same sense. Guy has a special significance in British folklore. In Europe, John and James are the Sons of Thunder, the equivalent of Castor and Pollux, and therefore characters with a sound Megalithic pedigree, but for some reason they undergo a coarsening in Britain. Not only does the phrase inescapably suggest Castrator and Bollocks but the very names *John* and *James* undergo a weird elision, for example a Tudor 'Jakes' was a toilet which we now call 'a john'. In English the familiar form of John is Jack whereas on the Continent Jacques refers to James! One of the stock characters in English mumming plays is Johnny Jack whose role is to collect money from bystanders but, whatever the actual origin, Jack is also synonymous with Everyman, as in Jack-of-all-trades. Jack O'

---

1 November 5th is the feast day of St. Emeric. Amerigo Vespucci was named after this Emeric which itself is a variation of Hermes. Readers by now will not be surprised to learn that America has a thoroughly Megalithic name.

Lent, also known as Jack O' Straw,[1] is the name of the straw effigy set up in public places, dragged through the streets and stoned before being burnt on a funeral pyre on Shrove Tuesday, the spring counterpart of the autumn festival when Jack O' Lantern is the central symbol of Hallowe'en. Folkloric Jacks tended to get festooned with Megalithic encumbrances. Jack O' Kent, for instance, was a famous wizard responsible for flinging immovable stones around the Welsh border area, but also finding himself entombed in various church walls, a common fate for standing stones. Jack's most famous journey was from his Welsh marches to London carrying hot mince pies, via such places as Worm Hill, St Michael and All Angels, Winforton and a now derelict St George's church erected by the Knights Templar on a beacon hill at Wormsley. Jack naturally had time to snag his garter on a church steeple on the way.

Jack-in-the-Green is a common character in traditional parades, resembling a bush or Green Man, who is killed at the close of play, a folk memory of the dying/resurrected year-god. In Rochester, one of the country's main entry points, a terminus of the Pilgrims' Way and hence a 'beacon' on the Kent coast, Jack-in-the-Green is woken at dawn on May 1st by 'chimney sweeps' who lead him through the town. Chimney sweeps themselves have Megalithic resonances. Blackened faces are part of the Morris dancing and mumming tradition and chimneys are etymologically linked to roads (*chemin* in French, *camino* in Spanish), harking back to the ancient connection between smoke signals and navigation. This is why sweeps are considered lucky, an otherwise perplexing attribute of such a disagreeable trade.

In Greek myth Hermes was said to have invented fire-sticks for kindling. In Britain, of course, the modern fire festival celebrates

---

1 Jack Straw features as one of the three leaders of the Peasants' Revolt of 1381 alongside Wat Tyler and John Ball. Their names were intended to evoke Everyman (Jack Straw and John Bull). Jack Straw's Castle is a highly visible Megalithic site at the highest point in London on Hampstead Heath. Oddly, but in hydraulic Megalithic terms unsurprisingly, there is a large body of water, the Whitestone Pond, at this eminent place.

that most famous would-be-kindler, Guy Fawkes. He is supposed to be a strictly historical character but various aspects of his 'life story' have inescapable Megalithic undertones. The real Fawkes is almost certainly the thirteenth century Guy Foulques, a native of Languedoc who rose from being Bishop of Le Puy-en-Velay to become Pope Clement IV and was the benefactor and patron of Roger Bacon, popularly credited with inventing gunpowder. Certainly somebody was tried for the crime of trying to blow up Parliament (with gunpowder) and inevitably, albeit lawfully, this person was executed by hanging, drawing and quartering, thereby undergoing the Triple Death. The name Guy Fawkes is properly, according to his signature, *Guido Fawkes,* or 'guide-o'-forks', that is the speaking signpost of Megalithic tradition. Just to make sure the Megalithic connection was underlined for the benefit of those in the know, the transcript of the trial carefully records the Christian name of Guy's adoptive father as being *Dionysus,* aka the Green Man aka Green George aka Jack-in-the-Green aka England's greatest hero, Robin Hood.

Foliate Head on Screen, Dore Abbey

Dore Abbey, Hertfordshire, is a former Cistercian abbey down the road from Wormbridge, which was owned by the Knights Hospitaller, successors to the Knights Templar, and has a well-preserved Green Man roof boss. A similar foliate head carving is at Hatfield House, also in Hertfordshire, given to

The emphasis of Hallowe'en on 'fall guys' and the spirit world is but a reflection of the wider struggle between Christianity and paganism, an extension of the age-old conflict between town and country,[1] literate versus non-literate, the centralised state against local interest. For instance, control of the pharmaceutical industry was always an arena for conflict between the formal qualifications of citified doctors on the one hand and the *folk* tradition of herbalists, apothecaries and wise-women on the other. The apothecaries were obvious recipients of Megalithic knowledge, given their origins as *spicers* and *pepperers*, i.e. they are at the end of long distance trade routes; the herbalists were the inheritors of the drug trade that underpinned so much of Megalithia; wise-women as practising midwives have a direct connection with the 'childbirth saints'.

A question that arises regarding Megalithic society is "What happens to Megalithics when they grow old?" Wise-women are so endemic in folklore as to suggest that the Megalithics solved the problem by giving their less active elderly members, a largely female group, sedentary employment as toll collectors, well-attendants, beacon-keepers, Watchers at the Ford,[2] who might conceivably be very unpopular on account of a) demanding tolls from people and b) cursing them if they failed to pay. Nor is the occasional persecution of these 'witches' very surprising because their crimes, contrary to the roseate view of wise-women held by anxiously non-misogynistic modern observers, are only too true. As Megalithics they had all the tell-tale marks: practising

---

1 Pagan, as already remarked, means rustic just as 'heathen' refers to heath, marking the gulf between religions (indeed cultures) that demand large-scale buildings and religions that, as it were, celebrate their absence.
2 They are called 'Washers at the Ford' in folklore and usually described as hags, washing blood-stained clothes, who could see into the future. They were said to be noisy creatures associated with 'keening' (i.e. 'knowing'). But the point is always the same: travellers ought to be wary of these apparently feeble old ladies. Paying the toll is cheap at the price.

an alternative religion, control over familiar animals, a working knowledge of powerful plants and holding themselves superior to and aloof from the common herd. A reputation for wisdom is never a bad thing but the supposed power to harm people is even more helpful as a means of ensuring provision in old age, worth the intermittent risk of hanging in the same way that communities continue living on the fertile slopes of a volcano.

The notion of witches as child-killers, cf. Hansel and Gretel, derives from the need for abortions in subsistence rural economies. Although this is a social necessity given the precariousness of the food supply, such activities are always kept behind closed doors because of the genuine and unavoidable guilt that derives from killing one's own, however necessary it may be. Megalithia is quite used to providing things that 'polite society' shuns and the antipathy of the Catholic Church to abortion and contraception is all part of their ongoing conflict with the rather more down-to-earth and life-affirming Pagans. This is why moon goddesses oversee the apparently contradictory practices of chastity and childbirth: it reflects the dual role of 'cunning-women' as both midwives and abortionists. The grimmer aspect of their work, the provision of abortions, is entwined with herbal lore. Cronewort is also called St John's Plant in honour of John the Baptist but its more popular name is Mugwort, *Artemisia vulgaris*; the *crone* part highlighting the plant's use by midwives as an abortifacient. Michaelmas is the traditional time to pick wild carrots, a plant described by Hippocrates as 'disrupting ovum implantation'.

The Druidic midwinter harvesting of mistletoe with a ceremonial golden sickle is generally assumed to be a 'fertility rite' but is more likely quite the reverse since both mistletoe and juniper berries are abortifacients, as of course is the sickle itself. Juniper appears to have a symbiotic relationship with mistletoe, a species of mistletoe being actually called 'juniper mistletoe'. Juniper berries are the main flavouring of gin, a drink named after French *genièvre* or Dutch *jenever*, both words meaning 'juniper'. Gin had the nickname 'Mother's Ruin' which socially-minded historians always assume to be because of the squalor and misery it created, but much more likely it was because gin (and a hot bath) was literally the ruin of motherhood-to-be. But juniper, if not gin, has a rather longer history, juniper berries having been found in Ancient Egyptian tombs. The Megalithic heartland of Wiltshire used to be covered with juniper but the plant is now more or less confined to the Porton Down chemical and biological warfare establishment. Make of that what you will.

Witches reputedly put vervain or 'flying ointment' on their broomsticks, a reference to shamanic mood-enhancing drugs. Vervain is an ingredient of *verveine*, a green liqueur made in Guy Foulques' Le Puy-en-Velay, one of the starting points for the Compostela pilgrimage *and* the First Crusade. The town is dominated by a St Michael chapel and has a Black Virgin made of cedarwood, the resin of which produces hallucinogenic incense. Historically vervain received a remarkable degree of 'official' approbation. It was a plant much prized by the Druids, and the Romans were said to dress altars with its leaves. A mysterious figurine called Verbeia was unearthed by archaeologists at Ilkley in Yorkshire, a strategic trading post on the notoriously dangerous River Wharfe. Usually described as a Romano-British 'water deity', Verbeia is unknown anywhere else and the Ilkley altar stone dedicated to her is also unique, so the "Romano" bit is highly dubious. She is a typical hag or 'watcher' at the ford, a prime site for toll collecting but perhaps here a suitable offering for safe passage. Vervain may have been cultivated for industrial purposes. In several European languages it is an 'ironherb' e.g. *ferfaen* is Celtic iron-stone, *Eisenkraut* in German and *IJzerhard* in Dutch means 'iron-hardener', all names that point to its use by smiths in metal hardening procedures, vervain acting as the carbon in carbon steel. This entire study of ancient metallurgy's use of vegetable alloys is a scandalously neglected subject.

Stone carving of Verbeia

This ancient relief carving had been incorporated into All Saints Church, Ilkley. The outlines of the carving are so indistinct that it is hard to determine if she is holding a pair of snakes or flaming torches or staffs, all of which have Hermetic associations. There may be a connection between Verbeia, the nearby Swastika Stone and St Brigid, the Irish patron saint of both blacksmiths and midwives whose cross resembles a swastika (sun) symbol.

What is hard to deny is that vervain is both 'witchy' and Megalithic and it is never difficult finding parallels between these two countryside (not to say, country-wide) traditions. The links are often via what we nowadays perhaps misleadingly call witches' familiars. Actually what is being referred to here is, as described in a later chapter, the close association between certain Megalithics and particular animals, so for example a toll keeper (i.e. a witch) might have a crow 'guarding' the crossing in her absence. The very word *crone* is etymologically related to crow (*corone* in Greek) and crows are universally associated with prophetic utterances. The crow family, *corvids*, are regarded as all-purpose omens, as in the popular rhyme used when magpies, rooks or crows (it varies according to region) are spotted. Not surprisingly the rhyme finishes on a Hermetic crescendo: "*One for sorrow, two for mirth; Three for a wedding and four for a birth; Five for silver, six for gold; Seven for a secret ne'er to be told*". Hermes is the god of birds of omen. His day of the week, Wednesday, has a corresponding day in Ogham, the ancient Irish tree-alphabet, 'Wednesday's tree' being hazel, the tree of wisdom and eloquence. Hermes' equivalent in the Norse pantheon, Odin/Woden, was usually shown with a pair of talking ravens acting as messenger-advisers named 'Thought' and 'Memory'.

The number thirteen, frequently associated with witchcraft, relates to the pre-literate Moon calendar of thirteen four-week months that was superseded by the Roman twelve-month system. Thus the thirteen was declared to be 'unlucky'. Birch twig brooms feature in witch tradition because twigs were used to write Ogham which, as the rival to the Latin of Christianity, was routinely blackened by association. Birch is the 'birth' tree, the first letter of the Ogham alphabet. If *Macbeth* is anything to go by, witches gathered on blasted heaths, the habitat best suited to birches (and heathens), and were 'by the pricking of their thumbs' versed in the Ogham finger-alphabet. Blasted heaths are also where fly agaric, the magic mushroom, grows best and circles of mushrooms are known as fairy rings, as are stone circles.

Witches were sometimes buried with their feet pointing backwards, recalling Hermes' trick of making his stolen cattle walk backwards to confuse their pursuers, a theme picked up by the *wryneck*, traditionally associated with witchcraft, which has two toes pointing backward. Owls, often seen as witches' familiars, also have convertible toes. A person being pursued by a witch was advised to scatter small objects in her path as she would be obliged to pick them up and count them (because of her true role as toll-keeper). The witch's cauldron is also part of this toll-keeping function so it is not surprising to find it too is accorded special powers in folklore. For instance, Mother Ludlam's Cave in Surrey is above a spring formerly called Ludwell, on a drovers' route leading to the Pilgrims' Way, and which traditionally housed the local hermit. Mother Ludlam herself was a wise-woman who owned a cauldron into which coins would be dropped "to persuade the fairies to grant wishes", typical of the legends that get attached to such sites because originally the cauldron was a receptacle for collecting tolls—it is much easier throwing tokens in than getting them out.[1] Mother Ludlam's cauldron is now in the local church at Frensham where there is a stained glass window of St George and St Michael.

Entrance to Mother Ludlam's Cave

The interior is inaccessible behind fancy grille-work but the spring to which the cave owes its importance can be seen trickling down from the entrance. Access from the path to the river Wey is obstructed by an alder swamp, possibly deliberately to enhance Mother Ludlam's earning capacity.

After Samhain the next great Megalithic festival is Yuletide, that is winter solstice, and as such had to be firmly expropriated by the Christians, though the join is always evident. The deeply ambivalent figure of Saint Nicholas/Santa Claus harks back to shamanic reindeer-herding, though he is admitted into Christianity as the patron saint of sailors, merchants, pawnbrokers, pharmacists and (repentant) thieves, all duplicating Hermes' portfolio. Santa's sack is the equivalent of Hermes' purse and leaving out mince pies and a glass of sherry is an unconscious extension of Megalithic

---

1 In folklore 'cold iron' wards off witches. Cold iron is clearly a play on the word cauldron (or vice versa) and reinforces the usual Megalithic injunction that paying the toll averts most supernatural punishments. This extends to the maker of the cauldron in the form of the 'tinker's cuss'.

butterstones just as Santa's grotto refers back to hermits' caves, and naturally requires a 'toll'. Even after fifteen hundred years of Christmas, the spirit of Yuletide is simply irrepressible and despite the annual urgings of clerics, the festival remains true to its roots. Even the most important church service, Midnight Mass, is on Christmas Eve rather than on the day itself, a specifically Megalithic way of celebrating. However, since Yule did become a Christian feast, the Megalithics largely transferred *their* festivities to the following day, Boxing Day, the feast day of St Stephen, the first Christian martyr to be put to death by *stoning*.[1]

Boxing Day is Wrenning Day, or the Hunting of the Wren, when a dead wren in a box, often attached to a garlanded pole, would be taken from house to house and in true Megalithic fashion a penny was demanded for its burial. This custom is still with us in the form of the Christmas Box, an annual toll 'requested' by tradesmen. Boxing Day may take its name from the wren's box, i.e. coffin, a ritualistic link with the death of the winter king who has to be sacrificed, which is why in folklore the unassuming wren is the King of Birds. Written as *dryw* in Welsh and *dreoilín* in Irish, wrens are associated with the *derw* or oak, traditionally sacred to the nearly homonymic Druids. Along with the robin, they are the commonest birds in Britain, their numbers suggesting that both birds have long been protected by folk belief. The robin is the spirit of the New Year who kills the wren, the spirit of the Old Year, but inevitably 'Cock Robin' has to be killed in his turn to make sure the cycle continues. Yule is associated with the white mistletoe berries which provide the two birds with a food source in winter. The other Yuletide berry, the red holly, completes the Megalithic colour scheme of red and white, which was adopted as heraldic colours by the later Megalithics, the Knights Templar, the Portuguese and Spanish navigators, the English, the Rosicrucians, the Swiss Red Cross and so forth.

Red dye, Kermes (Hermes) red or Carmine red, was made from the kermes beetle, a parasite of the holly oak (= kermes oak).

---

1 In Hebrew, *even* means stone, hence Steven is St. Stone! 26th December is the feast day of Pope Dionysius, the only pope named after a pagan god.

Carmenta was a Roman goddess who had the remarkable, but in Megalithia all too common, dual role of being the patron saint of midwives and inventor of the Latin alphabet. There seems to have always been a widespread prejudice against red-haired wet nurses, underlining an association between carmine and witchery (as in charm and karma). Carmenta is one of the three Muses and had a son by Hermes. Kermes dye was used for dying leather, especially buskins, scarlet half-boots, known as 'carmine leather' and which Hermes is always shown wearing (as is that other folkloric trickster, Puss in Boots).[1] Cinnabar, or vermillion in the powdered form, is the very poisonous 'red mercury' and was widely used for colouring.[2] All this emphasis on red and white seems to go back an extraordinarily long way. Red ochre is found in ancient burial sites in the Preseli Hills and on Salisbury Plain and provides the name of the 'Red Lady of Paviland', a ceremonial burial on the Gower peninsula dated to the Palaeolithic. Red ochre also features in the very anomalous midden culture on the Newfoundland coast. But it should not be ignored that red and white are also the highly visible colours on the fly agaric mushroom cap.

Folk customs are often related to trade and the attendant tolls necessary to maintain even primitive infrastructure. If folklore is to be believed the entire British countryside is populated by super-natural entities of one kind or another, though on inspection they generally turn out to be the usual injunctions to pay the toll. The supernatural agency varies with the terrain. Well-trodden and comparatively civilised places like river crossings in the Surrey stockbroker belt can be managed by relatively benign old ladies such as Mother Ludlam but wilder Britain needs fiercer guardians.

---

1 Dyeing has always been a Megalithic speciality. The commercial connection is best exemplified by the Company of Painter-Stainers making a bid for the Heralds' Office after the Great Fire of London. Needless to say, they were turned down.
2 Alchemists were essentially intellectualised apothecaries. The inclusion of mercury in patented medicines, particularly for syphilis, is attributable to the role of Hermes/Mercury. The stuff was so legendarily toxic that the name was used in a scam by Soviet ex-army types peddling "Red Mercury, the radioactive explosive".

Out on the open heathland and boggy marshes there lurk bogies, pixies, piskies, Scottish Red Caps, Jack o' Lanterns, will-o'-the-wisps, Black Dogs. The word pixie is related to *psyche*, the Greek for soul, returning us once more to Hermes conducting people. Pixies, though generally helpful, had a reputation for spitefulness if their assistance went unrewarded. Those unfortunate enough to be 'pixie-led' into bogs could escape by taking off their outer garments and turning them inside out, that is turning out their pockets.

In contrast to moors and fens, where the traveller needs help just getting across the treacherous landscape, wooded areas require a different kind of guide. The forest outlaw, Robin Hood, is the last in a line of comparable characters that stretch back into prehistory such as Robin Goodfellow, Jack o' the Green, Puck, Herne the Hunter. Herne is as his name suggests a horned god, the local version of Cernunnos, the stag-headed deity who is depicted on altars and cauldrons all over northern Europe from Paris and Rheims to Scotland, Ireland and Denmark. British representations show the god with two large ram-headed serpents for legs that rear up next to open purses of coins on either side. Herne is said to inhabit Windsor Forest, in many respects the 'heart' of England, and until the end of the eighteenth century there was an oak tree in the middle of Windsor Great Park called Herne's Oak from where he hanged himself 'to expiate a crime', a motif also central to the Woden and Jesus legends though Christians made sure horned figures would be automatically identified with the Devil. Windsor Forest was traversed by the main road to London which passed below the castle and the adjacent St John the Baptist church (it was blocked by Queen Victoria, presumably unamused by traffic in her backyard).

The earliest literary mention of Herne is in *The Merry Wives of Windsor* which was reportedly first performed at Windsor in the late sixteenth century on Garter Day, garter being a reminder of the wounded thigh of the hero. Robin Goodfellow is the British Puck. Puck is frequently conflated with Pan, half-man half-goat, who seems to be master of the Dionysian woodland revels, *pan*demonium and viticulture. Puck is synonymous with *fuck*—Pan, a son of Hermes, was associated with procreation, and portrayed with an outsize phallus. Whatever gloss is applied to these woodland folk, the fact of the matter is you need to find the way through the forest, and it will cost you.

Puck
[*Title page of* Robin Good-Fellow, his Mad Pranks and merry Jests *(1628)*]

Woods are particularly tricky places that require their own set of rules and thus a special category of guide in the Megalithic System. Just as Pixies provide assistance through treacherous moorland bogs, so Puck is their equivalent for the Wild Wood. Puck is embedded in English folklore, often in the guise of the Green Man, Herne the Hunter and latterly of course Robin Hood—all of whom alternate as protectors or persecutors of travellers, depending on whether they get paid or not. They have obvious Hermetic characteristics, all being folkloric tricksters. A recent Hollywood film is called Robin Hood: Prince of Thieves, *probably unaware the title belongs to Hermes, the patron saint of thieves. The legend lives on.*

Many of these themes are picked up in local festivals and played out against a backdrop of archaic practices. In Staffordshire the Abbots Bromley Horn Dance seems to be a version of the age-old trick of men disguising themselves as animals to lure prey and dates back to the Palaeolithic if cave paintings are to be taken at face value. The festival includes a Hobby Horse Dance in which six men carry sets of reindeer antlers which are not allowed to cross the parish boundary and are stored, through the year, now in St Nicholas' church but in earlier times at the Goat Inn next to the Butter Cross.[1] Ottery St Mary in Devon has an annual Pixie Day when its long-banished pixies return and imprison the town's bell-ringers who are then ransomed by the vicar. 'Bog guides' take centre stage in 'Throwing the Hood' at Haxey in the Lincolnshire fens on the Twelfth Day of Christmas when a 'bogan', a bog-sprite or Bogeyman, becomes Lord for the day and is given a caduceus with a red ribbon attached, but the Fool or 'fall guy', holding *his* staff and a leather purse, would be 'smoked' before being dropped into the fire. The Hood, made of sackcloth and also tied with a red ribbon, allegedly represents a bull's (severed) head and the opposing villagers have to get it to a nearby pub. Toll rights were a highly contested privilege between villages and the fierceness of the game is rather redolent of the real, if ritualised, tribal warfare of the Papua New Guineans, and it is not until quite recent times that these bloody affairs became the slightly more regulated medieval football matches. Though even these appeared to regard fatalities as all in the game.

Not everything was left to crotchety toll-keepers of course. Prehistoric routes such as the Peddars Way and Icknield Way are obstructed by dykes or ditches that forced travellers, and more to the point their animals, to follow pre-arranged routes. Typically these very substantial earthworks were said to be constructed by Woden, the Devil, giants or some other supernatural agency. It is noticeable that areas that have been extensively mined or been otherwise rendered infertile by man or nature are cited as the work-of-the-devil or wasted by a dragon. This tendency to conflate areas 'ruined' by human economic activity with supra-

---

1 Nicholas aka Santa Claus is borne by reindeer. Caribou, the Inuit word for reindeer, is the root of Cherubim, fierce winged creatures that guarded the temples and palaces of Sumeria and Babylon, called *Kar-i-bu* in Sumerian and apparently sufficiently iconic to make it into the Bible.

human retribution is a reflection of later 'civilised' governments' attitudes to the Megalithic past. Hence for example the Biblical condemnation of Sodom and Gomorrah which had actually greatly prospered from salt mining. The Devil's Punchbowl is at Hindhead on an intersection of the ancient London to Portsmouth road, now the A3, and has signs of being a former quarry. To the south is Torberry Hill, labelled an Iron Age hillfort, near an important trackway (now the South Downs Way), which was supposedly formed by the Devil throwing his spoon from the Punchbowl accompanied by fairies dancing at midnight on Midsummer's Eve. Hills in mining areas were popularly said to be haunted by fairies or 'little people' but this is because digging underground is so expensive it was always worth employing short miners who only required small tunnels. It has long been the case that traditional mining areas are populated by short people because it takes remarkably few generations, whether via selection or immigration, to produce a population that matches the major local activity.

Water is always significant in mining and in metallurgy, as well of course in the watering of livestock, all traditional Megalithic activities, so it is not surprising that local water sources often had religious overtones. The water from wells, under the tutelage of Megalithic paragons of chastity such as Ann, Margaret or Winifred (respectively the Baptist's mother, the Pearl of Scotland and Gwenivere), was considered to have healing properties and to be particularly efficacious for treating eye complaints.[1] Whether this refers to eyesight or 'inner sight' is not clear, though blindness was associated with underground professions in general.[2] Clear water has obvious health implications. According to Celtic folklore hazel nuts dropping into sacred wells were

---

1 In colloquial English 'lights' mean eyes and the French for eye, *œil* (*uel* in Old French), is very like 'well'. Wells seem to have an important role in surveying. The original Greenwich observatory was a well because formerly there needed to be a way of making long, plumb-line observations. Cf. Hooke at the Monument and Eratosthenes at Aswan.
2 Pit ponies often go blind.

eaten by fish and produced the Salmon of Wisdom but the real connection is that a fish in a well ensures the water is free of algae and therefore clear. It is likely that hazel nuts, easy to both carry and conserve, were used as toll currency to pay the hermit as well as being a convenient source of nutrition for long distance travellers. Traditionally British dowsers use hazel rods, a nod to Megalithic hermits who knew where the local water sources were. Unlike dowsers.

Michaelmas Eve is known in Surrey as Crack Nut Day when hazel nuts revealed the name of one's future husband but Christianity quite naturally frowned on such pagan connections and forbade the gathering of nuts on Sundays. The 14th September was termed Devil's Nutting Day and given the covering name of Holy Cross Day. Actually, what is really going on here is that this is the start of the Eleusinian Mysteries and the Egyptian Festival of Lights where people were 'transfigured'. The three subsequent Ember Days (ash/embers symbolise repentance) were therefore unlucky, a theme adopted by the Christians for their transformation story. Ashes, or cinders in the Cinderella story, symbolise a spiritual change or *metanoia*, literally 'rags to riches'. The transformation takes place in a pumpkin coach, bringing to mind Hallowe'en lanterns, and Cinderella herself is clearly a member of the traditional witchlike trio of sisters. The Scottish version of Cinderella is *Rushen Coatie*, the rush-coat signifying her poverty, and features a sacrificed red calf, comparable to the red heifer of Judaism, an animal at the heart of a mystical sacrifice whose ashes purify anyone coming into contact with the dead. Red leather in general is of course Hermes' apparel.

'Holy' wells are typically situated on ancient drovers' routes and tend to be next to chapels, churches, hermitages and pubs, often at crossroads. At Fornham All Saints, Suffolk, the village well was guarded by a mermaid who was reputed to devour children if they came too close. In folklore mermaids are the watery equivalent of witches. Fornham All Saints lies on a major cursus to prevent travellers bypassing Bury St Edmunds, a couple of miles to the south-east, an important staging post on the Icknield Way/Michael Line. However, wells obviously also have to be in quite isolated places and here a familiar custom, the wishing-well, was employed, i.e. travellers had to throw in a coin in exchange for its use. A little east of Guildford on the Pilgrims' Way is the bottomless Silent Pool just the sort of legend to deter would-be thieves from searching for toll items thrown in. Sussex Knuckers, legendary water dragons, lived in bottomless Knucker Holes, for example one lived next to St Mary Magdalene's at Lyminster, the water being of course curative. The Lyminster Knucker was outwitted by a commoner who fed it a pudding filled with stones and, once the dragon was unable to move, beheaded it with his axe.[1] Mention of dragons points to a mining connection, 'knockers' being fairy miners in many parts of the country, which indicates this well-guarded Megalithic watering hole in Sussex was formerly a quarry. Even today, once gravel pits have been converted to anglers' paradises, their original use is scarcely discernible after a bare few years. However, the residual 'mineral' properties of the water seemed to have been known to the Megalithics even though these qualities tend to escape modern, more chemically conditioned palates.

But the basic Megalithic activity was always the maintenance of droving routes with their attendant apparatus of maze signs, dolmens, stone circles and the rest. Of course many of the physical trappings have gone but place names, so long as they are understood without the benefit of the 'interpretations' of the Anglo-Saxon-crazed academic place name theorists, often provide

---

1 Pudding stones are highly coloured 'erratics', boulders that have been shifted by glaciers, so that later, when the glaciation is long gone, they stand out from the surrounding geology. It has been argued that Palaeolithic Man used these conspicuous objects as waymarkers. Obviously we would contend that Megalithic Man did this. A particularly vociferous but tiny minority argue that the Stonehenge bluestones are erratics that littered Salisbury Plain rather than having been taken there deliberately from Wales. This is another case of the difficulty of distinguishing between natural and artificial, a problem that would largely go away if specialists could only bring themselves to consider either possibility in all cases, irrespective of the preconceptions of their respective disciplines.

clues. Troy-related places crop up in all parts of Megalithia, e.g. Caerdroia in Wales, Troyes in France, Trojaborg in Scandinavia and Tyre in Phoenicia, right down to Troy Town in Dorset on the main east-west route and which is now less of a town and more of a goose farm. Trottiscliffe, pronounced Trozlee, is the site of the Coldrum (= cauldron) Stones on the Pilgrims' Way approaching Rochester in Kent. Just south of Rochester there is a Troy Town, on a crossing point of the Pilgrims' Way between Temple Manor and Temple Marsh. A group of stones south of Troy Town is known as Little Kit's Coty House, near a dolmen called Kit's Coty.[1] Little Kit's Coty is also known as The Countless Stones, following the tradition that the stones of a circle are uncountable. One solution was to place 'penny loaves' on top of each stone and deduct the number from the remaining loaves, a folk version of the former requirement to leave tolls at megalithic waystations.[2] Local legend claims that an object placed on top of the dolmen will disappear after the owner has walked round three times at the full moon, the stones themselves allegedly having been set up by three witches. Another Kit's Coty legend claims that a basin on top of the dolmen was supernaturally always full of water, a common motif in folklore, e.g. the Cheesewring on Bodmin Moor. All these folk beliefs go back to when the dolmens had the three economic functions of ensuring the payment of tolls, the leaving of goods for later pick up and the daily provision of water for the use of passing pack trains and droving animals.

The associating of supernatural forces with these pieces of Megalithic infrastructure serves to enforce the 'pay as you go' rules, as well as discouraging petty theft of toll items left for later collection. These general themes can often be sieved from a folk motif. For instance, at Wayland's Smithy on the Ridgeway (the Michael Line/Icknield Way) a short distance from the Uffington

---

1 A 'kit' was a wooden container or rush-basket used to carry goods. The term has been retained in 'kit-bag'.
2 In Yorkshire there is still a tradition of placing coins on top of moorland crosses.

White Horse,[1] travellers using the Ridgeway can leave their horse and a coin, traditionally a silver sixpence as in a Yule pudding, and the next morning the horse will be shod, the coin having magically vanished. Presumably people on foot were merely charged the usual penny. Wayland, the god of smiths and metalworking, was described as 'of the elven race' and he was associated with the Troy Game, drawing a parallel between the traditional lame smith trapped in his forge and a hobbled bird in the centre of a maze. Wayland, like all mythic smiths, had been crippled in the 'thigh', an allusion to the castration role of Hermes.

The notion of bad luck hedged about with sanctity is often applied to tolled river crossings, which consequently acquire suitable local legends. At Hoxne (pronounced *Hoxen*), a village in Suffolk on the Michael Line, the Anglo-Saxon King Edmund hid beneath the bridge when being pursued by the Danes but his whereabouts were betrayed by a newly married couple crossing the bridge on their way from the church. He underwent the Triple Death, being scourged, shot with arrows and beheaded. His severed head, surrounded by a bramble thicket, was guarded by a tame wolf which called three times 'Here, here, here' like a talking signpost to guide people to the spot. A spring is said to have emerged where the saint's head lay commemorated by an oak tree. Edmund was finally interred at (naturally) Bury St Edmunds, further along the Michael Line.

Festivals often take place around local megaliths and 'butter' is often associated with these sites presumably because butter and cheese can be both drovers' stock-in-trade and surplus village products, but in any case are suited to exchange, toll paying, taxes, transit-sweeteners and so forth. Out of the way places like Carn Menyn, meaning 'butter rock', at the top of the Preseli Hills, might serve but the more usual pattern is instanced by the Butterstone, between Bowes and Romaldkirk, which traditionally boasted a

---

1   The Uffington White Horse is often described as resembling a dragon. Dragon Hill, an artificially levelled mound just below the White Horse, is claimed to be the site of St. George's victorious battle.

large brazen container.[1] Historically the Butterstone was the site of a mini-mart used by farmers to sell butter and eggs, even sacks of wheat and tethered cattle, and their customers would leave money or trade goods. Megalithic commerce often had to be based on the honour system because in pre-literate times there can be no sophisticated organs of law and order so people get used to a way of life that requires little in the way of external enforcement. For some reason this very widespread and commonsense practice is looked at askance by modern academics who bizarrely but constantly claim these arrangements are only resorted to in times of plague when buyer and seller did not wish to come into personal contact. The Merrivale complex on Dartmoor, famous for its stone rows, is sometimes called The Plague Market as it was said that during a period of plague in the seventeenth century people left produce there for the townsfolk of Tavistock, which is most illogical since not only are there no nearby farms but Tavistock is five miles away. 'Honour systems' might be scoffed at by townies but over and over again rural people hark back to a golden age when "nobody locked their doors"—because thieves in rural settings rarely prosper such is the interest in everybody's business—and of course the system has been seamlessly re-introduced today in the form of roadside vegetable boxes without the slightest need for intervention by the organs of law and order.

In parts of Scotland cupmarks or grooves on top of megaliths would be filled with milk on or around Beltane, a practice often claimed to "ensure the herds' fertility", but a more likely explanation for this quasi-religious rite is that the Megalithics were the local animal specialists and the herds' fertility may indeed depend on 'paying the vet'. It is a mistake to suppose that farmers and drovers are invariably competitors, the strength of Megalithia being to ensure prosperous co-existence over the long run. Never-

---

1 Ancient free-standing stone crosses, associated with open moorland as well as town or village squares, are unique to the British Isles and Ireland. This astonishing revelation was obtained from the Victoria & Albert Museum so it may not be true.

theless, intertwined conflicts of interest become the stuff of local legend, especially dragon lore where a common motif is dragons' insatiable desire for milk, a curiously gentle request when set against their usual demands for sheep and/or maidens. But then again, drinking milk was (and is) recommended in the metal-working industries to guard against poisonous vapours ('metal fume fever'). Drovers could afford to pay with milk but presumably would rather not forfeit the other two. At Deeerhurst, where the Fosse Way meets the Salt Way, a milk-drinking dragon was killed by a smith, blacksmiths being masters of the 'dark arts'[1] and said to possess magical powers. The dragon of Mordiford in Hereford-shire, on the River Lugg (named for Lugh, the British Hermes), was hand-reared on milk by a local girl called Maud, seemingly a British St Martha, but like *La Tarasque* the Mordiford Dragon was unkindly despatched by the villagers.

Highways were sanctuaries with a distant aura of royal protection and this general air of sacredness extended to megaliths. It is only in quite modern times that the safety of travellers was guaranteed by statute rather than statue. As the megaliths' successors on the main routes, the churches were also places of sanctuary and, perhaps not very surprisingly, could also act as cattle marts. An annual cattle sale took place at Clynnog Fawr Church, standing by a well at a meeting-point of roads halfway between Anglesey and Bardsey, on a pilgrims' route.[2] The church is disproportionately large for the village and has a big coffer into which the requisite toll, nowadays alms, can be deposited. The coffer was originally a feeding resource for the passing animals, just as the font was originally for watering the animals. Their holy status evolved from the local duty of keeping both filled. It is noticeable how many churches proudly display 'original' fonts which like menhirs often have a remarkable survival

---

1 Chain mail is the blacksmith's business and blackmail is the charge.
2 The Latin for pilgrim is *peregrinus*, the peregrine falcon being a highly signif-icant Megalithic bird. Pilgrims were not above judicious thieving if the story that silk worm eggs were smuggled from China inside a hollow pilgrim staff is true. Though this is likely to be an apochryphal version of the story of Prometheus stealing fire from the gods using a hollow fennel staff.

rate. Welsh lore claims that Clynnog Fawr's church was built on top of ancient megaliths, the site of bull sacrifice, half the bull going to God and half to St Beuno, suggesting St Beuno had only a sideways connection to God. He was the uncle or father[1] of St Winifred, celebrated for restoring her own severed head through prayer, thus joining a long tradition in ancient Welsh myth and Megalithia in general. The name Winifred or Gwenfrewi (*Guinevere*) suggests a 'white goddess'. A standing stone, Maen Beuno, is next to the main road and just south of Luggy Brook opposite the village of Forden/ Ffordun. The Christian gloss is that this site commemorates the spot where St Beuno preached but its proper significance is that this is where Offa's Dyke and the Severn come together, the path itself passing between a St Michael's church and 'Nantcribba Castle'. Offa's Dyke has no connection with the Anglo-Saxon king of that name, it was constructed to ensure that animals went through designated toll points.

The wassail bowl (or 'vessel cup' or Holy Grail or, even more significantly, *mazer*) is, like the witch's cauldron, a collecting device for tolls but during the 'upside down' season of Saturnalia, the turn of year celebration of the winter solstice, the function is reversed and it is taken from house to house for people to sup from. Wassailing was always something of a West Country speciality, probably because the timetable of the apple harvest meant that cider was ready to drink around midwinter. Not surprisingly in the West Country where the apple is king,[2] the folk customs are peculiarly apple-based. In Somerset strips of common land, the Dolemoors, were parcelled out by drawing *lots* for al*lot*ments, using specially marked apples. Cider-making was the major industry both in the Megalithic West Country and in the equally Megalithic Normandy. Just as the 'beerage' was a set of very significant English families, so 'cider families' were important in the early development of

---

1 Saints, like popes, gradually came to be portrayed as celibate so fathers gradually came to be 'uncles'.
2 'Apples' were not necessarily apples, the term is used for commercial tree products generally, not just cider-making. For instance oak apples and sage apples were used in dyeing and ink-making.

both Britain and France, culminating in Sir Philip Sidney, a leading personage at the court of Elizabeth I, who died from 'a wound in the thigh' according to his biographer, Faulk Greville. Faulk is a Megalithic name and Greville is a village in Normandy. Sidney, *cidre* and Saint-Denis (Dionysus) are etymologically linked. But these esoteric matters need more exploration from scholars prepared to delve beneath the strictly historical record.

Whatever the Megalithic connections of the *modern* West Country (and let us not forget that the Elizabethan empire was triggered by West Country families) the ancient links are there thanks to the Michael Line. Glastonbury Tor, also known as the Isle of Avalon i.e. the island of apples (*aval* means apple in Cornish), is the alleged site of Arthur's last resting place. The point here is that *tradition* is actually no such thing but is in fact the Megalithics wishing to create widespread beliefs for their own purposes. It doesn't matter that Glastonbury was originally just a waystation on a now-disused trunk route, this conspicuous 'holy mountain' can be recycled to include Joseph of Arimathea, Arthur or anything else required from time to time by way of national myth (or to accentuate the importance of the Megalithic abbey there). The 'Glas' in Glastonbury suggests it was once a man-made island in a 'glass' lake, recalling the folk motif of dead kings lying in mysterious glass castles awaiting resurrection, a theme picked up by Snow White in her glass casket, waiting for resurrection after eating the apple.[1] Guinevere and Arthur are the First Couple found in myths everywhere. Guinevere is literally 'Queen Eve' and Arthur can be traced, admittedly by only tortuous etymology, to Adam. The Biblical version of these two is ambiguous about what the forbidden fruit was but the folkloric version makes no bones about it being an apple since it is the symbol of forbidden, i.e.

---

1 Snow White with her white face, red lips and black hair represents the colours of the three stages of the moon which in turn stands for the Triple Goddess, the steward of apple trees. Red and white are the colours of the skin and flesh of the apple, and of course of the Rosy Cross. Just to bring the story full circle, Hawkins, Drake, Frobisher et al. sailed under the Rosy Cross which was now the national emblem.

Hermetic, knowledge. This esoteric connection arises from the fact that when apples are sliced in half a pentagram is revealed and the pentagram is the enduring symbol of hidden truths.

Apple sliced in half

A pentagram is the axiomatic representation of a star and of a human stick figure, and is significant by virtue of Venus, the brightest light after Sun and Moon, taking five cycles, forty years, to return to its starting position. Forty years is a recurring Biblical motif. The Hesperides, the three goddesses of the sunset, were the mythical guardians of the golden apple tree and the British Isles were known to the Greeks as the Isles of the Hesperides.

Apples were originally cultivated for alcohol rather than for eating,[1] fruit and veg not being major components of the ancient diet, and one of the problems of large-scale alcohol production is always the need to keep it bacteria-free. Wormwood was widely used as a preservative, only being replaced by hops (for beer) in the fifteenth century. But the importance of wormwood in the ancient world is why it turns up so

---

1   The relationship between alcohol and technological advance is yet to be fully investigated. Mead, for example, was proposed as the agent of European intellectual development by Levi-Strauss. Nearer to home, whisky may have been the catalyst for the Scottish Enlightenment since production of good quality Scotch increased enormously in the early eighteenth century but, in response to a rise in English taxes since the Union of 1707, was consumed almost entirely by the home market. With the 1784 'Wash Act' taxation on whisky fell considerably as did Scotland's intellectual boom but this is masked because most of the nineteenth century savants were syphilitic (apart from those high on cocaine and opium products) and it is well known that the disease often has a 'genius' stage before everything falls apart (as with the drugs). It is noticeable that no further savants were produced after the discovery of antibiotics (and prohibition of drugs generally).

often in folkloric contexts. Its technical name, *Artemisia absinthium*, refers to Artemis the moon goddess but more popularly it was 'the blood of Hephaistos', referring to Hephaestus the god of blacksmiths and subterranean fire. The worm in wormwood can now be seen as being the worm/orm at the heart of the metal industry. Wormwood's various spellings have different translations but they all emphasise positive qualities rather than its actual bitterness, e.g. *wermuth* 'preserver of the mind' and *wermod* 'man-courage' or 'spirit-mother'. Worm/orm seems to be the same word as herm and wormwood/vermouth is linked to wisdom as well as Hermes.

Extract of wormwood was the main ingredient in absinthe, such a potent brew that it has been banned in modern times. The essential oil made from wormwood contains thujone, which has psychoactive properties and is therefore responsible for the notorious mind-altering effects of absinthe. Its potency was evidently known to the Ancients: Greek athletes were prescribed thujone, probably in the form of wormwood leaves soaked in wine, before taking part in the Olympic Games. Hermes, god of athletics, was especially honoured in Greek wrestling, a sport associated with the sacred thigh injury, the story of Jacob wrestling with the angel being a well-known example.

Sprig of Wormwood

*Wormwood thrives on roadside verges perhaps because the
Romans (or earlier road engineers) planted it for footsore soldiers/*

Another plant that contains thujone is sage, *salvia*, which also has connotations of wisdom. According to Culpepper, quoting Pliny, sage was a cure for 'stinging or biting serpents' as well as aiding the memory and 'warming or quickening the senses', all of which duplicates the wormwood effect. One of the things known about the Druids, which must also be true of any pre-literate intellectual caste, is that prodigies of memorisation were needed. An amphetamine-style drug such as ephedra which is in vermouth, wormwood wine, makes the process both enjoyable and multiplies the time that can be devoted to it without the brain seizing up in protest. No doubt the Ancients were prepared to pay a high price for mind-altering drugs which would include the cost of long distance transport. The Megalithic System not only benefited from transporting drugs as high value low volume cargo but the carriers themselves were required to walk such vast distances that drug-fuelled journeys, à la Incans on coca, were almost certainly involved. Secret, or Hermetic, knowledge would seem to be central to Megalithia since high value goods tend to remain high value only so long as the secret of their manufacture is kept. These secrets can be remarkably long held. Like 'Greek Fire', nobody now knows exactly how traditional absinthe was made but such ancient mysteries are hinted at in folklore.[2]

---

1 Or perhaps not. There is after all an entirely different means of drug delivery. It may be that the psychoactive substance in wormwood can suffuse through the sweaty skin of the sandalled foot, just as the laurel wreath relayed its message direct to the brain via the temples. In the Eleusinian Mysteries the head was nicked in order for the laurel to work better, probably the origin of Jesus' crown of thorns.
2 Alcoholic recipes were monkish specialisations and closely guarded secrets. The Cistercians' most famous abbot, Bernard of Clairvaux, built his first foundation in the *Val d'Absinthe* (later renamed Claire Vallée).

The modern term 'folklore' is often misleading, being generally coupled with 'popular', 'down-market', 'rustic' and similarly dismissive epithets. Yet somehow folk traditions have lasted a very long time without being formally recorded which indicates a practical, economically-driven significance beyond mere country sayings or quaint displays of merry-making. Today, folklore's mystique is often down to modish political and cultural fashions (in the nineteenth and twentieth centuries entire countries used folk tradition as national foundations) but a good rule is that the stranger the custom the more prosaic the likely explanation. In times when there was either no writing or little but official writing, it is surely the case that a great deal of business, of medicine, of everyday life will only survive in folklore, and customs and beliefs should certainly be viewed as rooted in *historical* reality and interpreted accordingly.

SEVEN

Paying For The System

Salt was the mainstay of the Megalithic economy. It was not only the most widely traded good, it was also the chief medium of exchange. The centrality of salt to the ancient economy is often given lip service in orthodox accounts—*salary* being cognate with salt is the usual example given—but the true importance of salt is rarely appreciated. It has great resonances with the various stages of human development:

1   Salt is not a *necessity* to pre-agricultural man. Whatever Man was doing before the coming of agriculture there will be plenty of salt in his diet.
2   It becomes a *near-necessity* when he switches to a cereal diet because, as animal saltlicks testify, just eating grass may not provide sufficient salt for large mammals.
3   When farming includes animals as well as cereals, salt becomes a *commodity* because the preserving of meat is best done using salt.
4   When preserved food, whether cereals or meat, forms the main diet salt becomes a much sought after *luxury* to make such an otherwise bland diet acceptable.
5   When civilisation begins, salt becomes a *raw material* since a large number of industrial processes require salt.
6   As a *traded good*, salt is plentiful in some places (the seashore, salt mines) but functionally absent everywhere else.

So, at all stages of human development salt is not only certain to be in demand but the transport of salt will also be necessary.

This is why it is difficult historically to define whether salt is a 'bulk item'. A bar of salt being moved across rough country on the back of a mule (or indeed the back of a man) seems to be a bulk item, but sticking some salt in a pannier to pay tolls along the way just makes salt somewhat heavy money. Salt can be both at once, at the same place. In Carthage salt caravans would head for the interior to exchange the stuff for gold but, being next to a salt lake, Carthaginians could also use it in vast amounts just to speed up the dyeing of cloth. The city was built on salt just as it was (according to the Romans) destroyed with salt.

Carthage was in many ways the epitome of the Megalithic city, that is one based on trade rather than territoriality, and just as Carthage used salt as its foundation so Megalithia in general used salt's peculiar properties to build its trading empire. Salt can either be absurdly cheap or very expensive. We *now* live in a society where salt is essentially free at the level of personal consumption and as a commodity only has the power to influence the whereabouts of various chemical industries. Salt is largely irrelevant as a political or economic factor. But how much would *you* pay door-to-door saltmongers if somehow they had managed to acquire a monopoly of the stuff? And how much more would you pay if you were reliant on salt for the preservation of your winter supplies? Of course the answer is 'a great deal' but, surprisingly, you might be prepared to pay it willingly if everybody else was having to pay the price and if all that aggregated cash went a long way to paying for the entire national infrastructure of transport and trade. Essentially, that was the deal that Megalithia offered. The entire system worked so long as the Megalithics could enforce a salt monopoly and unfortunately there is seldom a shortage of people willing to break it if merely visiting the coast and returning to one's village with a sack of salt on one's back is all it takes. So the Megalithics developed a twin-track approach to this central problem of their business, both of which have played a vital role in the course of history:

1   **Control the source**   Make sure that salt *production*
is in Megalithic hands and then freelancing can be kept
to a minimum. In any relatively primitive economy the
acquisition of capital is always the chief stumbling block
and the Megalithics, as a supranational organisation, are
generally in a position to deploy more capital than any
locals. Saltpans (in colder places) and salt evaporation
beds (where it is warmer) are not specially capital
intensive but the Megalithics can always build bigger and
therefore cheaper than anyone else. This model of building
large-scale works to produce goods suitable for long
distance trade became a signature activity for the various
Megalithic successor-organisations like the Cistercians and
the Templars.

2   **Control the government**   Many governments have
noted that salt is a) cheap and b) necessary and have tried
to use the manufacture and distribution of salt as a handy
method of taxation. The problem they all encountered
is that because salt is a) cheap and b) necessary, any
attempts to interfere with the salt trade is exceedingly
unpopular and governments do not like being unpopular.
So governments always look for cut-outs to do the
business and reap the opprobrium. The Megalithics made
a speciality of being, as it were, acceptably unpopular.

Even so, both methods of doing business are fraught. It is all
very well being the low-cost producer but that invariably means
the low-*profit* producer. Should the producer ever try to exploit
economies of scale to start making monopoly profits, they are
simply inviting in any and every local power elite into an industry
with low entry costs. The royal French salt tax, the *gabelle,* demonstrates what happens should similar tactics be tried with the power
of the state. The system works well enough if the tax farmers and
the state are prepared only to cream off a manageable surplus—
rather as a sales tax or VAT gets paid without too much trouble—
but whenever more than the cream is taken, and the temptation to

do so seems irresistible, then consumer resistance in the form of everything from wholesale smuggling to routine violence towards the tax collectors becomes so endemic that profits are severely dented. The Megalithics were peculiarly sensitive to the goodwill of the local populace among whom, *through* whom, they had to conduct their day-to-day transportation business.

The net result of these various prehistoric problems can be glimpsed as soon as history provides the evidence of the way the salt trade was organised later on. People that were like the Megalithics in that they had no obvious tribal limitations, 'the Celts' and 'the Saxons'—both names are etymologically linked to salt[1]—were able to seize control of huge areas and maintain a loose suzerainty sufficient for the kind of lucrative monopoly that anticipated the 'trade empires' operated by the Portuguese, the Dutch and the English. The Celts operated in the west of Europe using the sea salt that the conditions of the French Atlantic coast (still) allow to be made in vast quantities; the Saxons operated the salt mines in Saxony and exported the material up the Elbe (hence Old and New Saxony being at either end of the river). Both groups traded with northern Europe where it was too cold to evaporate salt from the sea economically and were especially active around the Baltic, which is so non-saline that even boiling seawater in salt-pans is impractical.

It may be that the Saxons and the Celts were 'Megalithics' in some guise, but more likely they simply adopted the trading model. Nothing lasts forever so it may be taken for granted that salt would cease to be a Megalithic staple at some stage. The Megalithic switch into metals can be identified by what historians call the Bronze Age and the Iron Age, but these eras should rather be thought of as the Rise and Fall of a Megalithic Industry. A lot of nonsense is talked about why bronze, an expensive and hard-to-find alloy, preceded iron, which is cheap and abundantly available. Usually some explanation involving higher smelting temperatures is cobbled together

---

1 Saxa salt is still the leading British brand.

to account for the fact that it required thousands of years to make the really rather minor technical adjustments that iron smelting requires.[1] The true explanation is that the Megalithics operated a very successful metallurgical monopoly organised at all levels from extraction to smelting to transportation to production of finished goods ('vertical integration' in modern business-speak). This is why there ever was a *Bronze* Age, because the production of bronze actually does require some kind of megalithic organisation in that tin and copper rarely occur together, and even more rarely close to where the demand is, so it requires long distance travel to make bronze production a reality. Anybody who has control over long distance travel will have control over bronze production. Iron by contrast can be mined, smelted and manufactured on one site and is sufficiently ubiquitous to provide access for all. Once the monopoly was broken, the 'iron states' replaced the 'copper states' or, if it is to be preferred, the territorial states overcame the trading states *or*, to use orthodox labels, the Hittites, New Kingdom Egypt, the Classical Greeks and the Romans defeated the Trojans, the Minoans, the Mycenaeans, the Phoenicians, the Etruscans and the Carthaginians.

But all this is Big Picture. How did Megalithia operate at grass roots level? How did the average village, nestling in some quiet inland spot minding its own business in the late Mesolithic, pay for its long distance goods like salt and superior flint axes? The salt has to be manufactured at the seashore a hundred miles away and the flint axes come from Norfolk a hundred miles in the other direction. Besides the transport costs, both the salt pan and the flint mine require the concentration of labour and capital on a scale that the village, even perhaps the state insofar as that existed, could scarcely contemplate. But that is the wonder of capitalism, the village doesn't have to concern itself with any of this, it merely purchases the finished goods. Actually, this being a pre-monetary as well as a pre-literate age, the village barters its own production,

---

1 The complete immolation of a human body, a routine practice in the Neolithic, requires comparable temperatures to iron smelting.

say clips of wool, or if it is strategically located the right of passage, for the salt and for the axes, but either way all the costs are in the price. The end consumer pays for the whole system. It is just like value-added-tax except it is entirely voluntary, the village is free to wallow in sheep clips and go without the value-added stuff if it prefers. But, also like value-added-tax, everybody has to vaguely give consent to the whole system to ensure everybody is to benefit from reasonably priced salt and axes. If the village regularly hinders the salt traders, and *every* village is potentially in a position to do so, then there will soon be no salt traders. Indeed, there is the further presumption that everyone has a clear interest in ensuring that nothing untoward happens *between* villages, all of which presupposes a minimum of co-operative law-and-order in any country where long distance trade occurs. Pre-history is silent on how precisely this came about. It may be that Megalithia is the immediate precursor of governments.

One of the problems of reconstructing Megalithia is that when Megalithia flourishes there are no historical sources and when historical sources become available Megalithia tends to disappear. Nonetheless there *is* evidence in situ. For example, consider the village green and the village pond. These are always treated as if they are the most natural thing in the world for any self-respecting village to possess, but that is not in fact the case. Animals are in fields and are watered there; they are moved from field to field; they are taken from the field to market. Where is there a requirement for communal animal facilities? On the other hand, the village green and the village pond are perfect for drovers bringing their animals through the village and needing somewhere to stop overnight. *Now* the green and the pond have become valuable communal assets since the drovers will not enjoy such facilities for nothing. But how does the drover pay? After all, the average drover, with meat animals on the hoof, will have nothing the village lacks and pack trains will likely be transporting goods for a quite different set of end-users. A constant theme of this book is to demonstrate that the Megalithics are the source of most of our religious practices and the curious but very widespread rite of sacrificing animals 'to God' gives us a clue as to one of the ways drovers repaid the village.

In agrarian economies, fresh meat is seldom on the menu. Meat of any kind is for high days and holidays and even then will normally be preserved. But for drovers fresh meat is all around so the calculated barbecuing of a lamb[1] for a village en route is to ensure a welcome at that village for drovers. Some animals seem to have been developed for payment purposes: geese for instance can waddle along happily for miles with juvenile imprinting relieving anybody of much in the way of supervision and their omnivoric diet means they can be left to their own devices along the way, all of which means dropping one off to a village en route is cheap indeed. A goose in every village is the Megalithic equivalent of "a chicken in every pot". The trading of meat for access can be an entirely routine exchange but the 'religious' dimension is emphasised should the village be 'en fete' in expectation of a communal barbecue. The village fete, and all the other annual intervals in the workaday life of the village, are often latter day survivals reflecting the regular ebb and flow of the drovers passing through on their perennial migrations. The drovers in turn reacted to their festive effect by turning up, not just with animals, but with a true motley. Something villages are peculiarly unable to provide for themselves is professional entertainment so the drovers brought along peripatetic show-biz in the form of circuses, funfairs, travelling theatres. Traditionally these were (for that matter, are) in the hands of the successors (or as may be, descendants) of the Megalithics: travellers, tinkers, gypsies and so forth.

It might be concluded that each side, village and drover, benefited from the other but this is perhaps an over-sanguine view as to the natural cordiality of the relationship. Taking strictly historical examples of where animals-on-the-hoof and farmers co-exist, say the sheep of the *Mesta* in medieval Spain or the cattle drives of the early American Midwest, it is certainly noticeable that mutual

---

1 But there are problems when freshly slaughtered animals have not been hung but are eaten immediately. This is the origin of *halal*, *kosher* and suchlike religious practices.

hostility is the order of the day. There is no attempt by either side to benefit the other *directly*; the relationship is policed by the state which understands both are necessary to the citizenry as a whole. Megalithia always assumes *there is no state*. It constructs its operations on the assumption that in good times the state will be so weak as to be of little assistance, in bad times there will be no state at all, and in the worst of times the state will be positively inimical. Hence the principle of strict mutuality, of parties benefiting directly from one another, was the Megalithic way.

Folk survivals are always good clues when it comes to ancient Megalithic practices. The song "Here we go gathering nuts in May" is a practice not advised since there are no nuts to be had in May, but is a reference to Megalithia because nuts, like salt, are the kind of high value, low bulk goods that can be used for exchange in a cash-free economy. But why would the Megalithics specialise in this when nuts are readily available everywhere? Firstly, it is because Megalithics are constantly moving from one geographic area to another so that with the seasons and with latitude they are shifting from places where certain types of goods are in supply to where they are in demand. Secondly, Megalithics specialise among other things in tree plantations. Nuts in peasant economies tend to be regarded as either a seasonal delicacy or as something best left for pigs, but that is because tree plantations are not a peasant activity other than on the small scale of coppicing for timber. Even fruit orchards are noticeably absent from the ordinary economy since it is just not worth going in for this kind of specialisation, local demand being too limited and transport costs of tree products being uneconomic. However, for Megalithics particular kinds of wood are required on a large scale, notably alder for smelting and oak for shipbuilding, so growing nuts on an industrial scale becomes another candidate. It may even be that our present large edible nuts are the product of Megalithic domestication efforts in the past.[1]

---

1   As perhaps are some oak species. The natural history of the oak, or the *un*natural history of the oak, is worth the attention of botanists with revisionist aspirations.

Another example of a folk survival commemorating a payment method is the wishing well. It is generally assumed that throwing a coin into a well is a modern form of the religious practice (vouched for by archaeological finds) of throwing offerings into 'sacred' water sources. It always pays to suspect 'it's for ritual purposes' explanations and in this case throwing gewgaws into water was originally an ingenious form of payment the Megalithics employed in places where it wasn't economic to have a fulltime toll collector. The drover simply threw his payment into the 'well' or a special pool. It is not generally speaking worth anyone's while robbing the well because wells are difficult of access and there might not be much in it anyway but the peripatetic Megalithic toll collector knows exactly when it is time to collect and, hydraulics being something of a Megalithic speciality, no doubt the means to do it came easily enough.

But wells are more typically associated with local activity, situated next to chapels, churches, hermitages and pubs, and at crossroads. As already noted, water impacts drovers in two respects—the animals need regular watering and they need to be able to cross water. It follows from this that particular places, say, water sources in otherwise dry chalkland or fords across major rivers, will become Megalithic centres. Indeed it seems that these 'centres' go some way to explaining how Megalithia is paid for at the *macro* level and how large-scale projects are paid for generally, something that is necessary alongside the smaller-scale day-to-day maintenance of the system via tolls. Taking a simple ford as a starting point it is possible to reconstruct the process by which a Megalithic complex can arise quite naturally. First of all there is no such thing as a *simple* ford. Rivers are forever altering their course and flow rate, through the year as well as over the longer term, so there is always a requirement for some form of continuing human intervention to keep a given ford operating. This is the origin of much of Megalithic hydraulic expertise, especially as the straight line system means that fords will be required in places that nature might not necessarily agree are suitable for fords. But having to undertake substantial terraforming with antler picks is sure to lead to explorations of more effective muck-shifting devices and, glory be! there's one right on site. The power of running water to make fundamental alterations in the landscape is a lost art today but the Megalithics regarded it as something of a Prime Mover. All chalk and limestone landscapes should be looked at afresh in the light of Megalithic activity, as should the course of rivers. Many 'natural' riverine features are no such thing—for instance, the presence of an *eyot* is normally a Megalithic giveaway since British rivers are not typically of the type that have islands in them. It can usually be inferred that eyots are artificial, for the purpose of river control. Any mention of a ferry should have researchers diving into the records to investigate their history and, while this will apparently go back no further than Domesday, various names of Megalithic significance will be thrown up along the way: saints, monastic orders, prominent families, pub signs.

Economic activity can change the course of a river since straightening a water course might be essential for navigation, for building water mills or 'streaming' for minerals. Once a local regime of water control is established at a particular point it follows that this in itself becomes an economic hotspot since, at the very least, toll collection and concentration of traffic is going to occur there. But the Megalithic take-off comes from economic exploitation of industries where water control gives an overwhelming advantage. The one that crops up most often in *historical* accounts is the fulling mill though textile works in general need access to water for virtually all processes. The Megalithics are associated with the textile industry not just because of the usefulness of flowing water but in their control over the salt trade and alum works. The *original* impetus derives from Megalithic long distance trade, especially in the need for leather and then cloth sails in the shipping business, and then because specially worked textiles are the sort of high value, low weight goods with a universal demand that so particularly appealed to the Megalithic business model. There is also a more direct dividend in interfering with river flow and that is in the catching of fish, weirs and fish traps being a Megalithic speciality. The transport of dried fish in large volumes becomes a lucrative industry when the fishermen become fishers of men and are able to insist that everybody must eat fish at regular intervals 'for ritual purposes'. The Catholics only got round to repealing the Megalithic injunction to eat fish on Fridays in the twentieth century.

It may be asked why locals are not taking over these obviously useful and profitable enterprises. How do the Megalithics stay in control over the long haul? In relatively primitive economies the state is never strong enough to provide capital-intensive services but even when the state is strong there may be difficulties. The Romans for instance blanched at the requirements of feeding the population of Rome and handed the task over to 'the Equites', aka the Megalithics, who organised a Mediterranean-wide system of corn imports.[1] The problem was not finally solved until the era of joint-stock companies and it is worth identifying the reason for the success of these entirely capitalistic corporations. Essentially, they solved the 'generational' problem. A family firm simply cannot exist for long enough to build and maintain major capital projects. Two generations of talent is difficult enough to guarantee but the requirements to maintain, say, even a modest ford go well beyond that.[2] No system of transport can rely on dynastic principles even in the medium term and in a cashless society there is no practical method of passing responsibility onwards by other means. It is worth pointing out that the most important 'family firm' of all, the royal dynasty, has problems in this regard too which is why the Megalithic System had to be proof against periods of dire instability. But by the same token Megalithia itself cannot be all-powerful, it cannot be a bureaucracy when literacy is absent. This internal structural problem seems to have been solved by

---

1 The Equites had run Rome itself during the early days when the Megalithic Etruscan kings were ruling.
2 This problem was mainly solved by attaching a pub to the ford (or the ferry), thereby creating a self-sufficient economic unit, a pattern that can still be traced in all parts of Britain today.

erecting something that from the outside looks like a priestly caste but built on what looks suspiciously like the franchise system: a highly successful organisation that is theoretically available to all but to which applicants have to bring something to the party, either cash or skills or, to judge from the early monastic saints, a connection with local royalty.

General characteristics can be more clearly seen from organisations operating in the historical era when evidence is available if not exactly copious, for instance in the records of the Cistercians, the Knights Templar and even Jewry. First off is their equivocal relationship to the state. Megalithics are always supranational by virtue of their roots in long distance trade and it is this primarily that allows them to stand-off the more powerful but more localised state (or sub-state in particularly bad times). There is a constant tension of course because the state has the power and the motive to take over Megalithic enterprises in its own territory, the question always becomes one of whether Megalithia can bring pressure to bear elsewhere on a scale to make these temporary local gains worthwhile. Most of the time the state discovers that once the capital gains of the enterprise have been added to the state coffers there is the small matter of maintaining the services that have also been taken over. The state is not normally a suitable vehicle for running fords, mills, ferries, fish farms, textile complexes any more than building roads and bridges (or schools for that matter) comes naturally. As late as the Reformation the Tudors discovered that it was easy enough spending the proceeds from selling off Megalithic assets after the Dissolution of the Monasteries but it was not so easy replacing the day-to-day services that these assets had been paying for.[1] The abiding problem is that royalty fights wars and only 'Megalithia' can pay for them. Large volumes of cash is not something that ordinarily 'comes with the territory' so, whether it is the Templars or the Fuggers, it pays the territorial state to be on cordial terms with 'them'.

---

1 So difficult indeed that the post-Tudors found themselves having to fight the English Civil War.

But how did the Megalithics themselves acquire the necessary capital? Again the Cistercians and Knights Templar demonstrate how it was done—by aggregating labour rather than capital, or to put it another way using labour *as* capital. Most human beings use their labour either to enrich themselves or to support their families, Megalithic organisations manage to persuade significant numbers of people to eschew this principle, by not enriching themselves (a vow of poverty) nor to support a family (a vow of chastity). The question is not how this trick was managed but rather 'What sections of the community can be readily mobilised to aggregate capital whenever it is the only way of doing this?' and it only requires an examination of the kinds of people who joined monasteries and knightly orders to understand that certain sections of the population—homosexuals, intellectuals, the very poor, younger sons, religious and militaristic fanatics—are always available once the correct buttons are pushed. It turns out that a surprisingly small proportion of the overall population is required to operate quite a sophisticated capital-aggregating economy. Once the enterprises are in full swing the profits from those enterprises are being generated in large amounts since the labour force is unpaid, and of course the profits are constantly re-invested because there is no other place for the profits to go. Unlike the family firm (and the dynastic state) there is little temptation to spend income on conspicuous display and other wasteful expenditure that otherwise seems to be part of the human condition. In fact the profits are so large as to practically enjoin an expansion in the form of new monasteries, new preceptories and extensions into new territories.

One seldom observed principle is that everything is strictly voluntary. This is not a moral question, it is because Megalithia does not possess the kind of local power that permits force. Large literate bureaucratic states *can* use force to set up an equivalent system based on slavery since slaves are necessarily subject to the vows of poverty and family-oriented celibacy. This can be highly effective because with this cheap labour-cum-capital the state can aggregate a surplus sufficient to support an army (which is also composed of de facto poor-and-celibate individuals in terms of not having a family to support) who can either themselves build really large capital projects or enforce the locals doing it or, by a similarly franchising effect, conduct campaigns in other states to bring in more slaves. Even quite modest states have the power to enforce the modified form of slavery known as 'serfdom' where, though neither poverty nor celibacy is present, there is at least enough 'force' available to get the most meagre local capital projects—roads, bridges, corn mills—up and running using forced labour. But this is small beer compared to the wonders that can be wrought by, say, a Cistercian monastery in terms of turning entire barren landscapes into highly profitable farmland in quick order, and then unleashing vast columns of pack animals bearing the agricultural produce to distant markets.

Eventually though these latter day organisations ran into a problem that Megalithia itself must have solved. No matter how enthusiastic the uptake during the early stages these 'Megalithic' organisations soon gave way to the human failings of sloth, personal financial gain and (according to all the records) non-celibacy. Even the re-investment of capital is no longer operative as profits are spent on grandiose but non-economic building projects. Soon the numbers of genuine 'monks' are few and the organisation is employing huge numbers of 'lay brothers' who are essentially normal employees slightly rebadged. When this stage is reached a Cistercian Monastery is now little different from a gentry estate and its good works and general contribution to the community are scarcely different from the normal by-product of noblesse oblige. There is certainly nothing very 'Megalithic' about them nor, taking the evidence from Cromwell's investigations during Henry VIII's time at face value, are they even very religious. Megalithia itself though lasted at least three thousand years so the question of how it avoided this apparently Iron Law of Decay remains to be answered.

In the first place it has to be conceded that Megalithic countries were inordinately static. One cannot very well commend the Druids for managing to spend the whole of the Iron Age keeping literacy out and generally making sure that Britain and northern Gaul did very little except to prepare themselves for being blotted out by Rome in a single generation. Nonetheless classical Megalithia had proved itself more or less immortal so there can be little doubt that it had managed to work its way into the warp and weft of north-west Europe. It might reasonably be concluded that by keeping literacy out and hence ensuring that government could not evolve higher than the rudimentary 'tribal' level, Megalithia was able to become a de facto supra-tribal government and thereby maintain itself in power indefinitely. In fact it was probably this ability to act as a shadow-government that allowed it to survive underground during the onslaught of the decidedly unMegalithic Romans.

EIGHT

Megalithic Terraforming

Geological and historical timescales are generally separated because the one rarely impinges on the other. But in the case of the British landscape this is not actually so. The whole of Britain down to the line of the Thames was covered by thousands of feet of ice up until about twelve thousand years ago and such ice sheets create a *tabula rasa* so whatever was there before in the form of surface features was completely erased and, when the ice retreated, a wholly new landscape emerged. Since the area immediately to the south of the ice will also be radically affected, it can be fairly said that the whole of Britain is a landscape only twelve thousand years old. *That* hill, *that* river valley, *that* lake, *that* plain have all been created by natural forces of weathering over the last twelve thousand years.

Human beings have been present all that time and it is only now that geomorphological ecologists—to coin an academic specialty that still hasn't come into existence—are realising that the earth's surface isn't necessarily what nature intended. The earliest human inhabitants, though few in number, would still have imposed themselves to a surprising degree since they hunt, or otherwise eliminate, large animals with 'un-natural' efficiency and large animals have all kinds of knock-on effects on forestation, erosion and eventually land forms. These chain reactions may be particularly radical in post-glacial areas because the local flora and fauna themselves are not yet securely established. Nonetheless the numbers of human beings in such conditions are sufficiently small to make the changes less than epochal, a situation that changes decisively with the coming of agriculture. Not only do overall numbers change from thousands to millions but these millions promptly set about consciously changing the post-glacial landscape for something *gentler*.

Other 'new' areas elsewhere on earth, that is landscapes that have only recently emerged from being covered by the all-scouring ice sheets, are universally forbidding terrain, unsuited to intensive agriculture. Areas like the Laurentian Shield in Canada or the Scandinavian peninsula are desperately poor in nutrients, littered with acidic lakes and generally not up to much in terms of any kind of human utility. This is also true of areas immediately south of the ice which are scarcely better in either North America or mainland Europe. None of this fits what we see in Britain, which has emerged from the ice just as recently but where conditions are best summed up as 'mostly benign'. Of course this may be entirely because of climate, subsoil or other local factors but the same effect *can* be achieved by Man, intentionally or accidentally, by fortuitous land alteration or deliberate action. Take, for instance, forest clearance. To read orthodox historical accounts, the impression is always given that the forest is somehow areas of the British countryside that the locals haven't quite got round to clearing. It is accepted from various lines of evidence that Britain was 'cleared' with considerable speed as soon as agriculture was established but then, for some reason, it is supposed that these same determined clearers weren't up to the task of finishing the job. This is obviously wrong. We may not know exactly why unfeasibly large tracts of forest were left intact but it must have been a deliberate choice on somebody's part to do so.

On the other hand, the landscape most readily identified with the Megalithics, the chalk downlands of southern England, are tree*less* but equally enigmatic. What exactly is a chalk downland? It cannot exist in nature since left to itself it reverts to scrub within a very few years so the mere fact of its existence today suggests two apparent 'facts' about the past: the southern English countryside has not been unsupervised even for 'a very few years' and somebody was once quite anxious that a large swathe of the countryside should be treeless. Again, why? At this remove all we can reasonably say is that chalk downland was caused by and steadfastly maintained by the Megalithics. By contrast, there are areas of the countryside completely denuded of trees but apparently left to their own devices, the British moorlands. These are routinely declared to be that way for natural reasons—soil type, altitude etc.—but human activity in the form of overgrazing, overfelling and industrial tailings are at least prima facie alternative explanations. These areas may be mute testimony to what happens when Megalithic principles are ignored or, perhaps more likely, the Megalithics regarded certain areas as 'industrial' and had few qualms about letting them go so far as agricultural use was concerned.

There is a loose correlation between moor and altitude e.g. Dartmoor, Exmoor and the Pennine moors. But altitude itself may to some extent be the consequence of human intervention. The mere act of clearing stones from the soil and using them for drystone walls can have remarkable consequences for the erosion of entire landscapes, comparable to the removal of trees. But in any case moorland is not necessarily high ground. There is a considerable extent of moorland between London and the New Forest, even though most of this is nowadays disguised by intense human activity, with only golf courses and army ranges peeping through. Here is William Cobbett of *Rural Rides* fame, writing about the Devil's Punchbowl at Hindhead, Surrey in the nineteenth century: "At Churt I had, upon my left, three hills out upon the common called the *Devil's Jumps* …. Will they (the Unitarians) come here to Churt, go and look at these "Devil's Jumps", and account to me for the placing of those three hills, or the placing of a rock-stone upon the top of one of them as big as a Church tower? For my part I cannot account for this placing of these hills. That they should have been formed by mere chance is hardly to be believed."

The only piece of major Megalithic terraforming recognised as such by academics is Silbury Hill, near Avebury. Though the mound is reckoned by archaeologists to have required six million man-hours, orthodoxy is reluctant to grant the Megalithics the capacity for the routine application of such vast forces to produce even more imposing interventions in the landscape. Similarly, since Silbury Hill has no obvious purpose, archaeologists are loath to

give the Megalithics any motives as to their monumental constructions other than the usual 'ritual purposes'.[1]

Silbury Hill

*Silbury Hill is the largest acknowledged man-made earthwork in
prehistoric Europe. Although it has been excavated, no clues to
its purpose have been found. Silbury, though free-standing, seems
to be pivotal in the Avebury-Overton Hill-West Kennet complex.*

When there *is* a historical record, terraforming is accepted as an
entirely straightforward matter. For example even run-of-the-mill
Georgian gentry families went in for prodigies of earth-sculpting
using methods—picks and shovels—scarcely more productive than
the tools available to the Megalithics, and did it in a single generation. Why then is it so difficult to contemplate an entire nation
with a timescale of at least centuries managing to Capability-Brown
much more extensive areas of the countryside? Especially if such
prodigious use of labour were in support of projects that were
more socially productive than the mere expression of family vanity.
Once it is accepted that, unlike Georgian gentry, the Megalithics'
terraforming was central to the British way of life, not only is the
mobilisation of six million man-hours unsurprising but much more
efficient methods of terraforming can be anticipated, utilising that
characteristic Megalithic speciality, the control of running water.
Just because the science of eroding (and re-depositing) chalk and
limestone is something *we* have rarely needed to do does not mean
that the Megalithics were not masters of how it was done. It should
never be forgotten that their brain power is identical to our own.

---

1   Even the astronomical purposes of Stonehenge required a civil engineer to measure
    them before archaeologists would reluctantly concede the point and even now they
    much prefer characterising the place as 'for the ancestors' and other vapourings.

162

The two most important Megalithic sites are Avebury and Stonehenge, the two being separated by but a few miles of Wiltshire countryside. So, given that Megalithia is country-wide, even Europe-wide, the sheer proximity of their two chief constructions is something requiring explanation. In fact the proximity *is* the explanation because they are essentially a single elongated complex even though, technically speaking, Avebury is a transport entrepôt and Stonehenge is a scientific establishment. Even a cursory examination of the Avebury environs will lead to the supposition that either Avebury was selected because it had a remarkable number of prominent features in the chalk landscape surrounding it, or Avebury was selected for some quite different reason and the surrounding landscape was sculpted to create prominent features all around.

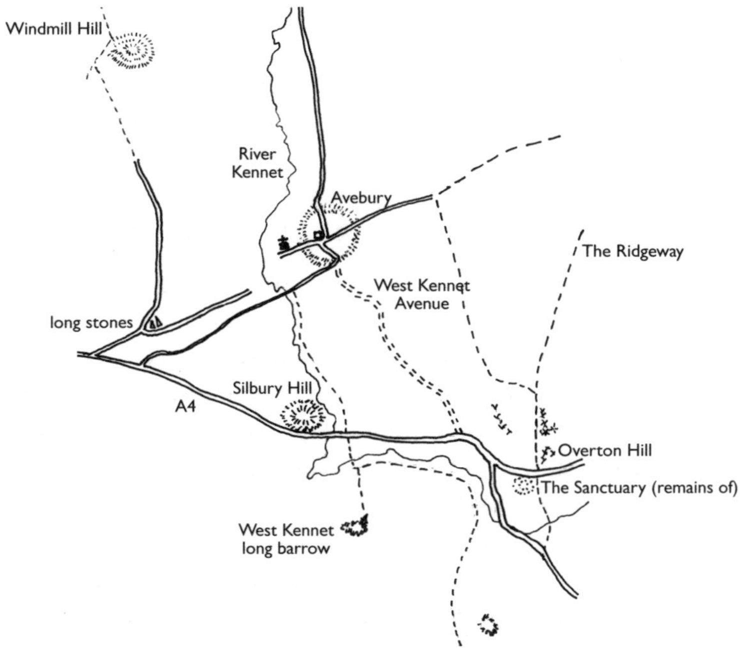

Avebury and its environs

Visitors to Avebury should allow for an extended stay because of the sheer number of extraordinary megalithic sites that are visible in every direction.

With Stonehenge, by contrast, there is a deliberate *lack* of prominent features surrounding it because the chalk landscape has been *planed* to create lines-of-sight for observational purposes. Since neither geographers nor archaeologists consider Ancient Britons capable of altering landforms on any scale and have declined to investigate the matter, the only evidence that Salisbury Plain has been planed is a statistical one: how many 'plains' are there in Britain apart from Salisbury Plain[1] and what is the probability that one of them would have the world's most famous prehistoric site on it? If the Avebury-Stonehenge complex *is* a complex, the sequence would then be:

1   Avebury was selected because of its geographic position at the centre of the trans-Britain straight-line navigational system
2   as such it became the de facto HQ of Megalithia and
3   therefore a convenient place for more detailed measurement
4   requiring the constructing of various earthworks on the horizon or in particular directions but
5   for astronomical computations an uninterrupted horizon was required so the nearest suitable site was selected and
6   'planed off' to create Salisbury Plain whereupon
7   the various stages of Stonehenge were constructed on it.

A small piece of supporting evidence is to be gleaned from the route *between* Avebury and Stonehenge, which passes between Milk Hill and Tan Hill. There has long been a local controversy as to which of these next-door neighbour hills is higher, a matter of some significance because these are the highest hills anywhere in this part of England. The BBC felt the dispute merited a half-hour of our time to decide which was in fact the taller and set about excitedly measuring them by the latest scientific techniques. No doubt terribly important but what everybody on the programme missed was the rather more pertinent question: what are the chances *in nature* of having the two highest hills in a given part of the country not only standing immedi-

---

1   The term 'plain' would seem to have been used *only* for Salisbury Plain. It became a technical geographic term only in the nineteenth century to describe for instance 'the Cheshire Plain' or 'flood plains'.

ately next door to one another but being of the same height? Statistically it is supremely unlikely but of course somewhere in the world it must happen, and presumably such a congruency might well excite the attentions of the local television station. But then what is the overall probability of this extraordinary situation happening halfway between the world's two most important Megalithic sites?

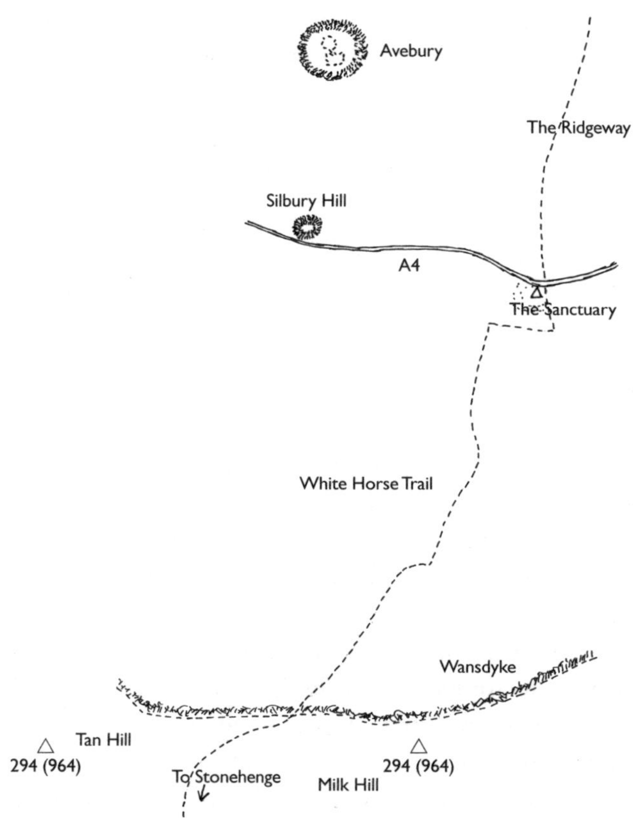

From Avebury to Stonehenge

Access to Avebury from the south is via the White Horse Trail, joining The Sanctuary below Overton Hill, from which a linear north-south link between Avebury and Stonehenge can be deduced. Note that the Wansdyke crosses this at right angles suggesting

*that it was originally intended to prevent pack trains avoiding toll
payment by going across country. But the entire Stonehenge/Tan
Hill/Milk Hill/Avebury complex seems to have outgrown its strictly
transport functions to become a Site of Special Scientific Interest.*

Should this in fact be no accident, the obvious inference is that the
Megalithics deliberately arranged for the two hills to be of equal height.
This is not physically a difficult task, merely a matter of lopping off a bit
from the higher one, but the challenging aspect is to be able to survey
their respective heights to within inches (ten, according to the BBC) in
an overall height of a thousand feet.[1] But then surveying, or some allied
piece of scientific endeavour, was presumably the reason for doing it
in the first place since striving for such pedantic accuracy seems a bit
extravagant if done for ritual or aesthetic purposes. The specific reason
though is unknown. The importance of latitude in the Megalithic
system generally might mean that having equally tall 'sighting posts'
would be a good way of calibrating cross-staffs but another possibility
is the timing of the sun behind one and then the other, which would
be useful data when measuring, for instance, the circumference of the
earth. Alternatively, having two hills of equal height, close enough to
be used as a giant spirit level, would make an excellent baseline for the
triangular surveying of the British countryside.

What would we expect of a system that lasted for at least three
millennia (4,500 to 1,500 BC) and more especially what would we
expect of a caste of characters who were operating a supranational
organisation based on navigational instruments and measurements?
It is reasonable to suppose that such people would become
inquisitive about matters not strictly limited to the requirements of
animal drovers getting about the countryside or indeed mariners
sailing the northern seas. Looked at sociologically, Megalithia Inc
would have to develop an intellectual elite at the top end in order
to provide the kind of all-embracing career structure open to 'all
the talents' so the development, however nugatory, of a megalithic

---

1   The fact that they are the same height *now* would seem to indicate an absence
    of erosion since Megalithic times. As we shall see, *preventing* erosion is yet one
    more tool in the Megalithic bag of tricks.

science based around their existing areas of expertise—surveying and astronomy—is not in itself at all surprising. There is intensive debate, both among academics and enthusiasts (but not of course *between* academics and enthusiasts), as to how 'nugatory' the science was. The starting point for everybody, the gold standard for theorising, is always to make head or tail of Stonehenge.

Since Stonehenge, in all its manifestations through time, is easily the most sophisticated of the stone circles but has no obvious practical function, its role is best understood as a kind of university, both in the sense of training neophytes and in doing basic research. A third role would be that of National Standards Institute. John Michell, of blessèd memory, pointed out that a national, nay international, surveying and astronomical measurement system would require a central standard and he made the case that the purpose of the cross-pieces of the trilithons, the lintels that stretch across from one sarsen to the next, safely out of reach and carefully cut to size (unlike the other megaliths at Stonehenge), were to act as the final repository of the basic Megalithic measure.

A Stonehenge trilithon

A trilithon, meaning 'three stones' (Tri – three, lithos – stone), a term coined by Stukeley in the eighteenth century, is used to

*describe two enormous upright stones topped by a horizontal
stone or 'lintel'. There are five separate Stonehenge trilithons in
a horseshoe setting at the centre surrounded by a continuous
lintelled circle, a construction unique in England and the world.
Allowing for subsequent erosion, both human and natural, the
uprights are apparently undressed stone and seem to be for
no purpose other than holding up the lintels. The lintels, by
contrast, appear to have been carefully shaped for a purpose
that is not obvious but is presumably central to the function of
Stonehenge itself.*

The rest of the monument, a series of near-circles radiating
out, though built at different times, would then be for ensuring
the accuracy of the calendrical and astronomical data required
for navigation. A valid objection to this theory is that cross-
staffs, stone circles and leylines just do not require this order of
exactness. However, there is one circumstance that does require
long-term monitoring of where precisely heavenly bodies are
situated and that is when dealing with the very long haul. The
night sky changes quite a lot over the centuries. For instance, our
Pole Star was not the Megalithics' Pole Star. As the earth's axis
wobbles via the so-called Precession of the Equinoxes so the star
that is directly over our North Pole changes. Before Polaris, it was
Drago, *Draconis*, the Dragon.[1] It is not just the Pole Star; when the
earth shifts its orientation in space, everything heavenly is up for
grabs so if you have a system that relies on where these objects are
in the night sky at any one time and that system is designed to last
for aeons, then somebody or other has to have something or other
to keep track of the changes.

But this is all so slow. Does it really take an entire Stonehenge to keep people abreast of such infinitesimal changes

---

1 How long these changes need to be tracked is still apparently of interest
to astronomers. That well-known Megalithic, Robert Hooke, used the
carefully sited Monument, designed by that other well-known Megalithic,
Christopher Wren, to measure the transit of Draconis and then abandoned
the Monument forthwith as an astronomical viewing platform, whereupon
it reverted to its official role as tourist attraction and commemoration of the
Great Fire of London.

when the end-user is operating to stone age margins? It may have something to do with how the Megalithics conducted their observations. Squinting at heavenly objects and marking their position via a back shadow off a standing stone with a stick is not the last word in scientific precision so it may be possible to improve matters by trading time for exactness, individual sightings will only be approximate but manifold sightings done over very many years might improve things. This would perhaps explain why Stonehenge was not only in use for such a long time but why, periodically, another circle-of-stones was built to replace the current one. And then there is the other possibility—trade space, not time, in the search for accuracy. Instead of doing two observations a long *time* apart, do two observations a long *distance* apart. The Michael Line for example can be a way of looking at the same sunrise several hundred miles apart and thereby producing a capacity for genuinely earth-wide, not to say solar system-wide, measurements. The oddly sophisticated stone circles to be found in the Orkney Islands suggest that north-to-south measurements were as important as east-to-west ones.

The Megalithics *thought big*. The Michael Line itself is evidence that the Megalithics were surveyors on the grand scale but the Line provides at least circumstantial evidence they were landscape engineers of epic ambition too. We are so used to the map of Britain that we can lose sight of the fact that it is suspiciously convenient in layout. How fortunate, for instance, is it that the longest landline across Britain should link the two most important megalithic commercial sites, the tin mines of Cornwall and the flintmines of Norfolk? Unless of course Britain was designed that way. A preposterous thought? Actually, re-sculpting Britain is surprisingly do-able in Megalithic terms. Here is a map of pre-Megalithic south-western Britain:

**Map of south-west Britain with
Somerset Levels undrained**

*The solid line shows the coast as of 4,500 BC. Most of the West
Country is now cut off, as judged by line of sight, from the rest of
the country.*

With this ancient coastline the greater part of Cornwall and Devon
is no longer 'plugged into' the rest of Britain, at least not as the
Megalithics saw things, with their requirement to have overland
leylines as their navigational system. So they drained what is now
the Somerset Levels and created a line-of-sight joining Britain's two
most distant east-west points, the Cornish west coast and the Norfolk
east coast. The evidence that the Somerset Levels are the product of
Megalithic intervention rather than natural forces is fourfold:

1   The Somerset Levels are highly anomalous since the
    nearest thing in nature would be made by a large river
    estuary, yet there is no large river here nor could there
    ever be given that there is no substantial hinterland in the
    narrow West Country peninsula.
2   It is agreed even by orthodoxy that the Levels date from
    4,500 BC, which is the same date Megalithia started.
3   They are formed by the *Polden* Hills; a polder is an area of
    land claimed from the sea.
4   The Norfolk Broads.

This last point arises because, while the Levels are unique in Britain (if not the world), there is one place that comes close in physical terms and that is the Norfolk Broads. By an otherwise astounding coincidence, the Broads are more or less bisected by the Michael Line, and not just any old bit of the Michael Line but the only other section that is directly affected by proximity to the sea. But just how 'proximate'? The North Sea erodes the east coast of Britain at a rate of about one mile per century, something we treat by shoring things up or alternatively letting things slide and the choice of what *we* do is dictated by three things: how we feel about any given part of the coastline, the level of our technology and the state of our finances. Not very surprisingly our ancestors took a similar view and protected those bits of the North Sea coast that were Megalithically valuable, of which the chief was their main trunk route, the Michael Line, and used their specialist technological expertise in hydraulic terraforming to do it. In other words they constructed the Norfolk Broads which have the happy effect of stopping sea erosion in its tracks. The process can be followed by a straightforward application of comparative cartography. Here is a map of the British east coast of six thousand years ago, i.e. before sixty centuries of coastal erosion @ one mile per century:

**North Sea coastline *c.* 4,500 BC
(shown as bold line)**

Now we draw in the longest landline across southern Britain, and protect it with 'the Norfolk Broads'

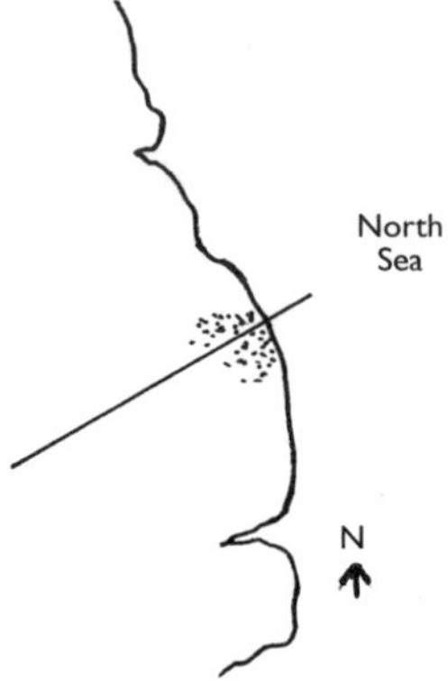

North Sea coastline *c.* 4,500 BC with Michael Line and Norfolk Broads protection

We apply sixty centuries of coastal erosion @ one mile per century except in the place where the Norfolk Broads have been constructed to prevent that erosion.

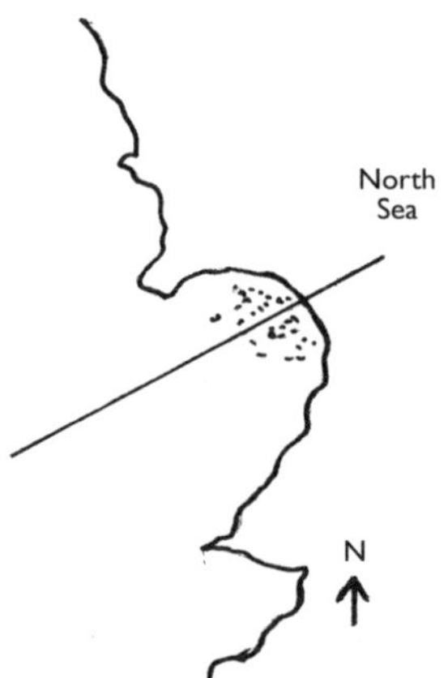

North Sea coastline after sixty centuries of erosion everywhere except the area protected by the Norfolk Broads

N.B. The Thanet peninsula also juts out for Megalithic reasons (q.v.)

There is an excellent piece of extant circumstantial evidence that this actually took place and that is the presence of two villages on the *present* coast either side of the Michael Line called Ormesby St Michael and Ormesby St Margaret. The fact that two dragon-slaying saints (plus Orme = worm = dragon) are still here facing the sea is eloquent testimony that they must have been there a very long time ago and that can only be true if *for some reason* coastal erosion has been stopped here 'a very long time ago'.

When it comes to the Megalithic countryside academics' under-standing is so inadequate that they are just as prone to make the opposite error, assuming something is deliberately engineered when in fact it is the result of inadvertent intervention. Take the famous phenomenon of the British 'Iron Age Hillforts'. These anomalous but often spectacular features of the countryside have been mapped in detail:

Map of hillfort distribution in southern England and Wales

Hillforts are mostly concentrated in the south and west. There are about two thousand known examples in the British Isles and Ireland. Some have signs of habitation, others none. No overall pattern has ever been discerned but as they were all on hills and

How do archaeologists define 'a hillfort'? It has to have two features: some kind of continuous enclosure and…well…um…be on a hill. The 'iron age' bit is not so defining—it is mostly archaeologists drawing a distinction between these prehistoric features and their presumed successors, the Roman camps and the Norman motte-and-baileys. Only a small proportion of 'iron age' hillforts have actually been investigated in any detail and while they are certainly present in the Iron Age, when they actually came into existence is not so easily decided. This is not the only puzzle.

1   Hillforts exist in staggering profusion. It is a curious society that demands a fort every few miles, and certainly not one that corresponds to what we know about Iron Age Britain, which was divided up into fair-sized and apparently effective political units.

2   Very few hillforts seem suited to actually keeping an enemy out for more than a few minutes. Either they are enormous, like Maiden Castle in Dorset, and would have required tens of thousands to man the ramparts, or they are so small as to be scarcely worth the bother. But even the middle-size ones seem curiously impractical. For the most part, the hills are not unduly steep and the walls not very formidable.

3   Contrary to widespread myth, building any kind of fortification on a hill is very unwise because a) the walls can be so easily undermined and b) water is hard to access. By contrast, building on a large *rock* can be very effective but almost no hillforts are.

4   Hillforts seem to last an unfeasibly long time. Most archaeological sites require a certain degree of work before their date and function become clear, but the Iron Age hillforts have, as it were, presented themselves for inspection, in contrast to the dearth of British Iron Age evidence in general.

It is this last point that betrays their true origin. These 'hillforts' are simply artefacts created by megalithic land use practices. The one thing that all ancient societies are obliged to do is to create 'kraals', places where animals can be penned at night. This is a requirement in any pre-modern society because the existence of large predatory animals (not excluding human beings) makes concentration and protection of domesticated animals at night an inescapable duty. Since domestic animals were introduced into the British countryside *c* 5000 BC the question then arises: what does five thousand years of kraals, up to the end of the Iron Age *c* 0 BC, do to a rapidly eroding landscape? As the entire British landscape has only been eroding for just twice that length of time, since the end of the last Ice Age, the effect of kraals will be very significant, should they in fact affect erosion. Let us see.

The most widespread building material in history is *wattle-and-daub*, the mixing and then compressing of soil, straw, hair and dung (on a wooden lattice, the 'wattle') to make durable house walls. But where does the wattle-and-daub technique come from? It comes from observing what happens when animals are penned together in purpose-built enclosures. They stir up the top soil on which lies hair, manure and straw and then they compress the surface with their hooves until eventually it forms a hard crust which lasts indefinitely despite everything the elements can throw at it. Hence the same formula is ideal for building house walls. Or to put it back the other way, when placed in a permanent enclosure, animals produce natural wattle-and-daub. It is perhaps difficult to conceptualise the process horizontally but penned-up animals will be creating artificial islands of especially durable, element-proof ground so, when general erosion of the entire area takes place, everywhere except that part protected by the animal 'wattle-and-daub' starts to erode and continues to do so *ad infinitum*, by anything from a few feet to hundreds of metres depending on local conditions. Since animal enclosures are necessary every few miles, it follows that ultimately patches of uneroded ground will remain standing proud from the surrounding landscape and, by definition, every one of these patches of higher ground will have archaeological evidence of a continuous animal-proof barrier all around them because that is how they were built originally, and the boundary enclosure will always surround the summit. The kraal itself of course was built at ground level originally. It is true that occasionally subsequent events *can* make correct identification tricky. What *we* mistake for hillforts are obviously potential sites for the *later* building of temporary defensive ramparts, and some may indeed have been used for this purpose. One or two (and the evidence suggests it was only one or two which is curious if they were built as hillforts) have certainly been the site of actual battles. Becoming places of local eminence, via differential erosion, some have latterly become convenient places for, in that famous phrase, high status dwellings, though again it is startling that thousands of 'hillforts' on investigation should turn out to be entirely bereft of human habitation. The one thing every last one of them has though is an animal-proof barrier.

The rainfall map of Britain is fairly decisive in proving that hillforts used to be animal enclosures. The greatest erosive agent of topsoil is rainfall, so it ought to follow that the more rain the more likely it is that kraals will produce these distinctive topological features. Here is the rainfall map of southern Britain which shows clearly that hillforts correlate more or less exactly with rainfall, except for the three areas of *greatest* rainfall—the Cambrian mountains, Exmoor and Dartmoor—which are all areas where local conditions are sufficiently extreme as to make the kraaling of livestock impossible in the first place. In these areas specially hardy breeds have always been left to their own devices and rounded up once or twice a year.

Rainfall map and hillfort distribution map

Natural wattle-and-daub is also the explanation for 'ridgeways'. It has always been something of a puzzle why ancient long distance paths are so often sited along ridges, rather than in the valleys. The usual explanation for this is that it is important to keep animals-in-transit separated from the local farmstock; that ridgeways are often drier and more negotiable than valley bottoms; and that it is easier to exact tolls from a specialised route. All this may well be true but it is equally the case that ridgeways are frequently cold, windswept and altogether rather unpleasant. There is also the small factor that naturally occurring ridgeways are hardly likely to be in the places and direction that animal drovers actually need to go. The explanation for this entire state of affairs is that what are now 'ridgeways' were originally specialised drovers' routes *at ground level* but that constant use by animals created the wattle-and-daub effect quite naturally and thus within a relatively short period erosion of the entire land surface will leave these artificially protected strips standing clear of the surrounding countryside, to create continuous elevated ridgelines.

This is not only a complete explanation for hillforts and ridgeways but explains why hillforts are so often to be found *along* ridgeways. The whole system is the end-product of millions of beasts tramping for thousands of years along the same restricted routes. It is the counterpart of the patchwork of organic paths that get made in and around the villages because once the wattle-

and-daub effect gets going it introduces the same self-reinforcing effect of each user finding the way ahead has been semi-forced on him by all those who have gone before. 'Green lanes' are formed in valley bottoms where the 'ridgeway' process cannot operate because material is being deposited rather than eroded. All this will be better understood by regular walkers than by either archaeologists or geomorphologists.

NINE

The Megalithic Control of Animals

Consider the pigeon hopping around on the platform of Hammersmith station, at the end of the Hammersmith and City Line. If you make a threatening gesture it will take to the air and alight a few feet away completely undiscombobulated. If it hops into an open railway carriage and the doors shut, it will wait with great serenity until the next station whereupon it will hop out and continue life much as before. What would happen to a sparrow in like circumstances? Utter panic, even though (British) sparrows have had nothing to fear from human beings for hundreds of years, unlike pigeons. So what accounts for the difference in behaviour?

There is no question that both the pigeon and the sparrow are wild animals but there is equally no question that the pigeon used not to be a wild animal. The pigeon, the British pigeon, is a feral animal, a species that used to be domesticated but has 'escaped to the wild'. We assume this for two reasons: (a) because its *present* behaviour, its easy familiarity with Man, is really only explicable if it has a *past* relationship with Man and (b) we have historical evidence (and archaeological finds and anthropological studies and the pages of *Pigeon Fanciers Gazette*) that Man domesticated the pigeon. But what if we lacked (b)? What if our only knowledge of pigeons was observing their present behaviour? We would *not* assume prior domestication. We would almost certainly put together some ethological theory to account for their behaviour or, though this would be highly unusual, we would say "Don't Know". Perhaps a few ornithological mavericks might suggest 'domestication in antiquity' to account for the 'odd behaviour' but this would be stoutly resisted by mainstream biologists who would a) demand specific evidence for such an outlandish theory and b) decline on general grounds any kind of human interference in their domain. Ornithologists, like all zoologists, have a professional reluctance to allow Man (i.e. the Humanities) into their Kingdom. But alas this state of affairs may not last much longer because, it seems, the Megalithics got there first.

There aren't many domesticated species. We tend not to think about this very much but the fact of the matter is that, taking all our familiar pets and farm animals together, not only are they few in number but they were all domesticated in vast antiquity. Here are our own particular local assortment:

**Dog Pig Sheep Goat Cow Cat
Chicken Duck Horse Goose**

'Vast antiquity' mostly means "we have no idea when" but in any case amounts to 'before civilisation' so purely *historical* evidence will always be lacking. One of the reasons we don't like to think about this, apart from hating not knowing, is because we no longer know how to domesticate animals and it irks *us*, who know how to fly to the Moon, not to be able to do something our rude ancestors could do. Now, several thousand years after The Golden Age of Domestication, we might be biologists of great acumen and know far, far more than they did about Life, the Universe and Everything but we can't domesticate for toffee.[1] But who exactly are 'they'? It may be the Megalithics since, after all, they specialised in animals but on the other hand Megalithics were not greatly interested in either farmyard or household animals because for the most part Megalithics possessed neither farms nor houses. Their interest was more in the *exploitation of wild animals* rather than strict domes-

---

1 Biologists (and everybody else) *think* we can domesticate animals if we really wanted to but if this were the case we would have domesticated zebras pulling kiddies round zoos. The Second Baron Rothschild had zebras pulling his carriage but then the Rothschilds are an extremely Megalithic family.

tication. This will be even harder to discover in the various records of the past. Suppose, for instance, that falconry had died out in about 1500 BC and had failed to get a mention in any historical document that had come down to us. What would be the average ornithologist's reaction (or yours, come to that) on reading this account:

The Megalithics were far in advance of ourselves when it came to the general domestication and induced behaviour of animals. For instance they could get any bird of prey (all the way up to the Golden Eagle) to sit calmly on their outstretched wrist until, with a quick forward motion, the bird would fly off, kill the prey and return to its owner who would reward it, if at all, with but a trifling morsel of meat. We are not entirely sure of the purpose of this, it may have been for hunting, for disposing of vermin or for keeping other predators away from the domesticated animals. Perhaps it was a sport—it certainly sounds like fun, if of a somewhat nervous kind. It is not known how this skill was achieved, whether by training, by breeding, by rearing wild chicks or some other method developed over the millennia by specialists.

A likely story. But suppose it were true and that the Megalithics really were able to do such an outlandish thing. Is the 'falcon' sitting quietly on the wrist of its owner a domesticated animal? Would we go further and say that 'falcons are domesticated animals'? Obviously not since, except for those 'tamed' by falconers, all falcons are wild animals. But what if it was claimed that Ancient Megalithics took one or other of the raptors and, by a special breeding programme, created a new species of raptor, which they termed 'a falcon' and which was entirely a domesticated species? This is perfectly possible in principle because it is a demonstrable fact that people in ancient times took various wild animals and created new, wholly domesticated, species out of them, and those animals included bird species. The evidence that they were able to do this is all around us in the form of our present domesticated species. But what would be the evidence if this 'falcon' were now no longer a domesticated animal? What happens when the 'domesticated raptor' is no longer required and, like the pigeons, has gone feral? Presumably evolution would take place as the falcon, as the new kid on the block, would be obliged to start competing with existing wild species, altering its behaviour and perhaps sub-speciating to cope with this rather strange new habitat free from (or bereft of) human control and sustenance. It is true that prompt extinction might be the normal evolutionary fate of such a species but it is equally the case that domesticated falcons were presumably bred to be rather good at their job which is after all tantamount to 'being good at being a raptor'. Competing with other raptors might well have been part of its human-bred skill-set.

But what would be taken as evidence *today* that this process actually happened? For example, does the statement "the peregrine falcon is the fastest-moving creature on earth" elicit the response, "Well done, peregrine, but *somebody* must hold the record" or is the better answer, "Well, yes, that is a tiny sliver of evidence in favour of the proposition that falcons were once domesticated and the peregrine falcon was bred specifically to be the fastest creature on earth." Or how would we judge the relevance of the 'factette': "There are thirty-seven species of falcon." It is a factette because we really don't know whether it is true or not—speciation is one of those areas where Life Scientists get a bit shifty and it is unlikely in the extreme that all thirty-seven identified types of falcon have been exhaustively tested to see if they are truly separate species. Instead we are told this:

> *The Gyrfalcon is a member of the hierofalcon complex. In this group, there is ample evidence for rampant hybridisation and incomplete lineage sorting which confounds analyses of DNA sequence data to a massive extent*

But even if we ignore taxonomic quandaries and just assume there are thirty-seven varieties of falcon we arrive at the following interesting but unanswerable questions:

1   Is thirty-seven a lot for branches of raptor families, if so
2   Would we expect great diversity if the falcon were
    originally a domesticated species and had been subjected
    to a great deal of artificial breeding or
3   Would we expect great diversity if a single domesticated
    species went feral and that species had to evolve
    very quickly to deal with a whole new set of natural
    challenges?

At this point mere revisionist historians have to throw in the towel. However, just to get the relevant academics, whether in the Humanities or the Life Sciences, interested in this ignored branchline of knowledge, just on the off chance it is a golden highway to somewhere significant, there are *things to look for*—characteristics that crop up with preternatural frequency in species that are suspected to have been meddled with (to use a term that includes practices that fall short of full domestication) by the Megalithics. Here are the top ten (not all characteristics apply to all animals, the term *domesticate* is used throughout for convenience):

1   **Smallness**   The domesticated version is smaller than the
    wild version even if, later, the domesticated version is bred
    to be larger than the wild original. The classic example
    would be the cow and the *auroch* (assuming that was the
    original domestication, which is not certain). Perhaps the
    largest cow (more strictly bull) still has not acquired the
    stature of the auroch but in the case of the dog and the
    wolf (again not a certain jump) the Irish Wolfhound is now
    bigger than any wolf. Why the domesticate *is* smaller is
    not known, perhaps it has something to do with breeding
    in gentleness or, more likely, prolonging the juvenile stage
    but the fact of it is sufficiently well attested to adopt this
    as a sign of domestication. Unfortunately it is also the case
    that nature alters the size of species so, whether examining
    the fossil record or living animals, it is not possible to
    definitively assign the hand of man as against the claw of

nature. Of course we are only dealing with the last 50,000 years so by definition all step changes will be 'sudden' by the standards of evolutionary biology, and therefore suspect. It is also the case that the last 50,000 years have seen massive climate change, a clear impetus to size change, and besides human behaviour other than domestication may have the same effect. Nonetheless any sudden downsizing occurring in any given species in the last 50,000 years can be provisionally regarded as at least a prima facie reason for suspecting domestication.

2   **Curious extinctions**   When domestication occurs it is often the case that the domesticated variant is sufficiently protected as to expand and oust the competing wild version. This can happen (from Man's perspective) wittingly or unwittingly, i.e. it might suit him to deliberately get rid of the wild version or it might happen, as it were, quite naturally via competition between a protected species and an unprotected one. The witting choice, that is the deliberate extinguishing of the wild version, may arise from wishing to expand numbers of the domesticate rapidly by cutting down on the opposition but there are also other good reasons, for example preventing cross-breeding or eliminating diseases arising in the natural population. Of course extinctions occur in nature and they certainly occur, again unwittingly, in the course of the general expansion of Man's peculiarly destructive activities, so it is not possible to equate either *modern* or *sudden* extinctions with domestication. That is why the term *curious* extinction is used here because it is only in very circumscribed circumstances that domestication is likely to be the cause. There is nothing curious about the dodo becoming extinct when Man first lands on the dodo's island home. It may be lamentable but it is not curious. Only large-scale extinctions would qualify though not every large-scale extinction in the last fifty thousand years is down to domestication.

3   **Peculiar habitat considerations**   When
domestication is introduced an artificial habitat will
probably be introduced too. This might stretch to an
entire ecosystem if the domesticated animal is sufficiently
important. The problem here is that nature and nurture
mimic one another so well, and it all happened so
long ago and in unrecorded times, that it is difficult to
recognise what is and is not 'peculiar'. For instance,
grassland is 'peculiar' in New Zealand—the plant only
being introduced by European settlers in the nineteenth
century—but if grass and grassland herbivores had been
introduced ten thousand years ago it is doubtful that
human agency would be suspected.

4   **Whiteness**   Not necessarily strict *albinism* though it may
be that albinism has some part in the story. Ditto *leucism*.
Why whiteness is involved at all is not known, it is just
that white or near-white animals so often occur among
animals suspected of being domesticated in antiquity that
it is unlikely to be coincidental. Whiteness can be useful in
itself, as making animals stand out, and white has enduring
connotations of royalty, beauty, purity and so forth. It may
be that simply choosing 'white' animals for special human
attention itself promotes domestic habits in the wild animal
over the long run. But the connection might be due to the
neo-Polar origins of the Megalithics generally.

5   **Usefulness**   The animal has a trait which is useful
to man. Obviously a particular species might be chosen
for domestication because it already has such a trait: for
instance, the honey bee. Or one species might be chosen
because it is particularly useful in an otherwise common
trait: every mammal gives milk but Man has chosen only
to domesticate a few mammals. Is it an accident that one of
them, the aurochs, now gives milk in amounts that is off the
natural scale or would any mammal, given several thousand
years of intensive breeding, manage this feat? Sometimes

the original use can be obscured. The pigeon has two uses—
providing meat and carrying messages—which interfere
with one another so it is impossible to tell which was the
original purpose. But of course there has to have been a
useful purpose originally though in the case of animals-
long-gone-feral this might have to be reconstructed.

6   **Odd behaviour**   All animals indulge in odd behaviour
(from our point of view) so to be truly described as 'odd'
it is necessary to show that the trait is not in keeping
with closely related species and therefore may have been
specially bred into the animal by humans. This special
purpose will still be present when the domesticate goes
feral especially if it proves to be useful in the wild. But,
as usual, this is going to be a matter of fine judgement
because individual species can evolve extraordinary
behaviour by natural selection—especially if it is 'useful in
the wild'. For instance, is building a dam odd behaviour
on the part of the beaver? It is odd insofar as no other
water mammal does it, nor is anything remotely similar to
be observed among the beaver's land relatives. Zoologists
will point out that dams are highly useful to beavers
in creating a 'perfect' habitat but revisionist historians
would equally point out that dams are enormously
energy-intensive capital projects that seem to add very
little to the beavers' requirements in terms of rearing
and eating, which would be encompassed perfectly well
by just pottering along the river bank like every other
riparian animal. "Who cares," say zoologists, "it obviously
suits the beavers who are, or at least were, mighty
successful in occupying most of the colder latitudes of
the northern hemisphere." Perhaps too successful since it
might equally be said that in both Western Europe and
North America beavers underwent rapid declines when
beaverian dam-building was viewed as a nuisance, hats
notwithstanding. It is a leap of faith even to hypothesise

that training an animal to build dams is a Megalithic achievement, but consider statements such as this and decide whether the behaviour is more likely to have evolved via natural selection or by human training

> *Beavers are most famous, and infamous, for their dam-building. They maintain their pond-habitat by reacting quickly to the sound of running water, and damming it up with tree branches and mud. Early ecologists believed that this dam-building was an amazing feat of architectural planning, indicative of the beaver's high intellect. This theory was questioned when a recording of running water was played in a field near a beaver pond. Despite the fact that it was on dry land, the beaver covered the tape player with branches and mud.*

7 **Appealing face**   One of the presumed routes to domestication is the human characteristic of enjoying the company of pets. A desideratum for pets is that they 'look cute' hence an appealing face is selected out in available animals. But this may be to confuse cause and effect as the desire for pets would seem to be minor compared to the general exploitation of animals for economic purposes. Since there are strong reasons to suspect that domestication involves the prolongation of the juvenile form, it may be this that is creating the 'look' because humans seem to like all juvenile forms (not just their own young) and this in turn leads to these attractive animals being adopted as pets. But however it arose, there is little doubt there is a correlation between domestication and 'appealing faces'.

8 **Aberrant genetics**   The problem here is that for the last two hundred years biology has been relying on the Linnaean System, that is mainly inspecting the physical form of an animal (morphology) to decide how to classify species. For the last twenty years this has been subject

to challenge from a completely different methodology, inspecting the genes. For *our* purposes each system is handicapped by the fact that both the appearance and the genes of a *particular* species vary to a degree that makes it impossible to be definitive when distinguishing that species from closely related species, making for difficulties in the context of domestication where there are relatively small variations among i) the wild progenitor ii) the domesticated version iii) the domesticated version that has subsequently gone feral and iv) the result of interbreeding between i), ii) and iii). Add to this the fact that neither morphology nor genetics can be precisely applied to fossils and the best that can be achieved is simply to point to situations which appear to be somewhat aberrant if the normal workings of evolutionary variation had been left to play out.

9 **A 'northern' dimension**   Since the Megalithics have their origin in the northern half of the great Eurasian steppes (and a little later in the North American grassland plains) and were kept 'up there' to a greater or lesser extent by Civilisation, there is good reason to suppose that most domestication events happened 'up there' also. Of course it is true that many of the domesticates were taken over by Civilisation, and have subsequently radiated worldwide as civilisation has radiated worldwide, and it is also true that domesticates-gone-feral have had plenty of time to make their way from their places of origin (especially birds). Nevertheless there is often a 'northern' bias that can still just about be discerned.

10 **Pack behaviour with dominant animal**   This factor is listed here because, unlike the previous nine conditions, this is put forward by biologists (and therefore adopted by prehistorians) as the main means of domestication. It is said that once Man is able to place himself as the alpha male, all the other animals in a pack (if a carnivore) or a herd (if a herbivore) or a flock (if a bird) will naturally follow him and that this natural behaviour, when allied

to other interventions, will lead to domestication. This
alpha male (or alpha female) aspect at the herd level can be
supplemented with, or indeed be produced by, 'imprinting'
with the mother (or occasionally with the father) at the
individual level to achieve the same effect.

These characteristics can help to identify animals that are not
ordinarily regarded as in any way domesticated *now* but may have
been in the past. Or at any rate have been subjected to human intervention in the past. To do this, all that is necessary is to run through
the ten-point checklist and see which applies. In this way, in this quasi-
scientific way, it is possible to set aside our zoological and historical
preconceptions in order to recognise potential candidates. Consider
for example the barn owl. How does it fare with the First Characteristic, *smallness*? The barn owl is not small by owl standards but
suppose the very largest owl, the eagle owl, is the wild progenitor and
that the small owls are either domesticated versions of the eagle owl
or are feral versions of the original domesticated 'small' owl. If this is
accepted *ex hypothesi* then the Second Characteristic, *curious extinctions*, is to a degree satisfied because the eagle owl is oddly absent from
the old Megalithic heartland in the British Isles and Western Europe.

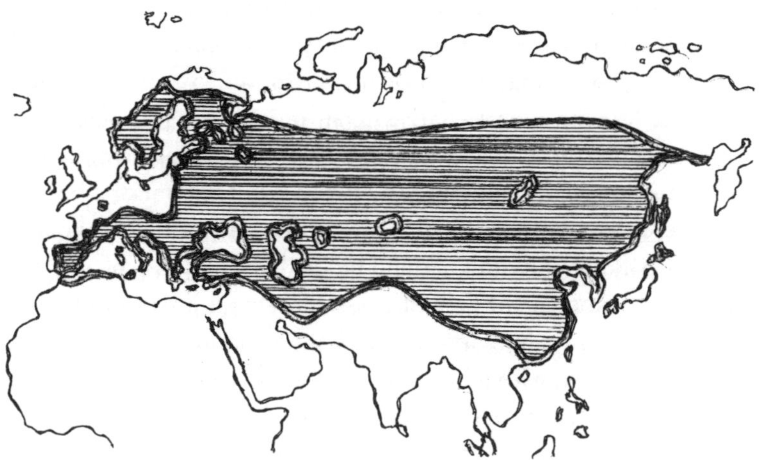

Shaded area: Eagle owl range

But this illustrates the challenging nature of this whole subject: what makes the eagle owl's absence from north-west Europe in any way unusual? No ornithologist has ever pointed to the fact as being noteworthy. It can certainly be argued that there is no obvious reason why the eagle owl could not flourish in Britain on strictly natural grounds but there is an obvious *un*natural reason and that is the eagle owl is a clear and present danger to a whole range of smaller domesticates, from rabbits to chickens (even, it is reported, to sheep and deer). Hence it is quite proper to contend, in a hesitant sort of way, that deliberate erasure by man, supplemented by artificially heightened competition from a protected, domesticated rival, would account for the absence of the eagle owl from part of its expected range. If so, this would also tick the Ninth Characteristic box, *a northern dimension*, since this range is very roughly speaking to the north of the eagle owl's present European range, and yet it is clearly not due simply to a more northerly climate.

However, to return specifically to the barn owl, does it satisfy the Third Characteristic, by having a *peculiar habitat*? It is widely reported that British barn owls have difficulty establishing themselves away from barns. Again, is this really very peculiar? Put neutrally it would seem so because the other owls don't much like barns and in any case barns are a 'peculiar' feature of the countryside insofar as they are, in animal evolutionary terms, an extremely modern one. Could such a situation arise in nature? Clearly it is possible to cobble together an explanation: one species of British owl started specializing in the (to an owl) rather wonderful habitat of a barnful of cereal-chomping rodents as soon as such an eco-niche became available, though why that should be the barn owl (as she was not called at the time) is not very obvious. Since owls are not otherwise noticeably fond of human company, the situation is much better explained by man, with a barnful of cereal to protect, giving a home to a rodent-killing specialist. This does not, after all, require domestication in itself because putting up nest boxes and messing about with nestlings (or whatever) might do the trick and after a few hundred, perhaps a few thousand, years such constant intervention might result in complete speciation of this exemplary bird. This could serve as a slogan for Megalithic best practice: "Full speciation without full domestication!"

The Fourth Characteristic, *whiteness*, is not only a feature of the barn owl but a strange one. It is all very well the snowy owl being white because it spends its life plunging out of the white background of the Arctic but why would the barn owl, which as a night predator ought to be any colour but white, be white? What is particularly baffling is that the white half, the underside, is the half that ought not to be white, looked at from the mouse's point of view. The barn owl chick is all white which might be significant if prolongation of the juvenile form is the key to domestication. Perhaps a better explanation, given the northern bias of the Megalithics, is that barn owls are ex-snowy owls, but the whole connection between whiteness and domestication is mired in mystery anyway. All one can say is that the barn owl ticks the fourth box.

The Fifth Characteristic, *usefulness*, certainly applies since the average barn owl kills around a thousand small rodents a year, in and around a barn. In strictly ethological terms, the barn owl's attachment to human buildings, which is unusual both in terms of owls and in terms of birds of prey generally, also satisfies the Sixth Characteristic, *odd behaviour* (not in keeping with close relatives) but another oddity is that barn owls do not hoot, as is the wont of owls, but screech in a rather unearthly way. This is the more significant because certain other avian candidates for Megalithic adoption—crows, geese, peacocks and so forth—have similar screechy attributes. It may be that 'scary' sounds are sought after attributes the better to keep domesticated and wild animals separate, quite apart from the legendary usefulness of giving warning to human beings.

There can be little doubt that the barn owl passes the *appealing face* test of the Seventh Characteristic. We tend to think of owls as being in any case rather sweet-looking but this is not necessarily so. At least one of them is downright horrible.

Eagle owl Barn owl

It is true that the other British owls are nicer looking than the eagle owl but none match the barn owl for cuteness. How the barn owl came by its particularly attractive looks may be to do with its status as the smallest of the available hunting birds. Falconers tend to treat their charges as pets (they would perhaps find this description insulting but it is obvious enough to lay observers) so if we assume that in Megalithic falconers' households, where domestication is an everyday business, it might well be that the smallest of the hunting birds hanging around the place would become something of a family pet. It is only a tiny step, indeed to a domestication-savvy society an irresistible step, to make this smallest bird a real pet and therefore to select for the a-a-ah factor. It is perhaps significant that cats, the major competitors of 'pet' owls in both barn and hearth, underwent a similar career trajectory.

Pussy Cat   **Lynx**

We tend to focus on the eyes and face but looking at both owls and cats, it may be the ear tufts that we react to subliminally. On the question of the Eighth Characteristic, *aberrant genetics*, the barn owl is truly in a class of its own:

> *True owl or Typical owl (family* Strigidae) *are one of the two generally accepted families of Owls the other being the barn owls (*Tytonidae).

The Tenth Characteristic, *Pack Behaviour and Dominant Animals*, would not on the face of things apply to owls or to birds generally since even those species that flock or who seek company when migrating do not necessarily have formal hierarchies. However, at the *family* level of organisation, at the level of choice of mate, selection of nest site, egg-laying, incubation, chick-rearing, fledging and so forth, human intervention is actually much easier with birds than it is with mammals because of the rooted nature of nesting birds' family life. This would appear to be true of barn owls in even greater measure since the barn owl, as it were, makes itself specifically available for human intervention by its choice of habitat.

So how does all this add up? At one level it may not amount to much one way or the other. Our own habit of feeding birds in our gardens has had a measurable effect on bird numbers (and perhaps even the start of speciation) in the short time we have been doing it, so it may be that just by fortuitously providing snowy owls with shelter against the harshest winters, at the southernmost limits of their range, might be enough over several thousand years to create the barn owl. We just do not know enough about bird speciation to rule this either in or out. But on the other hand there is clearly a prima facie case for regarding the barn owl as being to some degree a deliberate human artefact simply because we do know that such a change can take place under the conditions of domestication or at any rate of deliberate protection. There is no question that the barn owl is not *now* any kind of domesticate; at most it is a feral ex-domesticate that has managed to survive in the wild.

Ferrets and Their Familiars

One of the oddest of today's domesticated animals is the ferret. It is usually obvious why a particular animal was chosen for domestication but in the case of the ferret it is difficult to see what that reason was. Nowadays they are used more or less exclusively for hunting rabbits (aside from pets) but this seems a somewhat restricted activity in itself and unlikely to be the original reason especially if, as we are always being told, the rabbit is a recent introduction. However, if rabbits too are looked at with domestication in mind, the circle might be squared. If we assume that the European rabbit is itself a domesticated species then the sequence might plausibly be i) rabbits domesticated ii) warrens constructed to farm rabbits iii) polecats domesticated into ferrets in order to keep rabbits within the warren and then iv) to flush them out when required for eating. If so, Strabo, writing about first century BC Spain, seems to be referring to a time when things have got out of hand:

It is unlikely that rabbits would be such a nuisance unless they were something of an unnatural addition to the local fauna. Feral rabbits have continued to plague entire countries (indeed entire continents) ever since. But more on this when rabbits themselves are discussed.

A more intriguing use for ferrets is to be found in its meaning 'little thief', a usage still preserved in English by the phrase 'to ferret something away' and refers to the ferret's penchant for secreting away small items. This is sufficiently unusual as to constitute one of the Domestication Characteristics, *odd behaviour*, and if so this trait might be assumed to have been bred into the ferret specifically by the domesticators. The Megalithic purpose would then be for the ferret to ferret away toll items for later collection by the Hermit, thereby ensuring that permanent manning of the toll point was not necessary. Other members of the *mustelidae* family, to which ferrets belong, have what might be tenuously called 'Megalithic associations'. Here are some random but connected musings that may or may not have something to do with Megalithic control over one or other of these savage but oddly endearing creatures.

++ The term 'ermine' in English is used specifically to describe either the white, winter form of the weasel or, more usually, its fur. But the term seems to be applied further south without regard to whiteness and not even necessarily to weasels e.g. stoat in Spanish is *armiño* and in French *hermine*.

++ The 'ermine' changes from brown to white, a colour shift duplicated by the swan whose plumage also changes from the brown of cygnets to the white of the adult bird. Just as swans belong to the Crown and are protected, so ermine fur is reserved for royalty.

++ The stoat/ermine's white coat can be assumed to be natural, but what of the black tip of the tail? Ermine tails feature on the flag of Brittany (formerly Armorica, 'ermine-land'). The black tip of 'royal ermine' features on 'armorial' shields as chevrons.[1]

++ The stoat was thought to be the only animal that could kill a snake, giving it brother-status to Hermes' brother, Apollo, the Python-slayer.

++ "For as to the weasel, many still think and say that as it is impregnated through the ear and brings forth by the mouth, it is a likeness of the birth of reason (logos)." Plutarch.

++ The male stoat-weasel is a *dog*, the female a *bitch*, both 'dog' appellations; the young are called *kits*, short for kitten. These dog and cat references suggest sometime domestication.

++ An unusual stoat trait is *delayed implantation* which is when animals are able to prolong gestation in order to make sure young are born at certain times of the year. There is something of a correlation between the animals (some one hundred species) that are able to perform this apparently very useful trick and 'domesticates' which implies that the Megalithics were able somehow to use delayed implantation in their control of animals, presumably as another way of prolonging the juvenile form. It is always worth looking at animals that do use delayed implantation in order to identify candidates for human interventions (if that is not too circular an argument). For instance, the roe deer is the only deer species that can do it, though why it should need to do so is not obvious given that its natural range is wholly within a clement climate. It is more obvious why seals should have evolved the trait but it is still worth looking at various seal species for signs of Megalithic intervention.

---

1 According to Burke's *General Armory*, the earliest coat of arms yet discovered, belonging to a count of Wasserburg (d. 1010), is in the church of St. Emeran at Ratisbon, a major pilgrimage shrine. Hermes, aka Emeran, is the archetypal herald which is presumably why the whole business is termed heraldry. Lower down the social scale, in Cockney rhyming slang, weasel means coat ("weasel and stoat").

The harbour seal for instance is white in the juvenile form, has a particularly appealing face, is a smaller version of the grey seal and has 'domesticated' appellations attached: *bulls*, *cows* and *pups*. The fact that seals during birthing are completely at the mercy of human beings with boats (but have few other predators) make them ideal for 'protection'. It may be no accident that the harbour seal used to be the common seal but now isn't.

++ The otter, another of the *mustelidae*, is still kept by some river peoples today to help catch fish. The Chinese used to train sea-otters to herd fish; they even built their long-distance sampans with a special flooded compartment to keep their sea-otters in to provide a constant supply of fresh fish.

++ As those brought up on *Tarka* will know otters are relatively easy to tame and they crop up suspiciously often in northern mythologies—Norse and Native American—while Zoroastrians (always a good guide to Megalithia) are specifically forbidden to kill them.

++ "In Britain, the official records of the Pell Office show a payment of 66,13s.,4d. on 10th October to Robert Wood, "Keeper of his majesty's [James I's] cormorants, ospreys and otters" for making fish ponds and for building a house to keep the fishing animals in. Gudger (1927)"

Rabbits and Hares

Rabbits have a curious history in Britain. Although today they are treated as ordinary members of the countryside, they are always claimed to be an introduced species. The problem is that in the particular case of domestication, an animal might or might not turn up in the fossil/archaeological record in the expected way since if they are bred and consumed in very specific places they may escape detection in the ordinary course of excavation. As recently as 2000 AD it was confidently asserted that the rabbit was a Norman introduction but then a couple of Roman finds converted this to an equally confident claim that 'rabbits are a

Roman introduction'. How much further back this process might go is complicated by the fact that the most characteristic feature of a rabbit warren is the 'pillow mound', the central burrow of the colony, and this shape looks awfully like a great many other lumps-and-bumps in the prehistoric landscape. Palaeontology is not always to be relied on when, as is the case with domestication, morphology is on the move. Nor in this case does etymology help because the word 'coney', meaning something like rabbit (it really is confusing), turns up in equivocal circumstances. For instance Cunetio/Mildenhall on the Kennet in darkest Megalithic Wiltshire was a place for breeding rabbits, Cunetio being cognate with coney as well as Kennet. But then another Mildenhall turns up, also on a River Kennett, also surrounded by rabbit warrens, a hundred miles away in Suffolk, the two places being linked by the Ridgeway/ Icknield Way. Is this Roman, Megalithic, both or neither?[1]

Warrening, the keeping of farmed animals on a large scale in a small area under quasi-natural conditions, is a very specific practice used for creating large amounts of meat (or fur) and can be seen as a very Megalithic sort of practice, rather along the lines of fish-weirs, because creating a large supply of a reasonably valuable commodity suitable for trading over distance is a Megalithic speciality. Warrens may also be characteristic of mining areas because not only does mining tend to take place in terrain not suitable for farming but it requires large concentrations of people that need feeding. Contrariwise, rabbits are generally held to be unlucky by miners because their burrowing activities make mining walls vulnerable. It is a puzzle, and not only to readers of *Watership Down*, how rabbits are kept in their warrens. In the case of deer warrens, building a fence does the job but this cannot be done, except with very great difficulty, in the case of the burrowing rabbit. Fortunately—unless it was specifically bred into them—rabbits

---

1 Where the Romans themselves got rabbits from is another matter. It is generally argued nowadays that rabbits are a desert animal and that it was only Romans that bridged the gap twixt Britain and the desert. But of course the Carthaginians had been visiting Britain for many centuries and in any case the rabbit doesn't seem to agree that he is best suited to places where grass *doesn't* grow.

hate water and equally fortunately the Megalithics specialised in hydraulic engineering. Rabbit warrens are always surrounded by moats. That rabbits, unlike hares, burrow is what gives them their esoteric status: the normal mythological practice is to group serpents, worms and rabbits together because, as underground-dwellers, they are privy to 'underground knowledge'. Coney, pronounced 'cunny', is linked to 'cunning' (and 'conning'), Rabbit being a notorious trickster in folklore. But just why were rabbits 'bred to burrow'? The answer is clear enough if a *hare* warren is envisaged. Concentrating a whole lot of non-burrowing hares in a small area is also going to concentrate birds of prey, a damnably expensive nuisance. Why not train the hares to protect themselves by burrowing?

Ducks, Geese and Swans

Why do all these 'water fowl' have such a special relationship to Man? The chief reason is that any bird that spends its life floating around on water must have a large, compact body mass to conserve heat and any bird that has a large compact body mass will be of interest to human beings looking for food. Since these 'river-birds' live and nest in places where human beings can get at them relatively easily and since chicks have to be quickly and securely imprinted to make sure that they follow their parents on the water, the potentiality for Man to take over the imprinting, and with it responsibility for other aspects of the birds' lives, is obvious enough. From the birds' point of view this can be an excellent 'evolutionary career move'. For instance, just being able to avoid the extraordinary rigours of the annual migration might be a sound reason in itself to co-operate with Man, and north-west Europe is just the kind of cusp-territory where water fowl can exist the year round so long as Man adjusts conditions a little. How he does this is something best left to ornithologists but *that* he did it can sometimes be glimpsed in the later historical record in circum-stances which are significantly Megalithic. Interested observers should always be on the lookout for apparently trivial references such as "geese were specifically associated with *Michael*mas, and wild geese were penned by St Werburgh, an Anglo-Saxon princess/ saint from *Stone* in Mercia, the daughter of St *Ermen*hilda".

However, fully domesticated species (or for that matter wholly wild ones) are not being considered here so the strictly Megalithic contribution might best be summed up by consideration of the career of that very curious animal, the British swan, which is everywhere and always on the very edge of being either wild or tame. Perhaps the oddest thing about the swan is that it would appear, being the largest of the water fowl, to be the best designed for eating, but almost never is. This suggests it had a special status, and presumably therefore a special function. One thing everybody knows about swans is that they 'can break your arm' and it may be that swans were originally used as guard animals.[1] The swan is unique among British birds in being both tame and frightening. They are reported to rear up, wings outstretched, at fords to thoroughly frighten the horses which will encourage toll-paying no end. There is a Swan Hotel where the Michael Line crosses the Thames at the Goring Gap. But whatever its original use, the swan certainly has a very full list of Megalithic associations:

++ The swan always represents Mercury, one of the three prime alchemical elements and the only one specifically named for Hermes, Mercury being his Roman name.

++ Swans pulled the chariot of Aphrodite, the Romano-Greek moon goddess, even though the swan is an uncommon bird in the Mediterranean.

++ "The 30,000-odd year old finds included ivory figurines of mammoths and birds and flutes made from swan thigh bones" (*Nature* 18/12/03).

++ Angels are messengers in the Megalithic System and when taken over by Christian iconography they are always portrayed as having swans' wings. In northern European and Celtic mythology,

---

1 Including, as the largest of the water fowl, possibly the control of other water fowl. It is difficult to train, say, dogs to round up rapid swimmers.

swans are the vehicles for the soul's journey to the Otherworld just as Hermes accompanied souls to the Underworld.

++ At Wells Cathedral there is a flock of swans trained to ring a bell when they are hungry.

++ Although by no means silent, mute swans are less noisy than wild swans or geese. Were swans bred to be quieter in contemplative surroundings such as monasteries with whom they have long associations?

++ Whiteness is associated with domestication and a decrease in aggressive behaviour—black swans are reportedly more aggressive than white ones.

++ Transmutation, as with ugly duckling to beautiful swan, is the basis of alchemy.

++ Apart from the Crown and the occasional monastery, the only people legally permitted to own swans are the dyers' and vintners' guilds. This singular privilege reflects the alchemical associations of making chemical dyes and fortifying alcohol.

++ It is from the flight of cranes that Thoth was said to have invented the alphabet in Egyptian myth, Hermes did the same with swans.

++ The only (semi-)saltwater swannery in the world is at Abbotsbury behind the Megalithic Chesil Beach guarded over by a chapel dedicated to the Megalithic St Catherine.

++ Helen or Selene, the Greek moon goddess, was born from a swan's egg as a result of Zeus disguising himself as a swan.

++ The Cheremis, a Volga-Finnic people, would sacrifice a white goose, a white ram and a black ram in a *keremet*, a sacred grove. The ceremony was presided over by a swan couple who were then taken in a three-horse carriage to the river and set free after a silver coin was hung around their necks.

++ Swan-maidens, half bird half human, abound in folk myth. Actually, swan-maidens seem to be refined versions of goose-girls who similarly feature in these stories, presumably reflecting the fact that swans are 'refined geese'. The traditional female job of driving the birds along—as opposed to the males looking after the larger animals—reflects the very functional, non-hierarchical organisation of the droving life. The same informal equality can be seen when the drovers became canal families.[1]

Corvids (Crows, Ravens, Magpies, Jackdaws, Rooks, Choughs)

'Straight as the crow flies' has entered daily speech but why is straightness specifically equated with crows? Crows' nests in ships are so named because caged crows were taken on voyages; sailors used them to find land by releasing them and seeing which way they went. Since crows abominate open water[2] they head straight for the nearest land, an intriguing parallel with leylines which also abominate open water and travel in straight lines. Crows might have a direct input into leylines because in captivity they are reported to carefully lay out pebbles in straight lines and get very annoyed (and put them back) if the pebbles are disturbed. Such bizarre behaviour does not seem to have any natural evolutionary purpose but it would be terribly useful to surveyors if they could have an assistant who could plot and mark straight lines from fifty feet up. The most startling straight line/corvid association is with the otherwise etymologically weird *corvée*, the traditional method by which peasants worked off their labour obligations through performing communal tasks. These were overwhelmingly either the maintenance of local roads or by forming straight lines in ploughing and reaping the lord's domain.

The likely original cause of the man/corvid relationship is the raven's habit of following wolves in order to carrion feed on their kills, which is analogous to the man-and-dog partnership. The corvids' usefulness to Man, and the beasts that he follows/protects/domesticates, is

---

1   And perhaps theatre families, which were originally highly peripatetic. If so then panto should be mined for *in situ* evidence. The Megalithics are behind you.

2   Crows may originally have been aboard to catch rodents. Later domesticates used for this purpose, ferrets and cats, are notoriously water-shy. But then again so traditionally are sailors. The way crows walk is not dissimilar to the rolling gait of sailors, which may be an instance of crows' infamous talent for mimicry, unless of course crows were originally domesticated on a constantly shifting deck.

illustrated by for instance the fact that birds of prey will leave sheep alone when there are resident corvids about. Presumably this was not originally because the raptors were afraid of the corvids themselves but had learned to associate them with the more dangerous Man. Whatever used to be the case, it is certainly true that the corvids exploited this nervousness because today corvids mob raptors with routine aplomb, whether they need to or not. It may be that corvids were trained to attack larger birds (as dogs were with wolves) but such fierceness does not, it seems, mean that ravens will bother sheep though they will eat the afterbirth and dead lambs.

The outstanding characteristic of the *corvidae* in general is their intelligence. In terms of tool-using abilities they are ranked alongside chimpanzees but whereas chimps can be accepted as on a par with us because of genetic affinity, for birds to acquire such astonishing skills must surely be bound up with some other connection to Man. The question of animal intelligence is a tricky one when domestication is involved because we tend to give undue weight to the carrying out of tasks that we ourselves regard as important, and therefore 'intelligent'. So by training animals to do things for us, we start to imbue them with cleverness when really they are just exhibiting rote behaviour. On the other hand there is some evidence that the act of domesti-cation itself, and the consequent elongation of the juvenile stage, might enhance intelligence. Just being around human beings provides opportunities for 'learning', blue tits and milk bottle-tops being a good recent example, because human ingenuity, unlike nature, throws up new situations in less than evolutionary time. Crows are perfectly at home amongst crowds eating at roadside service stations where they have learnt to retrieve food from rubbish bags and are frequently seen patrolling the edges of motorways waiting for 'roadkill'. With tougher cases such as nuts and molluscs, they lay out the food to be opened by the wheels of cars, and even trains.

However, the corvids' truly remarkable ascent to the top of the animal IQ table might be from a quite different route, one which might account for Man's own remarkable rise from the hundreds of thousands of years when he could do little more than endlessly knap stone, a useful 'animal' trick but not in itself evidence of great intelligence. Every autumn reindeer gorge on fly agaric (*Amanita muscaria*, 'magic') mushrooms which pass relatively unscathed into their dung. In the tundra, where there are no trees and where the Megalithics hypothetically originated, campfires have to be made from this dung, meaning that both Man and Raven nightly sit around the campfires imbibing psychoactive smoke. If you can remember the Mesolithic, you weren't there. Ravens were there or at any rate they have somehow acquired the astonishing ability to filch burning sticks from a fire and pass it over their feathers, the smoke acting as an insecticide ridding them of painful ticks. Or so strait-laced ornithologists always claim. In Britain crows have been observed pecking fly agaric mushrooms, behaviour that has led these same ornithologists to claim the crows are after slugs on the cap but judging by the beak-sized chunks of mushroom carried off, it is for purposes other than satisfying hunger. Not necessarily for the buzz, because fly agaric, like many other psychoactive drugs, increases energy levels. The Siberian Koryaks have a hero, Big Raven, who unable to carry a heavy bag of provisions was told by the Great Spirit to go to a certain place to pick *wapaq*, little white plants with red hats (i.e. *Amanita muscaria*). After eating them Big Raven was able to lift the bag with great ease.

Carrion Crow

Notice the pronounced brow ridge. This is also present in anthropoid apes (in fact crows have been referred to as 'feathered

*apes' by zoologists) and would seem to be the product of rapid
brain development, the soft tissue of the brain evolving faster
than the brain casing, leading to the apparently unnatural but
necessary bulge. Neanderthal has the same prominent brow ridge
but we haven't. Make of that what you will.*

Corvids can, like parrots, be taught to speak.[1] Being given directions by a talking jackdaw might sound like a fairy story, in fact often *is* a component of fairy stories, but may well be harking back to a bygone reality. After all, it is no great feat to train a tame jackdaw to repeat simple instructions and place him at a crossroads (preferably perched on a standing stone), primed to speak his lines when any traveller shows up—a talking signpost in an age when there could be no written signposts. But it is worth considering all the ways that corvids could have assisted the Megalithics simply by listing the extraordinary range of corvid abilities and assuming that such singular ethologies could really only have come about via human intervention since it is difficult to see how some of these 'acquired characteristics' could possibly be useful in the wild. For instance, researchers have found that crows can recognise a human being even after an absence of many years, a trait so peculiar as to be good evidence that they were trained to recognise Megalithic travellers. 'The thieving magpie' actually applies to all the corvids who have a habit of removing shiny objects and placing them in caches. This unusual—and again apparently pointless—behaviour[2] is mightily useful to Megalithics needing unpaid toll collectors at out of the way places.[3] On the other hand toll-evaders might get the corvid treatment because it has been widely reported that specific individuals can be recognised and *attacked* by crows. Regular walkers will be aware that unlike all other birds corvids have the unsettling habit of staring quite unafraid at human passers-by. Naval corvids, the choughs, assist

---

1 As can starlings, an equally enigmatic bird but not one dealt with here. Tame corvids can conduct phone conversations with unwary callers. There are no current plans to employ corvids in the call centre industry.
2 Unlike for instance bower birds who do it to entice mates.
3 Crows have been trained to take coins out of slot-machines.

travellers by flying along cliff faces, mainly in Wales and Cornwall, warning approaching sailors away from danger. They are the only corvids that have bright red bills and feet. In Greek mythology choughs were called 'sea-crows', one of the sacred birds associated with the island of Ogygia, where Ulysses was rescued by Hermes.

Archaeological digs widely report that corvids are one of the commonest bird types found in Iron Age sites but for what reason archaeologists do not know. It is generally assumed that they were for eating but the true explanation can be deduced from 'Rook Sunday', the nearest Sunday to May Day, when "baby rooks were caught": not to be put in pies but because human intervention at the juvenile stage is the key to domestication techniques. Rookeries are often as old as the trees in which they are built because rooks will re-use their nests until the nesting trees become unstable. They have an uncanny ability to leave a tree long before its decay is apparent to humans which is presumably the origin of those folkloric associations regarding ravens abandoning castles, Towers of London, British Empires, just before their predicted fall. Farmers consider rooks to be birds of *good* omen, surprising in view of their forbidding appearance, ugly calls and hunger for seed.

Rooks keep to fixed timetables, their outbound and homeward journeys are as reliable as clocks, giving Megalithic travellers a time-check twice a day for their sun-sightings. Rooks that have colonised a particular copse will be as effective as any guard dog in alerting people to the presence of approaching strangers. It is noticeable that rooks appear to be wary of human beings but still choose to co-habit with them—no amount of rook guns can scare them away. Natural explanations for this odd state of affairs are possible but a close prior connection to the Megalithic System is an alternative hypothesis. Cobbett, in his *Rural Rides* of 1821, mentions regularly occurring hilltop copses on the downs and he noted approvingly the number of rookeries they contained. This has a double implication if hilltop copses were indeed Megalithic landmarks. Originally the rooks on sighting a traveller would rise up thereby indicating which copse was to be treated as the next waymarker—a copse is just a copse but a copse-plus-rooks leaps out of the auditory landscape. Later on, no doubt, the warning call would rather be for the benefit of the hermit to inform him that his services were required. The rook's most self-evident trait is *raucous*ness, raucous meaning harsh or rook-like, though of course it could be the other way around, the newly domesticated species being named as 'that which is raucous'. But in any event there would appear to be some correlation between raucousness and human-association since all the corvids possess the characteristic to some degree, as do parrots and peacocks.[1] Nevertheless, we cannot be sure whether the raucousness was bred in or was the characteristic that made corvids of interest in the first place. Dogs, the closest of all to humans, communicate with their owners and keep predators away by barking, something they do not do in the wild, so this trait was also presumably bred in.

Mythology underlines the role of the raven as consort of the gods. Woden is usually portrayed with two talking ravens, 'Thought' and 'Memory', on his shoulders acting as messenger-advisers, Apollo's messenger was a raven or crow and Lugh, the multi-skilled Celtic god and the patron saint of travellers and traders, had a crow as his messenger. Brân, the Welsh crow-god, *Brân* in Welsh meaning crow, is frequently conflated with *bryn*, the Welsh for hill. A hill called Caer Brân in Cornwall overlooks St Michael's Mount, the beginning of the Michael Line which at the Norfolk end passes *Brand*on close to Grime's Graves, from where flints were transported all over Britain. In Welsh legend the head of Brân (cf. Baphomet, the bronze 'talking head' reportedly worshipped by the Templars) was buried on London's Tower Hill, and it goes without saying that the Tower (of London) will fall should the ravens depart.

---

1 The 'treasure' guarded by peacocks shrieking from palace rooves is the royal family within. When the 'never-sleeping hundred-eyed Argus' was killed by Hermes, Hera transplanted his eyes into the tail of her favourite bird, the peacock. The fact that an Indonesian species crops up in early European folklore is testament to the wide hand of Megalithia.

Horses

Semi-feral ponies are a particular feature of moors, the descendents of working animals from the days of tin mining and stone quarrying. Similar ponies can be seen in other unproductive tracts such as Exmoor, the Gower peninsula and the New Forest. This reinforces the idea that moorland is often industrial wasteland. Dartmoor ponies have a reputation for being hardy but even so cannot survive the harsh winters on the moor without farmers' hay rations. They are clearly not 'wild ponies' if indeed such a species still exists. No-one knows when horses were first domesticated but since it is the animal best suited to rapid transit, the horse is likely to have been a major Megalithic preoccupation. However, horse *riding* as opposed to horse hauling is a much later development, of the Iron Age, and seems more associated with military use. Until the nineteenth century (AD) ploughing and carting were almost exclusively done by oxen (ignore the Hollywood version, American pioneers got there by ox-power). This leaves the possibility that horses were originally domesticated exclusively for mine work since these are places unsuitable for large, unwieldy beasts. You can't get an ox down a mine. If so, it would mean that 'horses' are in fact a later variant of ponies. The strictly palaeontological evidence of equine evolution certainly agrees that size is a very late development.

The Scythians were the horse-nomads of the southern European steppe who traditionally arrived in Ireland on May Day. May Day in the west of Britain is associated with hobby-horse parades and the Irish hobby horse is a breed now extinct but said to be the ancestor of the Irish draught horse *and* the Connemara pony. The hobby *bird* is a small falcon known to outmanoeuvre even swifts and swallows. Ireland is virtually tree-less (even though it is The Emerald Isle) and would appear to be something of an 'unnatural' landscape, the only other similarly treeless and unnatural landscape being the Mongolian steppe. Ireland is the last redoubt in Western Europe of the tinkers, travellers, gypsies, Romanies (whatever name is used), who are the last manifestation of the Megalithic tradition of combining the long distance movement of animals with metalworking.

The Case of the Eider Duck

Three things about eiderdowns:

1   The term *eiderdown* is an English word meaning roughly, and in recent times largely replaced by, *duvet*.
2   St Cuthbert protected the eider duck in the Farne Islands, because of its down which made for such excellent bed coverings.
3   A thousand years after he lived, the *eider duck* is still commonly referred to as the *cuddy duck*, i.e. Cuthbert's duck.

Which raises two questions:

1   How did a Dark Age churchman operating on a group of offshore islets manage to give his name to a duck and
2   How did that duck eponymously manage to stuff the bed coverings of all-England when it takes dozens of eider ducks to fill a single eiderdown?

As is so often the case with hitherto unconsidered oddities of British history, the answer lies with the Megalithics. Cuthbert was a leading Megalithic, one of the 'Celtic' saints that flooded out of Ireland in the Celtic Renaissance, after the Romans left. The fact that these saints set up 'monasteries' on offshore islands around the coasts of Britain, starting with Iona on the Scottish coast opposite Ireland, is usually explained by their need for security in those desperate times but the real reason, as any inspection of their sites will reveal, was to control the passage of the (literally) passing trade. However, these northern offshore islands in themselves are not great generators of trade and in fact tend to have just the one natural resource and that is seabirds who flock to the islands because the lack of natural predators allows for ground-nesting.[1] On the other hand ground nesting makes these birds specially vulnerable to

---

1   Whether the lack of predators in such nearby islands is truly natural is a moot point. Patrick 'driving the snakes out' is not the only case of Megalithics controlling ground predators. And meddling with *avian* predators is even more a Megalithic speciality.

human beings, always assuming that these human beings are clever enough to avoid simply wiping them out, the normal fate of such birds facing unrestricted human access. There is a long tradition of *hunting* seabirds as a staple but sustainable part of the diet, perhaps reason enough to set up a monastery amongst seabirds since feeding any number of unproductive people is a challenge during the Dark Age. But it is *control* of seabirds that is the real Megalithic ambition.

How can seabirds advance the Megalithic raison d'être, of promoting trade in high value, long distance trade? What is always in demand when the whole of north-western Europe is in the throes of the self-sufficient gloom of a Dark Age? Eiderdowns! Not just very high quality bed coverings for the rich and powerful but, since one lasts a lifetime, one per every upwardly mobile household. Lightness (per *tog*) becomes not only a desideratum for the sleeper but of course is directly linked to ease of transport and eider down is the very best substance in the entire known universe (still!) for this purpose. But is there evidence that the eider duck is a Megalithic 'breed', i.e. a bird selected in some way by humans for special treatment? Since eiders would seem to be unique amongst fowl in producing not only the highest quality down but down that, apparently, has a unique 'clumpability' quality, it is reasonable to assume either it was chosen from all ducks because it had the best down or the eider is a new species created by the Megalithics selectively breeding from some other duck species on the basis of producing better and better down. But however the eider duck arose, the real problem arises from the question: how many eider ducks does it take to make an eiderdown? Since the answer is 'a great many' it is pointless creating a super-duck if relying on the migratory habits of eider ducks visiting an island annually in 'natural' numbers. Hence when the sources opine that St Cuthbert 'protected the eider ducks on the Farne Islands' this should be read as 'the Megalithics had a programme for making sure that each year more and more eider ducks and fewer and fewer competing species used these islands, leading eventually to the creation of year-round eider-sanctuaries'. But two other characteristics were trained into the ducks and that is eider ducks pluck out their own down (somewhat labour-saving for their pluckers) and then line their nests with it (making it highly collectable). All in all, an excellent basis for an eiderdown trade. Small wonder that these now little regarded birds gave their name to the English language.

Cowboys and Indians

It is very easy to distinguish between grasslands given over to domesticated animals and grasslands that are 'wild' (insofar as anywhere today is in a 'state of nature'). It is simply a matter of counting the large herbivores, counting the large predators and inspecting the way of life of any humans that happen to be about. Let us take a very familiar example of a presently domesticated setting, a dairy farm in the Home Counties.

How many large herbivores?	Just the one, cows.
How many large predators?	None.
What are the humans up to?	Making their entire livelihood milking the cows.

Clear enough but compare and contrast with the Serengeti in darkest Africa

How many large herbivores?	Many different species.
How many large predators?	Many different species.
What are the humans up to?	Minding their own business and having very little, if anything, to do with the wild animals.

It could hardly be more different. On to our next example, the Texas panhandle a century ago.

How many large herbivores? Two, cows and horses.
How many large predators? None.
What are the humans up to? Ranching the cattle
by riding the horses.

Again, not very difficult to analyse, it is another domesticated situation. So it would seem that we have two very different types of grassland, the wild type with many herbivores, many predators and no human input and domesticated grasslands with one (or maybe two) herbivores, no predators and complete human engagement.

And so to our final example, the Great Plains of North America when the Europeans first arrived c 1800:

How many large herbivores? Two, bison and horses.
How many large predators? None.
What are the humans up to? Completely dependent
on hunting the bison
by riding the horses.

So clearly a domesticated situation. Except that everybody—historians, zoologists and palaeontologists—is unanimous that this situation was entirely 'wild' with the only 'domesticated' feature present being the horses, and even they were not domesticated by the human beings present but 'borrowed' from the Spanish in Mexico. Not surprisingly all these assumptions turn out to be the sheerest tosh once the Megalithic rule is run over them.

By the time the Europeans got round to observing the Plains Indians, the latter had achieved a complete 'horse culture', that is a completely nomadic lifestyle based on bison-hunting from horseback. If true, this amounts to one of the most astounding coincidences in the entire annals of recorded history. Taking every human culture that has ever existed and for which there is reasonable evidence, just two have managed the apparently demanding task of becoming horse-cultures: the Mongols and the Plains Indians. The former took several thousand years to achieve it whereas the latter took not quite several hundred years. This is remarkable in itself but what provides the very startling coincidence is that the

Mongols and the Plains Indians are, to all intents and purposes, the *same* culture. They look the same (and the genetics bear this out), they live the same way (yurts versus wigwams), their religion is the same (a sort of pantheistic shamanism) and in fact, according to academics, they *are* the same since the one relocated from Asia to North America in prehistory via the Bering Strait landbridge. But now a rather stupendous hiatus is introduced because while it is agreed that the Mongols and the Plains Indians *were* the same twelve thousand years ago, that was before the horse had been domesticated and horse cultures were even conceivable. So if the Plains Indians really did get their horses from the Spanish and if they really did develop their horse-culture after 1500 AD we are reduced to coincidence. Unless the Oglala Sioux had a hot line to the Buryat Mongols in 1500 AD, it has to be accepted that the two 'unique' horse cultures the world has ever seen had somehow given rise to one another by osmosis through a gap of several thousand years and several thousand miles.

It is tempting to bridge the gap by positing whether there is a 'horse culture gene' or that grassland steppes have a habit of creating horse cultures but, alas, neither of these arguments would account for the next set of astounding coincidences:

1   The Plains Indians studiously ignored their alleged Spanish
    mentors when it came to the tricky task of learning to
    ride horses from scratch—eschewing saddles, bridles and
    similar fripperies, and instead adopted the Mongol style
    even though they allegedly had no knowledge of Mongol
    horse customs.
2   In the available couple of hundred years, the Plains
    Indians were able to 'convert' the very large Spanish
    horses into very small Mongolian-style ponies even though
    no Mongolian-style ponies had ever been imported into
    North America.
3   Instead of using horses as the Spanish did in agriculture
    and transport, the Plains Indians adopted the Mongolian
    pastoralism model.

4   Somehow and for no obvious reason, in the same couple
     of hundred years, the Plains Indians managed to remove
     all the trees on the Great Plains just as the Mongols did on
     the Asiatic steppes.[1]

It is not only North American horse nomads that have a remarkable history, the North American *horse* has a remarkable history. The horse actually started life as a North American animal, which is not surprising since North America is something of a horse paradise. Then all of a sudden some twelve thousand years ago the horse disappeared from North America. Yes, it's a 'curious extinction'! Since Man first appeared in North America[2] about the same time it would appear the two events must be linked. The problem with this connection is that it is truly difficult to account for how (never mind why) Early Man managed to expunge the perfect animal from the perfect habitat. To hunt the horse to extinction over an entire continent without having a horse to hunt them with is a truly awesome undertaking. Orthodox accounts have always been troubled by this and the general explanation is most often 'The Ice Age', since that came to an end at the same time as both the appearance of Man and the disappearance of the horse. It seems not to matter to proponents of this theory that the end of the Ice Age made North America a *better* rather than a worse environment for horses and in any case it is doubtful that any horse would notice that its grazing area was a little to the north or a little to the south of last year depending on whether an Ice Age happened to be coming or going. 'The Ice Age' is always one of those standard academic explanations trotted out to cover any vaguely contemporaneous anomaly. Other explanations appear from time to time, usually featuring the phrase 'Clovis points', but these explanations tend to depend on whether Native Americans need politically appeasing at the time and in which direction—either emphasising their martial qualities

---

1 It is an article of faith for the Mongols that grassland plains should have 'uninterrupted views from horizon to horizon'. The reason for this belief is not known since even steppe nomads would benefit from the occasional stand of timber. Natural grasslands, e.g. the Serengeti, always have such stands.
2 Alaska is excluded from many of these statements because the critical barrier was the ice sheets covering western Canada rather than the Bering Straits.

or underlining their green credentials. Fortunately the true story takes everybody off the hook since it turns out the Native Americans *are* Continental change-makers but not to the point of deliberately fomenting an equine extinction event. This is what really happened.

The statement "Animal *x* went extinct ten thousand years ago" is misleading. What is really meant is "Animal *x* disappeared from the fossil record ten thousand years ago". Mostly of course the two statements amount to the same thing but palaeontologists are supposed to rule out other possibilities. However, they are busy people so mostly they don't. With this in mind it is possible to reconstruct two very different scenarios for what happened to North American horses and bison around 10-12,000 BC. Before that date, there can be no disagreement as to the facts because the grassland plains of North America were much the same as those of African grassland plains: the bison are the wildebeest of North America and can be numbered in their millions while the horse is the zebra of North America and can be numbered in the hundreds of thousands. Assuming these numbers produce a small but constant supply of fossils it is a racing certainty that palaeontologists will find a proportion of these fossils and extrapolate back the correct (and natural) situation that existed up until Man's arrival. Which is what they do find. But now the horse/bison fossil record changes sharply:

1   Man arrives on the grassland plains of North America
2   A little time later, the horse fossils disappear
3   The bison fossils continue but the animals themselves get markedly smaller.

Palaeontologists interpret this situation as follows:

1   Man killed off the horse for no obvious reason (presumably it was accidental)
2   Man omitted to kill off the bison for no obvious reason (presumably it was accidental)
3   The bison got smaller for no obvious reason (these things happen).

Such preposterously special pleading is only acceptable if the underlying assumption is that "it must have happened this way so we just have to accept our lack of knowledge in this area". And that really is the current position so far as academia is concerned, however much they dress it up. But the same set of palaeontological facts *can* be explained if we apply what might be called The Megalithic Option:

1   Man arrives on the grassland plains of North America
2   Man domesticates the horse
3   Man domesticates the bison.

This not only produces the fossil record the palaeontologists are actually reporting but this time there is an acceptable explanation attached and it applies to *both* animals. If Man domesticates the North American horse its *fossil record disappears*. This is in the nature of fossilisation, the sequence being

1   The wild population of horses disappears—and now there is not only a *reason* for Man to extinguish the wild horse but he has the *means* of doing so
2   The wild population can therefore no longer give rise to fossils
3   The domesticated horse is now present in relatively low numbers and since fossilisation is itself a rare event this will dilute the fossil record radically
4   But domesticated horses hardly ever die in circumstances that give rise to fossilisation anyway.

The 'alternative' bison story is equally robust. The overall fossil record for North America at this point in history shows that the fossils of *all* large animals, herbivores and carnivores, disappear completely which can only mean that these animals disappeared too. The single exception is the bison whose fossils turn up in large numbers and can only mean that the bison survived in large numbers. It is of course possible that Man's entry onto the Great Plains should cause mass extinctions of a range of animals by virtue of, say, Clovis points and hunting dogs, but what is not possible is that Man's entry onto the Great Plains should cause mass extinctions of *every large animal except the bison*. The only feasible explanation is that the bison was *chosen* for survival and all other natural competitors—whether large herbivores or the carnivores predating on them—were deliberately eliminated. It makes little difference whether the bison was formally domesticated, though the step change in size from *Bison antiquus* to *Bison bison* suggests it was, but anyway the North American steppes were converted into bison preserves. And this the fossil record 'proves'.

The North American bison, as observed by Europeans in the nineteenth century, were not at all 'domesticated'. But this is misleading. The Megalithics did not necessarily go to the lengths of domesticating a species, they exploited them by what might be called 'advanced management'. It may be for instance that the bison were meant to be wild but only in the way that deer are meant to be wild in hunting preserves. However, a more likely explanation is that the Plains Indians of the nineteenth century were not 'Megalithic' but only the inheritors of an earlier Megalithic culture. This would imply that the bison, whatever their status formerly, had gone thoroughly feral by the time the Europeans arrived. When the Europeans did turn up in appreciable numbers the bison underwent a rapid extinction though whether this amounted to a 'curious extinction' is a matter of argument. It is taken to be a sad but inevitable fact that European-scale hunting would lead to the extirpation of the bison but it is at least 'curious' that hunting should continue until there was actually none whatsoever left. It is understandable, by the standards of the day, that hunters would seek out large herds of bison to be killed on an industrial scale for meat, hides and so forth but there must have come a point when scarcity made hunting bison for these purposes uneconomic. It is just about possible to accept that scarcity itself would then make bison-hunting a sport and that would take care of the rest but a much more likely explanation for this 'total extinction' is that the bison population was not at all natural and, even in its feral state, tended to act as 'preserved animals' by a) staying in herds and b) not being particularly averse to human presence. Buffalo, as it were, continued to offer themselves in numbers for Buffalo Bills because that is what they were bred to do. And couldn't survive any other way.

This argument can be applied to another and much less publicised extinction which took place coevally with the bison, the disappearance of the passenger pigeon. Since the British pigeon is where this chapter started it might be satisfyingly symmetrical to close with its North American cousin. The passenger pigeon shares a very odd statistic with the bison: both went from being the most populous of their type (bird, herbivore respectively) *in the entire world* to total non-existence. The passenger pigeon's disappearance is even odder than the bison's. There is no doubt that the pigeon was hunted on the same industrial scale as the bison but the actual cataclysmic decline of the bird happened just at the moment, 1870–1890, when its chief reason for being hunted—to provide cheap meat for slaves—was no longer applicable. Since these two decades were also the precise time when the bison underwent its own spectacular demise, there may be some as yet undisclosed link between the two events. There is, after all, little likelihood that 'sportsmen' would start to seek out passenger pigeons when they too became scarce, and it is not the absolute decline of either species that is 'curious' but the fact that both species just ceased to exist on a continent-wide scale *totally*. It is as if two hitherto artificially protected species somehow could not survive when that protection was withdrawn. It is reported that, to the very end, the passenger pigeon presented itself in large flocks for the benefit of European hunters. But this is not the most peculiar aspect of this bird's ethology: passenger pigeon fledglings grow unusually fast, fourteen days to full-size, but cannot fly at that age, so these exceptionally plump birds are obliged to flutter down and spend a bit of time on the ground. This is frankly catastrophic behaviour on the part of any normal bird but is a remarkably useful trait for a domesticated bird whose domesticator has made sure no ground predators shall be at hand (except himself). What could be more convenient than birds that are entirely wild, requiring no human resources to flourish in vast numbers, but who present themselves oven-ready when the time comes?

TEN

The Origins of Megalithia

The very first Megalithics were dependent on an activity that still today stands right on the cusp of domestication, reindeer herding. It is not completely certain whether the reindeer was the original animal, nor that the Sami are the direct modern inheritors of the Megalithics, but *functionally* the general activity of 'following the herds' is how the Megalithic way of life came into existence. It combines the two key attributes of classical Megalithia: close association with animals and regular economic relocation over very long distances. The roots of Megalithia go back to *c* 40,000 BP with a bunch of reindeer 'followers' trekking back and forth, north and south, somewhere on the Eurasian grassland steppes. In orthodox academic language these people would be called *Cro-Magnons*, that is people who are anatomically modern (to distinguish them from the contemporary Neanderthals), but also culturally advanced (to distinguish them from other modern human beings elsewhere in the world).

Since The Sami Way really is quite an efficient method of going about things (now, never mind forty thousand years ago), it can reasonably be assumed that these reindeer-folk expanded wherever the grass allowed them to, which in Eurasia is very far indeed. There is little to stop them because, apart from economic efficiency, another factor in expansion is *military* efficiency. Compared to other primitive human activity models, the herding of reindeer allows for the concentration and organisation of individuals on a scale which makes it hard to contemplate any other group of hunter/gatherer/whatever people being able to prevent the expansion of the reindeer-herders wherever conditions underfoot allowed it. Grass would seem to be the only limiting factor so, for tens of thousands of years, The History of the World was The History of Grass.

Orthodox accounts of the 'discovery' of grass domestication often seem to involve a Palaeolithic housewife dropping wheat grains by accident at her back door and ... um ... discovering bread, but even more technical explanations for this epochal advance never address the central question: why, when choosing from a million plant species on offer, did Man decide on grass as the one he must domesticate first? Let us eavesdrop on the world's first Plant Domestication Congress to find out:

> **Man with long beard**: Dearly beloved, you have been gathered here today to decide what species we are going to begin our plant domestication programme with.
>
> **Man at back**: What are the choices?
>
> **MWLB**: The field is open. No pun intended. There are a million plant species out there and as far as we know they're all available. It's just a question of which one we choose.
>
> **Man with medium beard**: Obviously something that's good to eat.
>
> **Somebody else**: Some sort of fruit. Because a) they are delicious and b) trees are easy to mess with.
>
> **Somebody else**: I disagree. Fruits have very limited nutritional value.
>
> **Somebody else**: It must be a vegetable. They're good for you.
>
> **Somebody else**: Vegetables are no better than fruits, nutritionally speaking. It's got to be pulses—peas, beans, that kind of thing.
>
> **Somebody else**: What about tubers? Full of starch. Sugars, that's what we really need.

Man with long beard: It's all so very confusing. We'll just have to do what we always do when we can't agree, ask The Lunatic. What do you think we should domesticate first, Loonie?

Lunatic: Grass.

Chorus: Why's that then?

Lunatic: For a start, we can't digest it. The human stomach just can't process the wretched stuff.

Chorus: Fabulous. Just the job. What else?

Lunatic: Hopeless nutritional yield. One-ear emmer, just to take the local wheat variety, gives minimal calories per hectare.

Chorus: Does it get worse?

Lunatic: Sure does. Growing grass completely exhausts the soil. One crop is OK, next year the yield is down to a half, then … well … after that you might as well give up and move some place else.

Chorus: Oh no! We were really looking forward to settling down. Anything more?

Lunatic: Yes, growing grass is really difficult. You have to level the field, remove the trees, prepare the soil … it's all a complete bitch compared to growing fruit, veg, pulses, tubers or just about anything else whatsoever.

Chorus: So we're all agreed. It's grass!

Now for the real story. What is the chief limiting factor affecting reindeer numbers and therefore of reindeer-herder numbers? Given that there *are* reindeer-herders many of the natural limits, notably from predation, will be avoided and it is essentially only the grass supply that is going to dictate overall numbers. In summer, on the Eurasian steppe, there is for practical purposes an infinite amount of grass and therefore an infinite amount of reindeer; in winter there is not an infinite amount of feed, in fact so little that overall reindeer numbers are severely curtailed and, by extension, so are reindeer-herder numbers. So increasing the amount of *winter* grass will have a direct and dramatic effect on the fortunes of reindeer and their herders. As things turned out, the requirement to increase winter feed for reindeer was the key step not only in the rise of reindeer-herder numbers but in the Rise of Civilisation.

The normal internal structure of nomads is a determined lack of labour specialisation, what management theory calls horizontal organisation. Everybody does pretty much everything. As a system it is immensely efficient in countering the ordinary hazards of long distance transhumance but it has one drawback: no potential for development. Skidoos aside, the Sami haven't changed in forty thousand years. Given this one-for-all and all-for-one ethos it is not surprising that, as a point of honour, nobody is left behind. But to increase winter feed it is necessary to leave a bunch of people behind to maximise the southern grass when, at the end of winter, the herds and the herders move north. The people left behind in the south have the task of 'protecting' the southern grass, the future winter pasture, for when the herds return once again. That way the overall number of animals will be increased since the limiting cut-off point will be raised. This is a formidable technical task no doubt but *culturally* a great revolution will be required because this 'structural specialisation of labour' has for the first time created a body of people responsible for a job of work not directly concerned with looking after animals. Instead *they will be looking after plants*.

What sort of steps will they take? The first step is surely that just keeping other herbivores away from the southern grass will ensure more is available for the returning reindeer and saying 'boo' to nervous grassland herbivores is presumably well within the technical competence of human beings. It can safely be assumed that the southern grass will be relatively abundant but of course most of this ungrazed 'fodder' will simply go to seed. Methods must be sought that prevent or postpone (or exploit) this happening, and that is not naturally within the normal technical competence of human beings. Such things have to be discovered but, fortunately for the long term fortunes of the reindeer-herders, there is now a bunch of people whose year-round job is to do the discovering. Specialisation of labour not only produces efficiencies, it promotes innovation. Everything we think of today as *human* cereal consumption—from muesli to lager—should be reinterpreted as animal feed 'gone slightly wonky', that is as by-products of experiments to make grass animal feed storable for longer periods or to make it more easily transportable. In fact, the exploitation of surplus grass accounts not only for the development of most of our major foodstuffs but for the development of our familiar farm animals as well.

The important steps can be easily traced. It will not be long before the southern agronomists—for after all that is what these permanently settled grassland specialists are—will recognise that making sure 'other grass-eaters are kept out' is not the best way of ensuring the grass is in prime condition because, when the herds return in autumn, they will mainly find that the grass has gone to seed, withered, died and be of no use to man or beast. The solution is to allow *certain animals* to graze the grass without destroying it. Fortunately nature itself provides such specialised animals in the normal way of grassland competition because certain herbivores only graze new grass and it is only a matter of ensuring they serially crop the same area rather than constantly migrating to new areas, thus ensuring 'new' grass is still around in the autumn. This does not require domestication, just saying 'boo' selectively. Knowledge of herbivores' relationship to grass is something that reindeer-pastoralists can be expected to have a handle on, so it will not be long before the selection and development of animals that can exploit the stages of growing grass, or for that matter the seeds and chaff left on the ground, will be in full swing. This process itself will have profound effects on the kind of grasses that will flourish in such a regime and the new grassland specialists will presumably be on the lookout for grass types that seed late (or seed often, or seed seldom).

Well and good, but vast quantities of southern summer grass are still going to waste while the herds are away in the north. There must be a better way of storing the grass than simply feeding it through other animals. And with grass there is! Because the calories are overwhelmingly concentrated in the seed heads *and* these seed heads are designed by nature to be easily separated from the stalk at maturity *and*, for good measure, the seeds are also designed to last for several months if necessary whether on or under ground. This new source of 'concentrate' opens up vast possibilities since ears of cereals are potentially transportable and can be used as supplement for the main herds and once it is the ear that is the focus of attention it is relatively easy to select grass that maximises the number and size of ears. But the really revolutionary step happens when animal herders need to start lengthening the time before the natural forces of decay get to work on the ears. The reason why this step is revolutionary is because, for the first time, grass has to do something it has never been called on to do before: resisting the forces of ordinary decay and yet still be readily broken down in a ruminant's stomach. The reindeer's ordinary enzymes, evolved to break down ordinary grass, will have to keep up with this new development since it is no use developing, say, bran mash and then finding ruminants can't rumin it. Not to worry, the southern agronomists will just keep on experimenting until they find a process that preserves the grass but which some *other* enzyme in the reindeer's system can cope with. But now it is odds on that any nearby mammal will also be able to 'rumin' it since all mammals have digestive systems built along similar lines.

One nearby mammal is of course Man. What makes this new ingredient truly revolutionary is not its role as a long-lasting animal concentrate but what it does for human beings. Once humans can eat grass it is they directly who can expand to the full extent of Eurasian grasslands. We can see the process at work because we need only look at *today's* methods of long-term, high calorie cereal preservation to guess the upshot of these ancient experiments. Just to take two examples: ship's biscuit and alcohol, both of which are processes that ensure cereal calories last for months (if not years) so it is likely that both cereal-baking and cereal-fermentation were discovered this way. It cannot be an accident that yeast, an otherwise obscure fungus, is used in both processes but some *proper* experimental archaeology, carried out by archaeo-chemists, would be more than welcome at this point to flesh out the story.

The eating of grass (products) rather than the eating of reindeer (products) is a momentous step in itself but what is even more important is that the existence of these new artificial southern pastures makes reindeer themselves somewhat redundant. The whole point of reindeer is that they are naturally 'transhumance' animals, that is they are specially adapted (it is assumed by nature) to exploit grass over vast distances south-to-north. But as soon as there are year-round southern pastures it becomes obvious that constant movement is a ridiculous waste of energy. The Megalithics had the opposite view of animals to our own. We have lost the ability to domesticate animals so we are constantly looking for better feedstuffs for the animals we have; but the Megalithics tended to look for animals that could be domesticated to take care of the feedstuffs that were available. Nature after all has shown the way by providing herbivores who eat grass at all its stages of growth so it is a straightforward task for megalithic domesticators to look round for, say, a main grazer (cattle), followed by a short grass specialist (sheep), a rough grazer (goats) and an anything-goes mopper-upper (pigs). Indeed full domestication is one consequence of permanent pasture. Reindeer are not fully domesticated because there is no reason to domesticate them, transhumance being functionally the same as ordinary migration, but once there are animals feeding the year round on the southern grasslands there is a need to look after them in an increasingly unnatural way. Just as reindeer today are semi-domesticated quite naturally simply by virtue of generation after generation being exposed to human presence so cows, sheep, goats and pigs will surely and eventually become fully domesticated over the long haul if their entire ecology is artificial.

One critical step now triggers another, if triggering is quite the right term for a process spread out over thousands of years. As soon as there is a permanent division of labour between those who are staying with the herds and those who are staying in the south, the development of each will also divide. One branch leads to Civilisation and the other to nothing very much. There is little doubt, since there is the evidence from the living example of the Sami and other nomads, that the people who stayed with the herds did not do very much developing. True, the size of the herd is increasing since the winter feed problem has been overcome, but there is not much upside in learning how to control ever-expanding reindeer herds when nature itself provides examples of stupendous numbers. The people in the south by contrast are doing everything for the first time, not just in terms of the control of new animals and plants, but the building of an infrastructure. These are after all the first sedentary people in history with a built-in food surplus even if that surplus is supposed to be for the returning animals. There is a population functionally tasked with the creation of a surplus and the creation of a surplus is what generates (or as may be, permits) development.

It is not the case that mere 'settlement' promotes development. Human beings have for the whole of their modern(ish) existence been settled wherever a permanent food source is available year round, mainly shellfish according to midden mound evidence. But the midden-dwellers have not been specifically tasked to find ways of maximising the shellfish crop so they do not, as far as we know, do other than exploit what nature provides and do so indefinitely. The 'southern pasture settlers' do have a task and, it seems, carried out that task. But even so the process seems to have taken thousands of years without very great change, since the archaeological evidence indicates that 'grass-meddling' started about 10,000 BC but the real take-off did not take place until the coming of fully fledged cities *c* 3500 BC. Cities themselves can now be seen as the culmination of the southern agronomy experiments by a fairly straightforward analysis of where the first cities were founded.

A cradle civilisation is a discrete area with cities[1] which does not appear to be a product of another area-with-cities, but to have come

---

1 The defining characteristic of a 'civilisation' from *civitas*, Latin for city.

into existence more or less independently. There are five of these 'cradle civilisations', Egypt, Mesopotamia, the Indus Valley, north China and Mexico. What do they have in common? Two things: each of the five is at the southern end of a grassland steppe[1] and all five are associated with that rather odd geographic feature, a major river flowing through a desert: the Nile, the Tigris-Euphrates, the Indus, the Yellow and the Rio Grande respectively. This begs two questions: why should there be a river in a desert in the first place and why should there be such an apparently automatic triggering of a civilisation? As soon as the growing of grass is to feed people and animals direct rather than to supply the returning northern herds, then it follows that there is a simple need to maximise grass production in absolute terms and, it so happens, irrigated deserts are far and away the most productive of all agricultural land because by definition sunshine is a constant and the 'soil' tends to be friable sand which is not only easily worked but efficiently retains nutrients from riverine water. And irrigating deserts is sure to happen eventually as the cereal expansionists come to the *natural* southern limit of grassland, as defined by precipitation. It is a standing temptation to extend watered bits to nearby not-so-watered bits, and as sand deserts lend themselves rather well to terraforming it looks as though increasingly ambitious hydraulic schemes were able to green the desert. It is probable that what were originally artificial hydraulic schemes became what look to us now as natural rivers. It requires only a modicum of scepticism to spot that, say, the Tigris and Euphrates running parallel for hundreds of miles in an easily eroded landscape and never becoming tributaries of one another (before it is time for them formally to join and run into the sea) is not a situation that is likely to arise in nature. But one despairs of either geographers or historians ever doing other than accepting the world around them with stolid stupefaction. The dead hand of uniformitarianism is always with us.

Where do the Megalithics fit into all this? Their animal-droving expertise clearly comes from their original association with the

---

'northerners' though their tradition of hydraulic engineering can only have come from the 'southern' side. The Megalithics' later record suggests their natural habitat is to be at the cusp, exploiting both sides. Megalithics do not seem to fit naturally into the unvarying steady-state impoverished world of the transhumance nomads, while the settled but frenzied world of civilisation would seem to have little use for their particular talents. Yet making a living *between* the two contrasting cultures is not very easy because nomads and settlers do not have much use for one another. It is ironical given the origin of the southerners but nomads cannot benefit from the southern pastures once the southerners have settled agriculture simply because farmers are never going to grow grain to feed surplus transhumance animals when that same grain can feed vastly more productive human beings and fully domes-ticated farm animals. Nor have the nomads anything to offer the farmers since the only trade goods they have are animals and animal products, and both these can be produced in vast quantities much more economically using conventional farming methods. Once animals can be fed year-round the whole economic basis of transhumance is gone because it is the *movement* of animals that accounts for most of the energy (man and beast) and the vast energy expended in relocation over great distances is only slightly compensated by the fact that the pasturage itself comes free. This is why nomads are always such marginal characters. City states by contrast do have a great deal to offer the nomads in terms of material goods but since the nomads have nothing to trade it is an observable fact, i.e. all *present* nomad societies follow this pattern, that nomads live incredibly simple and self-sufficient lives. They make something of a fetish about it which is perhaps not very surprising since they have little choice in the matter.

The only way nomads can impinge on the civilised world is by taking what they want by force and this is one area in which nomads do have a natural advantage. Nomads are already de facto 'military' units organised on a single basis whereas farming societies are just as automatically diversified and atomistic. To some extent the whole of human history from *c* 3000 BC to *c* 1600 AD[1] can be viewed as the story of tiny numbers of nomads 'impinging' on the settled world and how the settled world came up with political organisations that addressed this often terminal dilemma. The act of civilisation itself might be thought of as one of the ways of coping with the problem since 'the city' is a way of aggregating settled human beings together as a counterpart to the way that moving large herds of animals congregates nomadic human beings. Civilisation is a phenomenally efficient process and, one would have thought, something that is capable of very rapid expansion. Yet the *other* history of the world is the story of how civilisation did *not* expand at all rapidly. Each cradle civilisation seemed to take an unconscionably long time civilising even the most promising parts—from Egypt to Central France (a tiddly leap o'er land and sea) took three thousand years!

But this is nothing compared to the really quite extraordinary time it took for cradle civilizations to make significant contact between one another. It might be supposed that 'like would call to like' in short order but history is eloquent that in practical fact it might take *thousands* of years to establish contact between, say, the Mediterranean and China or India and Mexico. For sure the Megalithics are ideally placed to interfere in such contacts because some control over either sea routes or land routes across the grassland steppe is necessary to make these links functional and there is reason to believe that both these spheres were the province of the Megalithics. Nomads are notoriously incapable of doing anything very much over the long haul, and certainly never in co-operation with one another, so they can be ruled out, leaving the Megalithic usual suspects who act *only* over the long haul, literally and otherwise.

Some attention might be paid therefore to the technical inadequacy of transportation methods over the first three thousand years of civilisation when horse, wheel, sail and wind were scarcely

---

1 Assuming the Manchu takeover of China to be the last splutterings of nomadism.

improved upon. Whatever the explanation for this remarkable lack of headway, the fact is that for the whole of the Megalithics' time, long distance trade, and especially very long distance trade between civilisations, could only be conducted in very high value, very low weight goods and therefore in astonishingly small volumes. Just the kind of thing easily controlled by vested monopolies. And not just the means of conveyance either, it was *where* people travelled that was so extraordinarily conservative. The very simple device of sailing round southern Africa or across the Atlantic (journeys, it is suspected, that were achieved in antiquity) was more or less sufficient not just to end the thousands of years of the Silk Road but the thousands of years of civilisation as it had been up till then. It would seem that nobody thought of doing either of these things earlier or perhaps they did but there were people around who gently discouraged anything coming of the effort. The suspicion is that the Megalithics had a hand in both the aeons of stasis as well as the revolutionary speed with which the entire *Ancien Régime* was swept away by the European voyages of discovery. The modern world is after all based on the nation-state, a type of political organisation that has proved to be both longer-lived than the territorial empire and more frenziedly developmental than the city-state. And the nation-state was the product of the Megalithics, or at any rate it was the Normans that began the process.

This book started with roads so let us finish with roads to show how difficult, or perhaps easy when the proper corrective spectacles are worn, it is to judge continuity and discontinuity. Everybody is slightly amazed on first learning that "the present A5, London to Holyhead road, is the Roman Watling Street" but people quickly get used to this kind of immense longevity in the road network because of the one unavoidable reason behind it: when everything is interconnected by roads it pays every generation of highway engineers to follow the path of their predecessors. Changing one part of a network means changing a cascade of other sections that no longer join but, more than this, life has grown up around the existing network for an indefinite period of time. A road is not just a road, it is a ford, a bridge, a route along a walled enclosure, inns, villages, towns—a whole nexus that will become unglued if you decide to go somewhere your predecessors did not go. So, on the face of things, there is nothing the least strange about saying "the present A5, London to Holyhead road, is the Megalithic Watling Street".

So which is it, Roman or Megalithic? Unless you are introducing a new technology, which the Romans were not, there is no reason to depart from what is already there. In the Romans' case, not just in Britain but over much of Europe, this meant the Megalithic trackways. Now the one thing everybody knows about Romans roads is that they were straight so it comes as something of a blow to learn that if a particular road happens to be straight, it is almost certainly *not* a Roman road. The reasoning is simple: the Romans were a) excellent civil engineers and b) had complete power over where to site their roads, and no civil engineer of even half-decent competence would ever build a straight road. There is no terrain in Europe (save perhaps the Campanian marshes) that lends itself to straight roads. British railway and canal engineers, who could afford to build straight if they really wanted to, almost never did. Neither did turnpike-makers. It just doesn't make any sense. But even if favourable terrain is present you would not do it simply because it is unnerving travelling in straight lines. If you doubt this, have a look the next time you are on a motorway: *it is never straight*. It proceeds in a series of sweeping curves that, put together, make for quite straight progress. This is not to keep drivers awake but to prevent them being driven mad. Marching along dead straight roads is even worse, they never seem to end. But more than that, wherever there is any kind of topography, which means everywhere except the Campanian marshes, going straight is never the quickest route. Soldiers who habitually marched *over* hills rather than round them would not be in a fit state to subdue the natives when they arrived.

Why then, despite what has just been said, are so many 'Roman' roads straight? It is because the Romans never arrive in a country that is *tabula rasa* even though their propagandists like to give that impression. Britain in AD zero already had a road network, the Megalithic tracks, which the Romans just adopted and adapted. Now the Megalithic network *did* have long straight sections, for reasons quite divorced from civil engineering: straightness is the only unambiguous direction when trying to conduct long distance travel in the absence of signposts. So looking at things through newly arrived Roman eyes, it was better to follow the existing infrastructure than to create one *de novo*. No doubt the Romans did forge new routes (though in truth we do not know a single one for sure) but mostly they built over existing ones. And how they built! Their technique was so good it completely obliterated all traces of the former Megalithic track, as surely as the meanest B-road obliterates Roman roads today.

Even so, the Romans had been making straight roads for hundreds of years before they got to Britain—they even had a name for it, the *Etruscan Discipline*—and they used this borrowed straight line technique when laying out their towns and cities. The Etruscans had been using a derivation of the Straight Line System because they were themselves 'Megalithics' or at any rate heirs to the Megalithic tradition. After all, in a Megalithic time-frame, the Etruscans are very *late*, flourishing in say 1,000 BC as opposed to Megalithia's debut around 4,500 BC. We do not know whether the straight-line principle was a British invention that spread to the Mediterranean and then got re-introduced into Britain in a new form by the Romans but it is doubtful that the Romans were responsible for anything particularly novel. Pre-Roman British towns were also laid out in perfectly straight lines, as archaeologists working on Silchester can testify. But let's not be parochial, Megalithia could be a Mediterranean invention. Either way, when the various *literate* civilisations were becoming established in the Mediterranean they would be faced with the same problem that all road builders face everywhere: either build on the existing system with minimum fuss, accepting a few inconveniences, or build it anew and find that nothing fits. By the time the Romans are building the Appian Way they will be following in the footsteps of several thousand years of people trading between Central Italy and Greece by a route which was initially a straight line. You may be sure that Appius Claudius was not so dim as to ignore this.

But this is the bane of all history. Because historians depend almost entirely on written sources they end up assuming that a road-plus-literacy is not just something laid over a road-minus-literacy. Once a road is *recorded* as being The Appian Way then it is gradually assumed to be *built* by Appius Claudius and eventually comes to be assumed as being *invented* by Appius Claudius. But for thousands of years before he ever lived generations of Megalithic Appius Claudii were busy on the route. It's not just roads that require historians and archaeologists to dig down a layer or two beneath their own preconceptions.

In these democratic times readers are permitted, even encouraged, to answer back. As it says in Chapter Six, Jack may not be as good as his master but generally speaking he is the master. Be that as it may, you can join in the debate on our website themegalithicempire.com where you can not only put the arguments in this book to the sword, if you think you're hard enough, but you can actually try them out yourself by going on various walks which have been posted up and where you can actually see Megalithic Principles in action marching across the landscape. When you are thoroughly indoctrinated you can even be allowed out on your own Megalithic Walks and these will be posted up in their turn. Eventually, one day, if reincarnation is true, Jack might be as good as the authors.

Index

abattoirs, 82
Abbots Bromley, 129
Abbotsbury, 75, 76, 106, 201
abortion, 121
absinthe, 141, 142
Achilles, 107, 109
Adam, 139
agriculture, 43, 44, 51, 100, 144, 160
  settled, 11, 12, 228; mixed farming, 13; stock raising, 213
Albi, 72
  Albigensians, 72
albinism, 185
alchemy, 81, 201
alcohol, 140, 142, 201
  – processing, 224
alder, 125, 151
Alfred, King, 87, 88
  Asser's Life of, 88
All Saints (All Hallows), 58, 77, 79, 104, 116, 123, 132
alpha male /female, 188, 189
alphabet, 54, 67, 127, 201
  tree-alphabet, 124
alum, 153
Amanita muscaria, 204 (*see also* fly agaric)
America, 117, 150, 186, 188, 208, 212, 213–17, 218

Meso-American, 34*n*; Native American, 197, 214
Anatolia, 80
Angel, The, 67, 106
angels, 23, 65, 66, 67–8, 74, 91, 94, 108, 141, 200
Anglesey, 8, 77, 137
Anglo-Saxon, 17, 57, 88, 93, 97, 133, 135, 138, 200
  Anglo-Saxons, the, 51, 55
animals, 16, 17, 43, 45, 102, 107, 111*n*, 115, 129, 130, 136, 137, 138, 149, 159, 219, 222, 226, 227, 228, 229
  domestic – , 68, 83*n*, 85*n*, 109, 144, 150, 175, 180, 181, 183–9, 193–8, 200, 202–3, 208, 211, 223, 224, 225, 228; – familiars, 121; feral, 179, 191; fossils, 215, 216; heavenly, 68; hunting bison, 216–7; packtrains, 10, 11, 13, 14, 16, 22, 43, 82, 134, 149, 150, 152, 157, 177; – sacrifice, 132, 150
ankh, 40, 41
antiquarianism, 25, 45*n*
Aphrodite, 89, 96, 115, 200
Apollo, 107, 207
  Python-slayer, 196
apothecaries, 120, 127*n*

Apparition of St Michael, 106, 107
Appian Way, 231
apples, 138, 139–40
– bearing sage, 100
Aquitaine, 70, 74
Arabs, 111*n*
Arabian horses, 106*n*
archaeologists, 1, 15, 20*n*, 25, 35, 42, 89*n*, 122, 131,161, 162*n*, 164, 174, 178, 206
antediluvian, 6
Ariadne, 109
Arians, 56, 97
Armageddon, 94, 107
Armorica, 196 (*see also* Brittany)
Artemis, 70, 78, 107, 109*n*, 141
Artemisia, 73*n*, 96, 121, 141
Arthur, 91, 139
Arthurian, 26, 52, 84, 98, 110
Artington, 73, 74
astronomy, 166
Aswan, 131*n*
Atlantic, 32, 34, 35, 41, 42, 47, 56, 82, 84, 147, 230
auroch, 183, 185
Avalon, 139
Avebury, 27–30, 35, 40*n*, 45, 70, 73, 77, 93, 110, 115, 161, 162, 163–4, 166, 167, 170
on Michael Line, 23, 27, 28–30; Central Clearing House, 28; Stukeley's diagram, 114

BBC, 79*n*, 164, 165
Bacon, Roger, 119
Baltic, 45, 147
bards, 67, 91
Bardsey, 137
Barford St John, 71
Barford St Michael, 71
Barwick-in-Elmet, 79
– Green, The *Archers*, 79*n*
Bath (Aquae Sulis), 110

Baume, 96
beacon hills, 15, 16, 35, 37, 69, 70, 72, 83, 101, 118
Beacon Hill, Rudstone Beacon, 104
beaver, 186–7
beer, 36, 74, 85, 113, 140
'beerage', 63, 138
Beowulf, 88*n*, 92*n*
Beltane, 116, 136
Bernard de Clairvaux, 96*n*, 142*n*
Bible, 66, 68, 96, 116, 130*n*,
birch, 124
Birmingham, 1, 2, 3, 10, 11, 20, 28, 29
bishops, 53, 55, 56, 57, 58, 59, 61, 81, 96*n*, 119
Bishopsgate, 80
bison, 212, 215–7, 218
Black Madonnas, 94, 95–6, 122
blacksmiths, 69, 110, 116, 123, 137, 141
Bodmin Moor, 25, 86, 134
bog sprites, bogies, 128, 130
bonfires, 101, 117
Book of the Dead, Egyptian, 86
Book of Revelation, the, 68
Bosphorus, 79, 87*n*
boundary beating, 112
Bowes, 82, 93, 135
Bowes-Lyon, 82*n*
Boxing Day, 126
Brackley, 93
Brân, 207
Brentor, 23, 65, 66, 67
Bretwalda, 46
Bridport, 83*n*
Brittany, 36, 83, 196
bronze, 3, 147
Bronze Age, 14, 30, 43, 45, 89, 90, 111, 147, 148; – foundry, 1, 2, 3, 30; as monopoly metal, 148; talking head, 207
Brough, 80

Brutus, 78
Buckingham, 93
Buffalo Bill, 217
bull, 82, 113, 130, 183, 197
   – cults, 83; – horns, 70;
   – running, 82; sacrifice, 138
bureaucracy, 46, 50, 53, 55, 57,
   154
Burgundy, 96, 97*n*
Burns Night, 91
Burrowbridge Mump, 23, 67
Bury St Edmund, 27, 133, 135
buskins, 108, 127
Butter Cross, 113, 130
   – stone, 126, 135, 136

Cádiz, 42, 77, 82
Cadmus, 112
caduceus, *vii*, 89, 104, 106, 107,
   111, 130
Caedmon, 112
Caerdroia, 134
Caesar, Julius, 47
cairns, 16
calendar, 42, 100, 124
Cambridge, 72
   Jesus College, 92
Canterbury, 72, 73, 92
   – St. Martin's, 78*n*
capstone, 6, 7, 9, 10, 92
Cardea, 103
Carmenta, 127
carmine, 126–7
Carn Menyn, 135
Carnac, 36, 37
Carthage, 32, 42, 45, 48, 88*n*, 145
castles, 17, 71*n*, 85, 91, 93, 118*n*,
   128, 138, 139, 206
Castor, 65, 93*n*, 108, 117,
Castor, Northants, 93
castration, 108, 111, 117, 135
Cathars, 71, 72
cathedral, 71, 86, 94, 110, 201
   Gothic, 60–2, 98, 99; – of the

Dales, 93
Catherine hills, 72, 73, 74–5
   – chapel, 72, 75, 76, 77, 201;
   – wheel, 72, 92
Catholic Church, 54, 55, 94, 99,
   121
cats, 192, 193, 196
cattle, 82, 124, 136, 150, 212, 225
   – marts, 137
cauldron, 124, 125, 128, 134, 138
Cecil, Robert, 120
celibacy, 156, 157
Celtic Christianity, 52, 56, 94
   – cross, 40, 41; – monks, 67; –
   Renaissance, 81*n*, 97, 209;
   – saints, 83, 209; traders, 147
cereal, 13, 144, 190, 223, 224
Cernunnos, 81, 82, 128
Chaldeans, 68, 80, 81
Chaldon, 75
chalk, 16, 26, 72, 92, 102, 152,
   153, 162, 163, 164
   – downland, 105, 160; – figures,
   17
chalybeate springs, 80, 85, 89
Channel Islands, 77, 82
Charles (Stuart), 105
Charlton-on-Otmoor, 105
Chartres Cathedral, 38
charts, 34, 42
Cheesewring, 25, 134
Cheremis, 201
Chesil Beach, 75, 76, 83*n*, 106,
   201
Chester, 49
chicken, 150, 180, 190
chimney sweeps, 118
Chiron, 109
choughs, 202, 205, 206
Christianity, 26, 56, 65, 75, 78, 79,
   83, 94, 120, 124, 125, 132
   in Roman Britain, 52
Christmas, 100, 109*n*, 126
   – Eve, 126; – stocking, 108;

Twelve Days of, *90n*
church spires, 15
cider, 138, 139
Cinderella, 132
circus, 150
Cissbury Rings, 95
Cistercians, 59, 142*n*, 146, 155,
    156–7
civilisation, 49, 50, 52, 55, 144,
    180, 188, 226, 228, 229, 230
    cradle –, 226, 227, 229; Rise of,
    222
Clairvaux (*see* Bernard of
    Clairvaux)
Classical Greece, 42
Clement IV, 119 (*see also* Guy
    Foulques)
clews, 109
clothes, 12, 120
Clovis points, 214, 216
Clynnog Fawr, 137, 138
Cobbett, William, 161, 206
'Cock Robin', 126
cockle shell, 89, 115
Cole (Good King), 78–9
compass, 4, 6, 7, 8, 10
    leather, 8, 10, 18, 24; magnetic,
    42
Compostela, Santiago de, 77, 78,
    92, 96*n*, 115, 122
coney, 93*n*, 198, 199
conspiracy theories, 47*n*, 60, 61
Constantine, 52, 78–9, 83
copper, 1, 3, 44, 69*n*, 148
copse, 16, 18, 206
    copse-plus-rooks, 207
coracle, 82, 89
Cornwall, 1, 2, 8, 9, 14, 21, 24, 25,
    28, 32, 34, 44, 45, 83, 84, 89,
    106, 109, 169, 170, 206, 207
corvée, 202
corvids, 123, 202, 203, 205–7
    – intelligence, 203–4
cow (*see* cattle)

Cranbourne Chase, 93
cranes, 67, 201
Cro-Magnon, 219
cronewort, 121
Cronos, 77
crossroads, 17, 72, 77, 78*n*, 84*n*,
    85, 95, 110, 132, 152, 205
cross-staff, 40, 72, 92, 104, 165
crow, 76, 77, 123, 191, 202,
    203–4, 205, 207
    as the crow flies, 202; carrion
    – , 204; crow's nest, 202
Crusade, First, 122
    Second –, 96*n*; Third –, 33, 96*n*
Culdees, 81*n*, 89
Culpepper, 142
Cuneburga, 93
Cunetio, 198
cup-and-ring markings, 17, 18–19,
    93
cursus, 17, 20, 93, 104, 105, 132
cyan, 23

Dandelion, John, 95*n*
Dark Ages, 55, 64,
Dartmoor, 66, 86, 93*n*, 136, 161,
    176, 208
De Clare family, 85, 90*n*
    Richard – (*see* 'Strongbow')
De Vere family, 85
dead reckoning, 34, 39, 40
deer (*see* reindeer), 70*n*, 190
    preserves, 198, 217; roe deer, 196
delayed implantation, 196
demotic languages, 54, 59
    langue d'oïl, 59
desert, 70, 85*n*, 198*n*, 227
Devil, 70, 83, 105, 128, 130, 131
    – Dykes, 17; as dyke-builder, 75,
    130; Jumps, 161; Nutting Day,
    132; Punchbowl, 131, 161
Devon, 24, 25, 65, 75, 130, 170
Diana, 80
Dionysus, 76, 98, 109, 119, 139

Dissolution (of the monasteries),
    155
dodo, 184
dog, 90, 128, 180, 183, 196, 200*n*,
    202, 203, 206, 207, 216
dolmen, 37–9, 40, 92, 133, 134
Domesday, 153
domestication, 83, 84, 151,
    179–84, 187–9, 190–2, 194,
    195, 196–8, 201, 203, 206, 219,
    220, 223, 225
Don Giovanni, 109*n*
Dorchester, 70
Dore Abbey, 119
Dorset, 75, 93, 106, 134, 174
Dover, 71, 72, 73, 92, 94
Draconis, 34*n*, 69, 168
dragon, 15, 23, 34*n*, 53, 65, 68,
    69, 70, 71, 74, 80*n*, 83, 84, 106,
    116*n*, 130, 133, 135, 137, 173
    – associations, 53, 65, 69, 130,
    133; in China, 84; Draguignan,
    96; fear of iron, 116*n*; hills, 69,
    74, 135; *La Gargouille*, 74; *La
    Tarasque*, 96, 137; insatiable
    desire, 137; links to Pole Star,
    34*n*, 68–9, 168; – saints, 23, 70,
    74, 84; – slaying, 66, 68, 70,
    79*n*, 83, 89, 92, 96, 112, 133,
    173
drovers, 40*n*, 43, 50, 135, 149,
    150, 152, 165, 177
    access to villages, 149, 150;
    competition, 136, 150; payment
    of tolls, 137, 149–50, 152;
    – roads, 13, 14, 43, 44, 50, 71*n*,
    82, 124, 132, 177, 202
drugs, 73*n*, 122, 140*n*, 204
    in dung, 204; mind-altering,
    142; – trade, 120, 142
Druids, 25, 30, 44, 45, 46, 47, 48,
    50, 54, 77, 122, 126, 142, 157
duck, 180, 199, 209, 210 (*see also*
    eider)

dyeing, 127*n*, 138*n*, 145
    dyers' guild, 201; red dye, 126,
    127
dykes, 17, 75, 130, 167

Easter, 56, 90, 91, 100
eclipses, 42
Eden Centre, 21*n*
Edinburgh, 91
Edith Swan-neck, 58
Edmund, 135
Egypt, 40, 83, 101, 148, 227, 229
    Ancient – , 68, 86, 102*n*, 122,
    132; – Point, 72
eider (Cuddy) duck, 209, 210
    – down, 209, 210
Elbe, 147
Eleanor of Aquitaine, 74
Ellen of the Ways, 77 (*see also* Helen)
Eleusinian Mysteries, 132, 142*n*
Elizabeth I, 139
Elmet, 79
Ember Days, 132
Eostre, 90
ephedra, 142
Equator, 22
Equites (*see* Romans)
Eratosthenes, 81, 101, 131*n*
Ermin(e) Street, 45, 77, 80, 81, 82,
    84*n*, 85, 90, 93, 95, 106, 120,
    142
ermine, 195–6
erosion, 16, 25, 35, 75, 159, 161,
    166*n*, 168, 171, 172, 173, 175,
    176, 177
erratics (*see* pudding stones)
ethology, 179, 218
Etruscans, 148, 154*n*, 231
    Etruscan Discipline, 231
Euphrates, 227
Everyman, 75, 117, 118*n*
Exmoor, 161, 176, 208
extinction, 182, 184, 189, 214,
    215, 216, 217, 218

eyot, 153

Faerie Queene, the, 92
fairies, fairy tales, 101, 124, 131, 205
    – miners 133; – rings 124
falcon, 84*n*, 89, 181, 182, 183, 208
    falconers, 181, 192; gyr – 182; peregrine – 89, 137*n*, 182
Farne Islands, 209, 210
Feast of Guardian Angels, 74
fens, 128, 130
Fermain Bay, 82
ferrets, 194–5, 202*n*
Ferrières, 95, 96
ferry, 36, 91, 117, 153, 154*n*
    Ferry Lane, 74
Findon, 95
Finistère, Finisterre, 22*n*, 76
fire, 15, 88*n*, 101, 117, 118, 130, 137*n*, 141, 204
    beacons, 16; corvids' use of, 204; – festivals, 117, 118; Great Fire of London, 127*n*, 168*n*; 'Greek Fire', 142
Firth of Forth, 91
fish, 85, 94, 132, 154, 155, 197, 226
    on Fridays, 154; as trade goods, 85; – traps, 154; – weirs, 198; in wells, 132
Fisher King, 103
fleur de lys, 102
flint, 4, 207
    – axes, 148; – mines, 95, 148, 169
fly agaric, 124, 127, 204
folk tradition, 100, 120, 143
Folkestone, 92, 94
football, 113, 130
fords, 16, 17, 18, 22, 85, 152, 155, 200
forest, 128, 129, 160

– clearance, 160; forestation, 159
Fornham All Saints, 132
Fosse Way, 95, 137
fossils, 183, 188, 197, 215–16, 217
France, 22*n*, 29, 30, 55, 59, 71, 76, 78, 79, 80, 81, 82, 84, 86, 92, 95, 96, 97, 102*n*, 134, 139, 229
Franks, 55
Frensham, 125
Freya, 41*n*
fulling mill, 153

gabelle, 146
Garland Day, 106
Gaul, 42, 46, 47, 48, 52, 54, 56, 57, 58, 81, 158
Gaunt, John of, 110
geese, 150, 191, 199, 200, 201
    goose girls, 201; goose quills, 67
geezers, guisers, 117
genetics, 187, 188, 193, 213
Geneva, 86*n*, 97*n*
Genoa, 97*n*
Geoffrey of Monmouth, 78
geologists, 15, 25
Ggantija, 94
giants, 25, 69, 75, 83, 93, 130
Gildas, 52
gin, 86*n*, 121, 122
Giza, 95*n*
Glastonbury, 23, 27
    – Abbey, 27, 139; – Tor, 26, 27, 67, 75, 139
Gnostic, 68, 78*n*
goat, 128, 180, 225
    Goat Inn, 130
Godolphin family, 106*n*
Gog Magog, 106*n*, 142
Goring Gap, 70, 200
Goseck, Thuringia, 92, 114*n*
Gothic cathedrals, 60–2, 98, 99
Gower peninsula, 127, 208

Gozo, 94, 95
Grail, 59, 81, 103, 138
grass, 144, 185, 198*n*, 219, 220–5,
    226, 227
    domestication, 220, 223–5;
    grassland, 185, 188, 211, 212,
    213, 214*n*, 215, 216, 219, 222,
    223, 225, 227, 229
Greece, *vii*, 42, 59, 100
green lanes, 178
Green Man, 62, 98, 99, 118, 119,
    129
Greenwich, 81, 131*n*
Gresham College, 80*n*
Greville, Faulk, 139
grey wethers, 111
Grime's Graves, 4, 207
Grotters, 113, 115
Grubstones, 112
Guernsey, 82, 83
Guildford, 73, 74, 75, 133
guilds, 63, 201
Guinevere, 138, 139
Gulf of Lion, 96
Guy Fawkes, 117, 119, 120
    'fall guy', 120, 130
Guy Foulques (Clement IV), 119,
    122
Gypsey Race, 105
gypsies (*see* tinkers)

habitat, 124, 182, 185, 186, 187,
    190, 193, 214, 228
Halal, 150*n*
Hallaton, 113
Hallowe'en, 79, 105, 116, 117,
    118, 120, 132
hallucinogens, 73*n*, 122
Hansel and Gretel, 121
hare, 90, 91, 113, 195, 197, 199
    Hare Pie Scramble, 113;
    three-hare motif, 86
Harold, 58
Hastings, 58

hawthorn, 101–2, 103
Haxey Hood, 130
hazel, 89*n*, 124
    – nuts, 131, 132
heath, 124, 128
    heathen, 120*n*, 124
Hecate, 72, 78
hedges, 16, 102, 112
    cavorting under, 111
heelstone, 5, 6, 7, 8, 9, 10, 11, 24,
    106
Helen, 78, 79, 201
    Sarn Helen, 77; of Troy, 78,
    79
Helston Furry Dance, 106
hemp, 83
Henry VIII, 87, 157
Henry of Huntingdon, 45*n*
Hephaestus, 69, 86, 141
heraldry, 102, 196*n*
    Courts of Heraldry, 33*n*; Lords
    Lyon, 82*n*
hermai, 103, 104
Hermes, *vii*, 10, 23, 31, 45, 67, 72,
    76, 79*n*, 80, 82, 91, 101, 102*n*,
    104, 106, 108, 109*n*, 110, 111,
    116, 117, 124, 125, 126, 127,
    128, 129, 132, 135, 137, 141,
    196, 200, 201, 206, 207*n*,
    aka Emeran 196*n*, St
    Emeric 117*n*, Fermin 82, St
    Hermentaire, St Hermes 23,
    Mercury 23, 67, 127*n*, Michael
    67, Thoth 67, 110*n*; escorting
    souls 109, 117, 128, 201;
    inventor of fire-sticks, 118; –
    pillars, 77, 103, 104; purse,
    125; stealing cattle, 124;
    – Trismegistus, 72; wisdom, 141
hermits, 10, 18, 30, 45, 47, 50,
    58, 69
    hermitages, 18, 26, 66, 72,
    91, 132, 152; reputation
    for wisdom, 18; 'servants of

Hermes', 10, 18, 45; as speaking
signposts, 18, 46, 119
Herne Bay, 82, 113
– the Hunter, 82, 128, 129; –'s
Oak, 128
Hesperides, 140
High King, 46, 47, 49, 52, 54, 103
Hilda of Whitby, 112
hillforts, 17, 18, 35, 82, 131, 173,
174–6, 177
Hindhead, 131, 161
Hippocrates, 121
Hittites, 80, 148
hobby horse, 84, 109, 110, 130,
208
– falcon, 84*n*, 208
Hocktide, 110
Holderness, 81
Holy Grail (*see* Grail)
Holy Roman Empire, 57
Holy Well, 90
Hooke, Robert, 168*n*
Hooker, Richard, 87
horse, 106*n*, 115, 135, 180,
200, 201, 208, 229; hobby
– , 109–10, 208; in America,
212–6; – nomads, 208, 212,
213–4; white – 116, 135,
165
Hospitallers, 91
Hoxne, 135
Hull, 45
Humber, 28, 80
Hungerford, 110
hunting, 77, 84*n*, 89, 90, 126, 181,
192, 194, 210, 216, 217
bison –, 212, 217
Huntingdon, 85
hydraulics, 60, 118*n*, 152, 171,
199, 227, 228

ibis, 67
Ice Age, 175, 214
Icknield Way, 29, 45, 77, 84*n*, 85,

87, 106*n*, 130, 133, 134, 198
Ilkley, 122, 123
Indus River, 227
Iona, 91
Ireland, 25*n*, 40, 46, 49, 50, 52, 53,
54, 58, 59, 81*n*, 83, 89, 90*n*, 92,
107, 128, 136*n*, 173, 208, 209
Druids in –, 48, 49, 54; first
alphabetic demotic, 54
Irminsûl, 104
Iron Age, 13, 14, 35, 43, 45, 131,
147, 158, 173, 174, 175, 206,
208
ironherb, 122
Isis, 87*n*, 102*n*
Isle of Man, 86, 88, 89
Isle of May, 91
Isle of Wight, 72, 92
Ivinghoe Beacon, 70

Jack, 110, 117, 118, 128, 231
and the Beanstalk, 75; as
Everyman, 75, 117; – in-the-
Green, 118, 119; – o' Kent, o'
Lantern, o' Lent, o' Straw, 118
jackdaws, 202, 205
James I, 77, 120, 197
Jerusalem, 62, 107
Jesus, 65, 76*n*, 78, 97, 128, 142*n*
joint-stock companies, 154
Joseph of Arimathea, 139
Judaism, 97, 132
juniper, 86*n*, 97*n*, 121, 122

Kelmarsh, Northants, 98
Kennet, Kennett, 162, 163, 198
Kent, 29, 78, 113, 114*n*, 118, 134
keremet (sacred grove), 201
kermes beetle, 126
– dye, 127
King of Birds, 126
Kit's Coty, 134
Knights Hospitaller (*see*
Hospitallers)

Knights Templar (*see* Templars)
Knuckers, knockers, 133
Koryaks, 204
Kosher, 150*n*
kraals, 175, 176

labyrinth, 73, 109
Land's End, 22, 76
Langdale, 4
Languedoc, 97, 119
Latin, 20*n*, 54, 59, 80, 124, 127,
    137*n*, 226*n*
latitude, 39, 40, 41, 72, 151, 166
Le Puy-en-Velay, 119, 122
leather, 82, 127, 130, 132
    buskins, 108, 127; – compass,
    7, 8, 10, 18, 24; – sails, 82, 153;
    smelliness, 82
lee shore, 33, 34
Leggin'-down Day, 110
Leith, 91, 95
leucism, 185
leyline, 8–9, 10, 11, 13, 14, 15, 17,
    18–20, 22, 24, 40, 45, 47, 93,
    168, 170, 202
    trans-European – , 107
Lihou Island, 77
Llandudno, 3, 69*n*
logan stones, 15, 25
Lollards, 93, 110
London, 9, 73, 76, 78, 80, 81, 87,
    90, 110, 118, 128, 131, 161,
    206, 207
    as Trinovantum, 80
longitude, 81
Loveny river, 86
Luftwaffe, 75
Lugh (Lud), 76, 77, 137, 207
Lundy Island, 77*n*
Lyminster, 133
lynx, 193
Lyonesse, 76
Lyons, 76
lyre, 72

Ma'at, 67, 110*n*
Mab, 102
Mabinogion, 87, 102
Macbeth, 124
Magdalen Hill, 73
    – College, 93*n*
Magic Flute, The, 109*n*
magic mushroom (*see* fly agaric)
magpies, 123, 202, 205
Maia, 91, 101, 102
Maiden Castle, 174
Malta, 94
Maplebeck, 92
maps, 47
 pre-literacy, 1, 2, 4, 7, 94, 111
Marazion, 23, 24, 109
Margaret of Scotland, 91, 131
    Margaritifera margaritifera, 91
Margate, 72, 73, 78, 114
    'sea-gate', 78, 82, 95
maritime, 22*n*, 31, 34*n*, 35
    ship, capital-intensive, 39;
    – trade, 32, 47, 48, 54; – travel,
    32
Marlborough, 73
Marseilles, 42
Martha, 74, 75, 96, 97
    St Martha's Hill, 73, 74, 75; in
    Provence, 96
masons, 61, 62, 109*n*
    – lodge, 73*n*, 112
May Day, 84, 100, 101, 104, 106,
    111, 206, 208
maypoles, 79*n*, 104, 105, 107, 109
    dancing round, 104 ; tallest in
    country, 79
mazes, 17, 19, 74*n*, 107, 109
    – Hill, 58; Mizmaze, 72, 73
Mazey Day, 109
mead, 140*n*
Mechlin, 94
Mediterranean, 21, 22, 32, 33, 34,
    41, 42, 44, 48, 83, 94, 96, 154,
    200, 229

Megalithic, *vii*, 8, 9, 10, 18, 21,
  22, 27, 32, 34, 36, 37, 39, 40,
  44, 47, 49, 50, 52, 53, 54, 55,
  56, 58–9, 64, 68, 69, 73, 77, 78,
  79, 89, 92, 105, 107, 109, 110,
  112, 115, 122, 125, 138, 154,
  156, 157, 161, 163, 169, 170,
  189, 191, 195, 198, 200, 201,
  205, 206, 208, 209, 210, 217,
  219, 229
  – anti-canon, 65, 66, 68, 106,
  126; – art, 61; – colours, 102,
  126; esoterica, 75, 76*n*, 79, 80,
  81, 85*n*, 86, 91, 94, 98; 109,
  111*n*, 116, 117, 118, 119, 139;
  landscape features, 14–20, 22,
  25, 27, 35, 38, 40, 66, 75, 80,
  83, 89, 206; – families, 82*n*,
  85, 90, 103, 180*n*; forgery, 99;
  – franchise, 83; infrastructure,
  12–13, 60, 131, 133, 134, 152,
  153–4, 198; – missionaries,
  50, 56, 57; payment, 115,
  116, 117, 125*n*, 125, 134,
  152; – politics, 97, 155;
  professionals, 10, 39, 41, 43,
  62, 110, 129, 132; – science, 81,
  87, 101, 120, 162, 166–7, 168*n*;
  slogan, 56, 191; – trade, 83, 95,
  96, 97, 136, 142, 144–6, 147,
  148, 150–1, 153, 169, 209–10;
  – travel, 5, 7–11, 18, 20, 21, 24,
  28–9, 30, 34, 36, 42, 43, 90, 92,
  95, 118; – women, 71, 89, 120,
  123, 131
Menai Straits, 17
menhir, 35, 36, 71, 75, 76, 88*n*,
  103, 137
Mercury, 67, 79*n*, 127
  – as Hermes, 23, 127*n*; metal,
  in alchemy, 81, 86, 200; planet,
  41*n*; cure for syphilis, 127*n*
meridian, 58, 80, 81, 82, 95, 104
mermaids, 132

Merrivale, 37, 136
Mesta, 150
metallurgy, 44, 65, 69, 115, 122,
  131
metanoia, 132
Michael Line, 23–7, 28, 29, 45*n*,
  66, 67, 70, 95, 101, 133, 134,
  135, 139, 142, 169, 171, 172,
  173, 200, 207
Michaelmas, 58, 74, 121, 132, 200
Michell, John, 93, 167
midden, 127, 226
Middle Ages, 60, 64, 71, 78, 115
Midsummer, 100, 104, 131
midwives, 71, 120, 121, 123, 127
migration, 150, 199, 225
Mildenhall, 198
milk, 70, 136, 137, 185, 203
  Milk Hill, 164, 165–6; – pails,
  106
millstones, 83, 84
Minehead, 77*n*, 109
mining, 69, 70*n*, 131, 133, 198
  salt – , 131; tin – , 86, 106*n*, 208
Minoans, 83, 148
mistletoe, 121, 126
Mithras, 79, 97
moats, 17, 199
monasteries, 55, 57, 60, 66, 78,
  99, 155, 156, 201, 209
Mongols, 212, 213, 214
Mont Saint-Michel, 65, 107
Monte Gargano, 107
Monument, The, 131*n*, 168*n*
moon goddesses, 70, 72*n*, 77, 89,
  91, 102, 115, 121
  Aphrodite, 200; Artemis, 70,
  73*n*, 78, 141; Catherine, 71;
  Diana, 80; Ellen, 80*n*; Hecate,
  78; Helen, 78. 201; Margaret,
  71; Melangell, 90; Selene, 78,
  201; Sin, moon god, 23*n*
moorland, 129, 134*n*, 136*n*, 161,
  208

Mordiford, 137
Morris dancing, 74, 107, 118
Mother Ludlam, 124, 125, 127
motte-and-bailey, 17, 174
Mount Carmel, 107
Mount Sinai, 23
Mozart, 109*n*
mugwort, 96, 121
Muslims, 97, 111
mustelidae, 195, 197

Nantcribba's Castle, 138
Native Americans, 197, 214, 215
Navarre, 82, 116
navigational systems, 4, 13, 40,
    101, 164, 166, 170
Neanderthal, 205, 219
Neolithic, 12, 13, 14, 30, 51, 148*n*
Neoplatonism, 99
New Forest, 161, 208
Newfoundland, 127
Nile, 227
nitre, 86*n*
nomads, 208, 214, 222, 226, 228,
    229
Norfolk , 4, 21, 70, 148, 169, 170,
    207
    – Broads 170, 171–2
Normans, 51, 58, 71, 72, 74, 76,
    85, 90*n*, 92, 197, 230
    – castles, 17, 85, 174;
    – Conquest, 58, 64
Normandy, 58, 74, 83, 95, 107,
    138, 139
Northgate, Canterbury, 92
Northgate, Oxford, 77
nuts, 132, 151, 203
    hazel –, 131, 132

oak, 126, 128, 135, 151
    – apples, 138*n*
obelisk, 35, 36, 37, 40, 72
Odin, 58, 70, 124
Odyssey, 3*n*

Offa's Dyke, 138
Ogbourne St George, 70
Ogham, 124
Ogygia, 206
Olwen, 102
Olympic Games, 141
orchards, 151
Order of the Garter, 110
Orkneys, 36, 40*n*, 169
orm (worm), 173
    Great Orme, 69*n*; ormests, 69
Ormesby St Margaret, 70, 173
Ormesby St Michael, 70, 173
ornithologists, 109, 180, 181, 190,
    199, 204
Ortygia, 109*n*
otters, 197
Ottery St. Mary, 130
Overton Hill, 162, 163, 165
owls, 190–3
    barn –, 189, 190–1, 192–3, 194;
    eagle –, 189, 190, 193; snowy
    – , 191, 194; *Strigidae*, 193;
    witches' familiars, 124
oxen, 36, 208
Oxford, 72, 85, 86, 87, 88
    and Bosphorus, 87*n*; centre of
    Britain, 78*n*, 85, 87; earls of – , 85
    (*see also* De Vere); East Gate, 93*n*;
    Northgate, 77, 93*n*; seventeenth
    Earl (Shakespeare?), 85*n*
Oxford English Dictionary, 111
oysters, 113, 115

packtrain, 10, 14
Padstow, 84, 109
pagans, 50, 65, 94, 98, 99, 104,
    120, 121, 132
Paganus de Beauchamp, 85
palaeontology, 198
Palestine, 59 (*see also* Phoenicians)
Pamplona, 82
Pan, 128
pantomime, 84

Paris, France, 72, 76, 79, 81, 96*n*,
    102*n*, 128
Paris of Troy, 79
Parisii, 79, 80, 81
parrots, 70, 205, 207
partridge, 109
Paulinus, 48
peacock, 86, 191, 207
Peddars Way, 130
pedlar, 1, 14
pentagram, 140
Pentridge, 93
Pen Troydin, 90
Penzance, 109
perambulation (*see* boundary
    beating)
peregrine falcon, 89, 182
    peregrinus, pilgrim, 137*n*
Petuaria (*see* Brough)
Phoenicians, 22, 23, 24, 42, 59,
    77, 83, 148
    as 'Saracens', 111; trading
    model, 48, 53
picks, 70*n*, 153, 162
pictogram, 17
pig, 151, 225
pigeon, 179, 182, 186
    – *Fanciers Gazette*, 179;
    passenger – , 218
pilgrimage, 72, 78, 122, 196*n*
Pilgrims' Way, 29, 72, 73, 74, 75,
    78*n*, 90, 95, 114, 118, 124, 133,
    134
pillow mound, 93*n*, 198
pirates, 70, 89
pixies, 128, 129
    Pixie Day, 130
plains, 164, 188, 214*n*, 215
Plains Indians, 212, 217
Pliny, 142
Plutarch, 196
Poitiers, 77, 92
Polaris (Pole star), 34n, 68, 69,
    168

Polden Hills, 170
Pollux, 65, 93*n*, 108, 117
ponies, 20, 36, 131*n*, 208, 213
Porton Down, 122
Portsmouth, 30, 131
Portugal, 97*n*
Postling, 92
pre-literate, 3, 34*n*, 94, 111, 113,
    142
    – calendar, 124; – organisation,
    9, 52, 54, 136, 148; – sailing, 39
Preseli Hills, 77*n*, 90, 127, 135
Prometheus, 137*n*
Protestantism, 56
Protomagia, 100
Provence, 95, 96, 98
Prussia, 57, 97*n*
Pseudo-Dionysius, 99
pubs, 16, 62, 67, 70, 132, 152
Puck, 128, 129
pudding stones, 133
Puritans, 105, 109
Puss in Boots, 127

Queensferry, 91
Quiberon Bay, 32, 34
quipos, 34*n*

rabbits, 90*n*, 91, 93*n*, 197–9
    hydrophobic, 199; introduction
    of, 194, 197, 198*n*; in Spain,
    195; underground knowledge,
    199
Ramsgate, 73, 78, 82
raptor, 181, 182, 183, 203
ravens, 86, 202, 203, 204, 207
    – messengers of Odin/Woden,
    70, 124, 207; – at Tower of
    London, 206, 207
Red Caps, 128
Red Cross, The, 126
Red Lady of Paviland, 127
'red mercury', 127
Reformation, The, 35, 76, 155

reindeer, 130, 204, 224, 225
  – antlers, 130; caribou, 130*n*;
  – dung, 204; – herding, 125,
  219, 220, 221–2, 226
relics, 78, 85, 99
religious rituals, 42
rhombus, 93
ridgeways, 177
Ridgeway, The, 29, 70, 134, 135,
  163, 165, 198
Ring of Brodgar, 5*n*
roads, 2, 11, 12, 13, 14, 42, 47,
  50, 52, 67, 80, 104, 118, 137,
  155, 157, 230–3
  organic network, 11–12
robin, 126
Robin Goodfellow, 128, 129
Robin Hood, 119, 128, 129
Robin Hood's Way, 92
Rochester, 73, 118, 134
rocking stone (*see* logan stones)
Rogationtide, 58, 111
Rohesia's Cross, 85
Romaldkirk, 93, 135
Romans, 42, 48, 49, 50, 52, 53,
  54, 64, 67, 103, 122, 141, 145,
  148, 158, 198, 209
  – in Britain, 44, 46, 47, 48, 49,
  50–4, 122, 198; – calendar, 124;
  – camps, 17, 174; vs. Druids,
  47, 48; – Empire, 49, 52, 53, 57,
  71, 94; Equites, 154; – roads,
  47, 50, 90, 231–2; villa system,
  50, 51
Romanies, 208
Rombald's Moor, 93, 112
Rome, 42, 53, 54, 56, 154
rood cross, screen, 104
rooks, 123, 202, 206, 207
  Rook Sunday, 206
Rosicrucian, 77, 85, 86*n*, 126
Rosy Cross, 45*n*, 139*n*
Rothschilds, 180*n*
Rouen, 74, 76

royal families, 65, 154, 155, 207*n*
  Irish, 89, 90; Northumbrian, 93;
  Welsh, 89
Royal Society, the, 80*n*
Royston, 45, 77, 95
Rudstone, 104, 105
Rufford Abbey, 92
Rushen Coatie, 132

sage, 100, 138*n*, 142
saints, 80, 83, 94, 99, 138*n*, 153,
  155
  bull – , 83; dragon-slaying, 173;
  Irish, 83; Megalithic, 77, 89, 90,
  92, 94, 209; patron – , 58, 85,
  86, 88*n*, 89, 90, 91, 94, 106,
  108, 115
  St Andrew, 91; St Anthony,
  84, 85*n*, 91; St Augustine, 48,
  52; St Beuno, 138; St Brigid,
  123; St Catherine, 23, 71, 72,
  74, 77, 201; St Cecilia, 72*n*; St
  Claus, 125, 130*n*; St Columba,
  96; St Crispianus, 108; St
  Crispin, 108; St Cuthbert, 209,
  210; St Cynog, 69; St David,
  89, 90, 91; St Denis, 87, 96*n*,
  98, as Dionysus, 76, 98, 99,
  139; St Eloy (Loy, Eligius), 86;
  St Emeran, 196*n*; St Emeric,
  117*n*; St Ermenhilda, 200; St
  Fermín, 82; St Gatien, 78; St
  Germain, 81; St George, 70,
  89, 125, 135*n*; St Goar, 70; St
  Helen, 78, 80; St Hermentaire,
  96; St Hermes, 23; St Hilda,
  112; St James, 65, 77, 93*n*,
  115, 116, 117; St John, 93*n*,
  117; St John the Baptist, 65,
  93*n*, 94, 95, 100, 109, 121,
  128, 131 ; St Lucy, 88*n*; St
  Luke, 76*n*; St Margaret, 70,
  71, 131, 173; St Martha, 65,
  73, 96, 97, 137; St Martin, 78;

St Mary (Magdalen), 65, 73, 92, 94, 95, 96*n*, 133; St Mary (Virgin), 65; St Maughold, 89; St Mawrel, 113 (*see also* Melangell); St Melangell, 90, 91, 113; St Michael, 23, 26, 58, 65, 66, 67, 68, 70, 71, 89, 94, 106, 107, 125, 173; St Michael & All Angels, 113, 118; St Millán, 116; St 'Monday', 108*n*; St Neot, 85, 87, 88; St Nicholas, 125, 130*n*; St Non, 89; St Patrick, 83, 89, 209*n*; St Paul, 65, 110; St Peter, 76*n* ; St Petroc (Perran, Piran), 83, 84; St Radegunde, 77, 92, 94; St Romanus, 74; St Rombald, 92, 94; St Sampson, 83, 84; St Stephen/Steven, 126; St Werburgh, 200; St Winifred, 131, 138
Saint-Denis, 78
– en-Lyons, 76
Saints' Way, 84
Salisbury Plain, 93, 127, 133*n*, 164
Salmon of Wisdom, 132
salt 48, 144–7, 149, 153
in alchemy, 86; – mining, 131; – pan, 148
Salt Way, 137
Salvia (*see* sage)
Samhain, 79, 94, 105, 109*n*, 116, 125
Sami, 219, 222, 226
Sandgate, 78
Sangatte, 78
Santa Claus, 125, 130*n*
Santiago (*see* Compostela)
Saracen, 111
sarsens, 111, 167
Saturnalia, 138
Savoy 97*n*, 110
Saxon Shore Way, 82
Saxony, 147

scallop shells, 115
Scandinavia, 45, 49, 50, 57, 58, 134
poor in nutrients, 160
Scientific Revolution, the, 80*n*
Scotland, 54, 56, 59, 81*n*, 91, 103, 128, 136
Scottish Enlightenment, 140*n*
scriptoria, 87 (*see also* monasteries)
Scruton, 92
Scythians, 208
seabirds, 209–10
seals, 196, 197
Selby Abbey, 81
Septimania, 97
Serengeti, 211, 214*n*
serpents, *vii*, 95, 104, 128, 142, 199
severed heads, 80, 130
Baphomet, 207; Edmund's, 135; Winifred's, 138
Severn, 28, 138
Shakespeare, 67, 85*n*
shamanism, 125, 213
sheela-na-gigs, 77
sheep, 103, 137, 150, 180, 225
looking like, 12; wethers, 111; attacked by eagle owls, 190; protected by ravens, 203
Shell Oil Company, 115*n*
shoes, 108
Shoeing the Colts, 110
shroud, 109
Sicily, 59, 88*n*
Sidney, Philip, 139
Silbury Hill, 73, 110, 161, 162, 165
Silent Pool, 133
signposts, 1, 2, 4, 7, 18, 25, 26, 30, 44, 45, 47, 119, 135, 205
Sion Abbey, 23
Skellig Michael, 25*n*, 107
snake, 68, 83, 106. 111, 112, 123, 196, 209*n*
Snow White, 139

Somerset Levels, 26, 170
song-lines, 3
Sons of Thunder, 65, 116, 117
Spenser, Edmund, 92
St Clears, 90
St David's, 89, 90
St Ives, 85
St Michael's Mount, 22, 23, 65,
    67, 107, 109, 207
St Neot(s), 85
St Paul's Cathedral, 110
standing stones, 15, 19, 83, 111,
    112, 118, 136n, 138, 169, 205
starlings, 205n
Steiner, 101
steppes (*see* grassland)
stoat, 195, 196
stone circles, 1, 4, 5, 6, 24, 31, 38,
    39, 40, 41, 43, 47, 104, 124,
    133, 167, 168, 169
Stone Street, 92
Stonehenge, 5, 40n, 43, 77n, 90,
    92, 93, 95, 114n, 133n, 162n,
    163–4, 165, 167–8, 169
Strabo, 77, 194
streaming, 86, 153
Strongbow, 92
Stuarts, 87, 103
    Charles, 105
Stukeley, William, 114, 167
Suffolk, 132, 135, 198
Sumeria, 23n, 130n
surveying, 21, 34, 40, 101, 103,
    112, 131n, 166, 167, 169, 202,
    231
swans, 67, 81, 86, 195, 199, 200,
    201
    – maidens, 201; property of
    Crown, 196, 201; Swan-neck,
    Edith, 58; swannery, 75, 106;
    Swan Hotel, 67, 200; Three
    Swans, 110; at Wells, 201;
    – wings, 67, 200
swastika, 123

Switzerland, 86n, 97n
Sylvester I, II (popes), 79n
Synod of Whitby (*see* Whitby)
syphilis, 127n

Tan Hill, 164, 166
Tara, 49
Tarascon, 96
Tarasque, La, 96, 137
Tarka 197
Tarot cards, 110n
tarragon, 96, 97
Tavistock, 136
Templars, 60, 63n, 80, 83, 85, 91,
    97n, 118, 119, 126, 146, 155,
    156, 207
terraforming, 153, 159, 161, 162,
    171, 227
Teutonic Knights, 97n
textiles, 153
Thames, 29, 67, 73, 87n, 159, 200
Thanet, 172 (*see* Margate)
theatre, 150, 202n
thigh, 86, 200
    – wound, 69, 110, 128, 135,
    139, 141
Thor, 41n, 116
Thornborough, 40n
Thorney, 82
thorns, 90, 102
    Jesus' crown of – , 142n
Thoth, 67, 86n, 110n, 201
three-hares, 86
three-legged stool, 87
three-legged table, 86
thujone, 141, 142
Tigris, 227
tin, 1, 3, 10, 14, 18, 20, 21, 22, 24,
    28, 44, 84, 85, 86, 106n, 111,
    148, 208
    – mine, 2, 3, 10, 30, 169;
    – streaming, 86
tinkers, 125n, 150, 208
Tiw, 41n

tolls, 17, 46, 47, 50, 71*n*, 82, 84,
    89, 110, 112, 115, 120, 123,
    124, 125*n*, 126, 127, 130, 132,
    133, 134, 135, 137, 138, 145,
    152, 166, 177, 195, 200
    – collecting, 18, 96, 102, 110,
    120, 122, 152, 153, 205
Tolvan, 106
tor, 75, 78
Torberry Hill, 131
Tory Island, 25*n*
Tours, France, 78
Tower Hill, 67, 78, 94, 207
trackways, 1, 14, 16, 102
transhumance, 222, 225, 228
transmutation, 201
transport, 4, 8, 12, 13, 39, 43, 50,
    97, 144, 145, 147, 148, 151,
    154, 163
    long distance – , 10, 13, 95, 142,
    210, 213, 229
trefot (three feet), 86, 88
trilithon, 167, 168
Trinovantum (London), 80
Triple Death, 108, 119, 135
Triple Goddess, 72*n*, 77, 102,
    139*n*
Trojaborg, 134
troubadours, 59, 72*n*, 74, 84, 97,
    98
Troy, 78, 79, 80
    – Game, 90, 135; – Town, 134
Troyes, 79, 80, 134
    Chrétien de, 81
Tudors, 83*n*, 87, 88, 155
Tyre, 23, 134

Uffington White Horse, 134, 135
underworld, 67, 72, 110*n*, 117,
    201
uniformitarianism, 227
universities, 60, 87, 88, 98

Venus, 89

planet, 41*n*, 140
Verbeia, 122, 123
vermouth, 141, 142
vervain, *verveine*, 122, 123
Vézelay, 96*n*
Victoria, 128
    Victoria & Albert Museum,
    136*n*
Vikings, 58
villages, 11, 12, 82, 130, 149, 150,
    173, 177
    antiquity of, 11, 51; boundary
    marking, 112; – green, 104,
    113, 149; in pairs, 71; – pond,
    149; water rights, 113

Wales, 1, 23, 28, 44, 77, 83, 89,
    90, 92, 134, 206
Waltham Abbey, 58
Wansdyke, 165
warehousing, 39
warrens, 93*n*, 194, 198, 199
Washers at the ford, 120*n*
Washington, George, 81
wassailing, 138
watermills (*see* hydraulics)
Watling Street, 231
wattle-and-daub, 175, 177
Wayland, 135;
    – 's Smithy, 134
weasels, 195, 196
weirs, 72, 154, 198
wells, 16, 18, 74, 75, 80, 83, 91,
    92, 113, 115, 132, 152
    and eyesight, 131; wishing – ,
    133, 152
Wells Cathedral, 201
West Country, 138, 139, 170
Wharfe, river, 122
whisky, 140*n*
Whitby, 112
    Penny Hedge, 112; Synod of,
    56, 57
white horse, 17, 116

White Horse Trail, 165;
    Uffington – , 135
whiteness, 185, 191, 195, 201
Whitstable, 113
Whitwell, 92
Wiltshire, 122, 163, 198
Winchester, 72, 73
Windsor, 128
Winestead, 81
Winforton, Herefordshire, 118
Winteringham, Lincolnshire, 80,
    106
Wintringham, Huntingdonshire,
    85
wise-women, 120
witches, 102, 120, 121, 122, 124,
    125*n*, 132, 134
    –' s familiars, 123, 124
withy, 111
Woden, 41*n*, 79, 82, 124, 128,
    130, 207
Woldgate, 105
wolf, 135, 183
    Loup names, 96*n*
wood circles (henges), 43
woodland, 79*n*, 128, 129
wool, 60, 149
    – carding, 103

Worlebury Hill, 95
Wormsley, Herefordshire, 118
wormwood, 96, 141, 142
    as preservative, 140; – Hill, 142
Wren, Christopher, 168*n*
wrens, 126
    Wrenning Day, 126
wrestling, 141
wryneck, 124

yeast, 224
Yellow River, 227
Ynys Ellen, 77*n*
York, 79, 80, 83, 92
    York Minster, 80
Yorkshire, 28, 79, 80, 81, 93, 104,
    112, 122, 134*n*
Ys, 102
Yuletide, 90*n*, 125, 126
    – pudding, 135

zebra, 180*n*, 215
Zeus, 65, 201
zoos, zoologists, 180, 186, 205,
    212
Zoroaster, 98